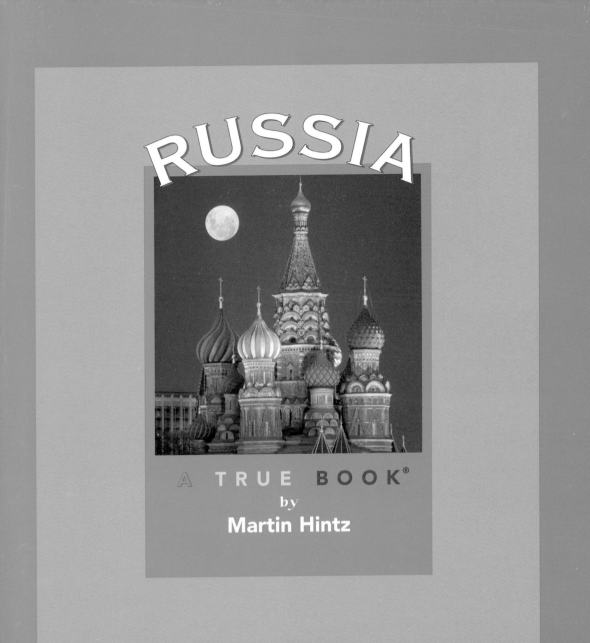

RUSSIA

A TRUE BOOK®

by
Martin Hintz

Children's Press®
A Division of Scholastic Inc.

New York Toronto London Auckland Sydney
Mexico City New Delhi Hong Kong
Danbury, Connecticut

Content Consultant
Dr. Amy J. Johnson, Ph.D.
Berry College

Reading Consultant
Sonja I. Smith
Reading Specialist

A young Nenet woman
from northern Russia
harnesses a reindeer.

Library of Congress Cataloging-in-Publication Data

Hintz, Martin.
    Russia / Martin Hintz.
        p. cm. — (True book)
Includes bibliographical references and index.
Contents: Finding Russia—From Czars to Commissars—After the
Revolution—Life at home.
    ISBN 0-516-22814-5 (lib. bdg.) 0-516-27929-7 (pbk.)
    1. Russia (Federation)—Juvenile literature. [1. Russia (Federation)]
I. Title. II. Series.
DK510.23.H56 2004
947—dc22

                                                        2003018663

CHILDREN'S PRESS, and A TRUE BOOK™, and associated logos are
trademarks and or registered trademarks of Scholastic Library Publishing.
SCHOLASTIC and associated logos are trademarks and or registered
trademarks of Scholastic Inc.
1 2 3 4 5 6 7 8 9 10 R 13 12 11 10 09 08 07 06 05 04

Contents

Arctic Ocean

East
Siberian
Sea

Barents
Sea

Kara Sea

Laptev
Sea

White Sea

ESTONIA

LITHUANIA

FINLAND

LATVIA

BELARUS

● St. Petersburg

UKRAINE

☆ Moscow

Volga

Ural Mountains

RUSSIA

Sea of
Okhotsk

Black Sea

● Volgograd

GEORGIA

Caspian Sea

KAZAKHSTAN

● Novosibirsk

CHINA

MONGOLIA

CHINA

0   1000 miles

0   1500 kilometers

N
W   E
S

RUSSIA

Finding Russia

Russia stretches across the top of Europe and Asia. The country is almost twice as big as the United States. It is so large that Russia shares its frontier with fourteen countries. Russia's largest neighbors are Kazakhstan and China to the south and southeast.

The Arctic Ocean forms the country's northern border, where it can be very cold during the long winters. But winters in the capital city of Moscow in western

Russia are no colder than those in the midwestern United States. The weather in southern Russia is usually warm and pleasant. Rain falls on the rich earth, making southern Russia a prime farming region.

The rugged Ural Mountains stretch along Russia's western frontier. Gold, salt, and coal are mined in this mineral-rich region. At the foot of the mountains are the steppes, the vast rolling plains of central Russia. This land is also very **fertile**, perfect for

Farm workers harvest cabbage, a vegetable that is popular among Russians.

growing wheat and corn. Russian farms there also produce sugar beets, sunflower seeds, fruit, beef, and milk.

Part of the vast Caspian Sea washes the coastline of southern Russia. It is the world's largest body of water surrounded by land.

A fish market in Astrakhan, a city in southern Russia near the Caspian Sea

Fishers catch sturgeon, perch, and herring in the Caspian Sea and sell them in busy outdoor markets throughout Russia.

Russia's Volga River is the longest waterway in Europe. It winds its way south from northwest Russia to the Caspian Sea. Many

A village along the Volga River

tributaries pour into the Volga, causing its swiftly flowing blue-green waters to rush even faster. Through the centuries, the river has been a major transportation route. Even today, barges carry goods to and from factories along the shore.

Who Are the Russians?

Almost 145 million people live in Russia. Most people have homes in **urban** areas of the European part of the country, or western Russia. This is where most jobs in factories and offices are found.

Due to its location, Russia has always been a crossroads

Crowds of people make their way through the streets of Moscow, the largest city in Russia.

nation, a place where people from many different backgrounds passed through. Among the earliest people to arrive were the Slavs. They settled between the Baltic Sea to the northwest and the Black Sea in the southwest. Over the centuries, other ethnic groups arrived on the scene. They may have been members of an invading

As in other parts of the world, young Russians enjoy a good joke and a laugh.

army or traders from faraway lands traveling there to sell their goods. Some of these people decided to live in Russia rather than return to their original homelands.

As a result, groups such as the Tatars, Ukrainians, Chuvash, Bashkir, Belarusians, and Moldavians also call Russia their home. They each have their own languages and customs, yet all of them also speak Russian. Today, many

A Bashkir family drinks tea in their backyard.

foreign businesspeople live in the big cities, where English, German, and Japanese are frequently spoken.

Russ to Russia

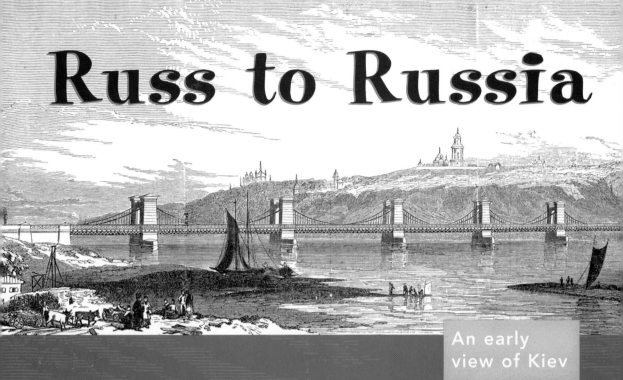

An early view of Kiev

In ancient days, the term *Russ* or *Rus* was often applied to the eastern Slavs who lived on the great steppes, or fertile plains, around the fortress of Kiev. This powerful city was very important from the 800s to the 1100s. Although it is now the capital of Ukraine (with a modern-day spelling of *Kyiv*), it is still referred to as the Mother of Russian Cities. From *Russ* comes the word *Russia*.

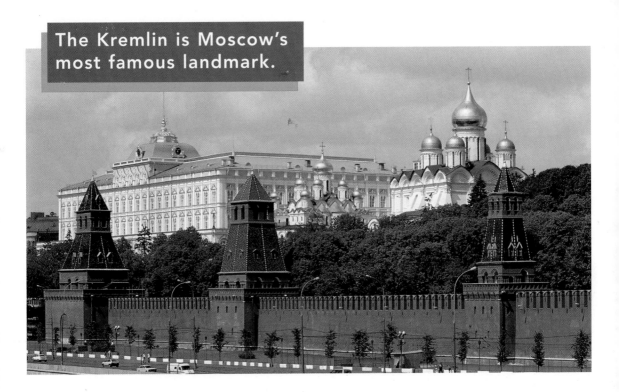

The Kremlin is Moscow's most famous landmark.

Moscow is one of the world's largest cities, with about 8.3 million people. A massive fortress in Moscow, called the Kremlin, is the traditional seat of Russia's head of state. This part of the city is surrounded

The Winter Palace was home to Russia's royal rulers until 1917.

by thick walls and includes many palaces and **cathedrals**. St. Petersburg is another important Russian city where the early rulers of Russia once lived. The city's beautiful Winter Palace is a world famous art museum.

From Czars to Commissars

Russia is a very old nation, dating back at least one thousand years. By A.D. 988 its princes ruled over the territory of present-day European Russia, Ukraine, and Belarus. Over the centuries Russia continued to expand its territory and gradually became a world

19

power. The strongest male rulers were called czars, and the female rulers were known as czarinas. These titles were similar to those of kings and queens in other countries.

Peter the Great was one of the most important czars. He took power in 1689, when he was only seventeen years old. Peter wanted his country to be as **modern** as western Europe. He built ships and expanded his army. Catherine II, who came to the throne in 1762,

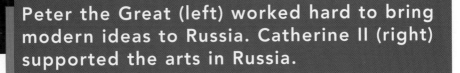

Peter the Great (left) worked hard to bring modern ideas to Russia. Catherine II (right) supported the arts in Russia.

was another strong ruler. She continued to spread Russia's influence and is remembered for supporting her country's arts and culture.

The Russian Circus

The circus has always been one of the most popular forms of entertainment in Russia. Everyone loves going to see the highly skilled circus performers. Daring acrobats, or gymnasts, balance on thin wires high above the arena floor. Clowns make the audience laugh with their jokes and funny costumes. Bears, camels, dogs, horses, lions, and even hedgehogs perform under the watchful eyes of their trainers.

The Russian circus features tiger tricks, acrobats, and clowns.

Many Russian peasants lived in extreme poverty.

Some Russian leaders were not good rulers and paid little attention to the country's many peasants, or farm laborers. The rich people in the ruling class owned most of the land, while other Russians remained poor and uneducated. Many people objected to the way in which the country was governed.

People who supported an extreme change in the way Russia was run were called Communists. The idea of communism is that all goods should be held in common so that no one has to go hungry or do without. In practice, the state would run the country's businesses, farms, and schools. Commissars, or Communist Party government officials, would be in charge of everything. The

Communists hoped that this system would help the peasant class of Russians.

As World War I (1914–1918) wound down, a **revolution** broke out that resulted in the czar being toppled. A civil war followed, in

Russian revolutionaries attacked the Winter Palace in October 1917. This event marked the start of civil war.

which the Communists gained the upper hand. The new Communist government believed that Russia had to deal with its own problems first and could not afford to remain in the war. So, Russia signed a separate peace treaty that withdrew the country from fighting.

After the Revolution

Russia took a new name in 1922, officially becoming the Union of Soviet Socialist Republics (USSR). The original Russia then became just one of fifteen republics in the country. The new USSR was the largest country in the world.

The Communists had promised big changes and a

Police arrested people suspected of plotting against the government.

better government. Instead, they focused on dreams of world **domination**. The government oversaw the **economy** and ran all aspects of people's lives. To keep control, secret police closely watched what everyone did. The Communists murdered millions

of people who disagreed with their ideas. Others were exiled, or sent away, to Siberia, a remote part of the USSR.

During World War II (1939–1945) the USSR was attacked by Germany. Joseph Stalin, the leader of the USSR,

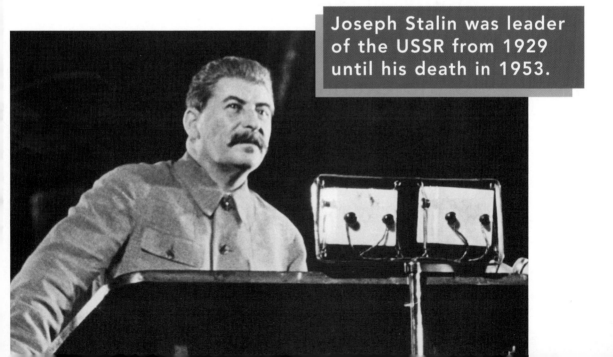

Joseph Stalin was leader of the USSR from 1929 until his death in 1953.

appealed to the people to defend "Mother Russia." Seeking help, the country became a major **ally** of the United States.

After the war the USSR set up rigid Communist governments all over Eastern Europe. Free Western nations objected to the Communists' methods of running the territory they controlled. This difference of opinion was called the Cold War. Yet over the years the

By 1991, most Russians were not satisfied with the Communist government. In August 1991, a crowd of people gathered in Moscow in support of democracy.

economy of the USSR grew weaker because it could not compete with the West. The Communist system collapsed, or failed, in 1991. The republics of the USSR split from one another, becoming independent nations. Russia became Russia again.

Today, the Russian government is headed by a president elected by the people.
The president is helped by a cabinet of ministers. The lawmaking body is known as the Federal Assembly.

Russia is trying hard to strengthen its economy. Industries are being updated

Members of the Russian government meet in Tavrichesky Palace.

so the country can produce goods to sell in other nations. Russian factories make airplanes, ships, trains, and electronic equipment. The country is also a leader in exploring outer space and operates scientific workstations far above the earth.

The Russian space station *Mir*, shown here in orbit above Earth, played an important role in the history of space exploration.

Money Counts

Russian rubles and kopeks

The ruble is the basic unit of Russian money. In 2003 about thirty rubles equaled one United States dollar. A ruble is divided into one hundred kopeks, which is similar to a dollar being made up of one hundred pennies.

Life at Home

Many Russian people live in crowded city apartments. Few families can afford a large home. Some people have a dacha, which is a small house tucked into the forest or near a lake, where they can relax on weekends. It is expensive to own a car, and many Russians

Dachas and gardens near Petropavlovsk

take the bus to their jobs because public transportation is efficient and costs less.

Russian families start their busy day with *zavtrak*, or a simple breakfast. This is often just a cheese or ham sandwich with a cup of tea. Children love *kasha*, any cooked grain served with milk, sugar, and butter. Sausages, fish, and stew are some of the foods served during the main meal in the middle of the day. Later, families gather around the kitchen table for supper, called *uzhin*. Together they talk about their day at school or at work. A popular evening meal consists of potato cakes with mushroom sauce.

Borscht (right) is a popular Russian soup made from beets. Children look forward to eating freshly baked bread (below).

Children play in St. Petersburg's Dvortsovaya Square. A picture of Grandfather Frost, similar to Santa Claus, is in the background.

Celebrations and holidays are important parts of Russian life. Many towns hold a snow festival in the town square on New Year's Eve. Children and parents dance and sing around bonfires, which ward off the chill. December 6 is the Feast of St. Nicholas, a holiday when gifts are given. Most Russians celebrate Orthodox Christmas on January 7. Eating a big meal is part of the fun. A priest is invited to bless the home, and he sprinkles holy water in each room.

On Easter Sunday, mothers give a loaf of bread to the priest for blessing. This special bread has a round top layered with sugary frosting that makes the loaves look like the domes on Russian churches. When the bread is served at home, older members of the family are the first to be served the delicious crust.

Russian Independence Day is on June 12. During this celebration parades of youngsters carry red, blue, and white flowers. These are the colors of the Russian national flag.

Russian Writers

Alexander Pushkin

Anton Chekhov

Marvelous Russian authors are noted for their very real portrayals of the lives of their fellow citizens. Alexander Pushkin, Fyodor Dostoyevsky, and Leo Tolstoy are among the nation's best-known writers. Stage plays by Anton Chekhov are gripping and true-to-life. Writer Alexsandr Solzhenitsyn won the Nobel Prize in 1970 for describing his life in a prison camp twenty years earlier. He had protested against the Communist system and was jailed for his beliefs.

To Find Out More

Here are some additional resources to help you learn more about Russia:

 **Books**

Harvey, Miles. **Look What Came From Russia.** Franklin Watts, 1999.

Marquez, Heron. **Russia in Pictures.** Lerner Publications Co., 2003.

Murrell, Kathleen. **Eyewitness Russia.** Dorling Kindersley Publishing, 2000.

Nickles, Greg. **Russia: The People.** Crabtree Publishing, 2000.

Streissguth, Tom. **Ticket to Russia.** Carolrhoda Books, 1997.

Organizations and Online Sites

Russian Culture Center

1825 Phelps Place NW
Washington, DC 20008
202-265-3840

For details on Russian history, heritage, and customs.

Russian National Tourist Office

http://www.russia-travel.com

For information on travel to Russia, as well as details about historic sites, cultural activities, holidays, and art.

Peace Corps Kids World— Russia

http://www.peacecorps.gov/ kids/world/europemed/ russia.html

Features country facts and a map as well as information about geography and every-day life in Russia.

Important Words

ally a friend or helper; in this case, a country that helps another during a war

cathedrals churches

domination ruling power

economy management of the income and spending of money and resources

fertile capable of producing crops

modern up-to-date, current

revolution the overthrow of a government by those who are governed

tributaries streams or rivers that flow into a larger river

urban of or belonging to a city or town

Index

Meet the Author

Martin Hintz lives in Milwaukee, Wisconsin. He has written almost one hundred books, including many in the Enchantment of the World and America the Beautiful series for Franklin Watts and Children's Press. His works have won major national awards.

Hintz is active in numerous journalism associations, including the Society of American Travel Writers, the Society of Professional Journalists, and the Committee to Protect Journalists. Hintz has a bachelor's degree in journalism from the University of St. Thomas in St. Paul, Minnesota, and a master's degree in journalism, with an emphasis on international affairs, from Northwestern University, Evanston, Illinois.

The Pirates

ALSO BY LOU SAHADI

The Long Pass
Len Dawson: Pressure Quarterback
Miracle in Miami
Pro Football Gamebreakers
Broncos!
Super Sundays I-XIII
Year of the Yankees
Steelers! Team of the Decade

The Pirates

Lou Sahadi

Times BOOKS

Cover and color photographs courtesy of Mickey Palmer

Published by TIMES BOOKS, a division of
Quadrangle/The New York Times Book Co., Inc.
Three Park Avenue, New York, N.Y. 10016

Published simultaneously in Canada by
Fitzhenry & Whiteside, Ltd., Toronto

Library of Congress Cataloging in Publication Data

Sahadi, Lou.
    The pirates.

    1. Pittsburgh. Baseball Club (National League)
2. Baseball players—United States—Biography.
I. Title.
GV875.P5S23   796.357′64′0974886   79-3813
ISBN 0-8129-0917-8

Manufactured in the United States of America.

For My Mother
Who knew my love for baseball as a
child by providing many summer
nights of late dinners waiting for me to
come home.

Contents

Acknowledgments

The author wishes to express his sincere thanks to Joe Safety and Tom Bird of the Pittsburgh Pirates; Sam Corman and Nancy Crespinel, who assisted in the research; Bert Rosenthal in editing and Marian Ciaccia who contributed unselfishly in final manuscript typing; and last but not least, Tony Giglio who designed and completed the lay-outs under an excruciating deadline.

Introduction

They are a colorful bunch. There's Pops, Cobra, Scrap Iron, Mad Dog, Rooster, Candy, Teke, Hammer, Buck, and any other number of nicknames. They are unique to say the least; but more than that, they can play baseball. Certainly no other team in baseball played better than the Pittsburgh Pirates in 1979. Their dramatic World Series triumph over the Baltimore Orioles has earned them a valuable chapter of Series lore in the years to come.

It was much more than winning that made the Pirates a household word last year. It was the way they played the game. They played baseball the way it was intended, for fun. It was a refreshing approach, too. Undaunted by pressure, they played and won in a manner that captured the hearts of baseball fans everywhere.

They did it all within a family syndrome. Baseball had never been played in that atmosphere before. It was one big Pirate family inside and outside the clubhouse. What made it work was that it was genuine. It withstood skeptics and even at times critics who looked upon the Pirates' family theme with a jaundiced eye.

There is no other team in baseball that plays in such a wholesome environment. It's believable because the Pirates made it work. They believed in each other, and together they won a world's championship—family style!

The Pirates were proud of their family-like feelings for each other. Their informal clubhouse blared with the disco sounds of Sister Sledge's "We Are Family."The players knew the words and, even more important, knew its meaning. It was their theme song. Their leader was Willie "Pops" Stargell, a lovable 38-year-old veteran who had been with the Pirates his entire 17-year major league career. He looked over "his family" and rewarded their efforts of achievement with little gold stars that the players proudly displayed on their caps.

It's only fitting that one more great big star be presented, to Pops Stargell and the entire Pirate family for making 1979 so meaningful.

Lou Sahadi

The Pirates

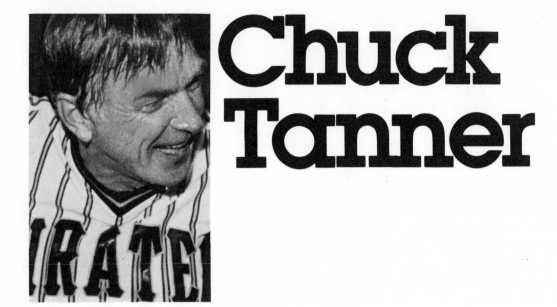

Chuck Tanner

He stood there bareheaded. He had both hands in his hip pockets as he looked up at the sky. Rain was falling although not with the intensity it had earlier. Still, it was a steady, persistent rain, one that threatened to postpone the opening game of the 1979 World Series. The tarpaulin covered the infield, but the outfield was wet and soggy and there were small puddles of water in some spots. After turning to survey the field for a moment, he was convinced he had seen enough. Only then did Chuck Tanner leave the field, walk into the dugout and retire to the warmth of the clubhouse.

Yet, he wasn't the least bit perturbed. Sure it was raining, but he couldn't do anything about the weather. A short time later, the game was officially postponed and the opening of the Series was delayed until the following night in Baltimore. But even if it were delayed a week, it wouldn't have mattered to Tanner. He was where he wanted to be, where he had dreamed about all his baseball life . . . in the World Series. That was happiness enough for Tanner and rain, or cold, or snow didn't make any difference to him.

"It's not an irritation," remarked Tanner. "It's not a disaster. It's an inconvenience. We're going to stay here until we play two games, we know that. Actually, we were concerned about the condition of the field. We're disappointed, but we didn't want anybody hurt on either side. The World Series is supposed to be fun."

That is what Chuck Tanner is all about. He is low-keyed and self-assured. He approaches his work as fun because that's the way it always has been for him. Yet, despite his calmness, he has a deep inner strength. He brought his relaxed approach to baseball to Pittsburgh in 1977, and in 1979 the Pirates were playing in the World Series for the first time since 1971. That, indeed, was as happy as Tanner could get.

"Here is the big thing about baseball," added Tanner. "Kids want to grow up to be

3

big-leaguers. Then they get there and don't
enjoy it. Why? Because they're pressing.
They're fighting themselves to do well.
They're depressed if they lose a game. They're
depressed if they go 0-for-4. They have to remain the same people mentally. They got here
because of their physical talent. If they maintain their natural mental outlook, they can
enjoy the game and they'll succeed."

Tanner's simple philosophy easily reached
his players. The players were for the most part
colorful, free-spirited and carefree. Tanner
understood them without having to make
certain demands on them. The players
understood him. That's all that was necessary
for Tanner's method of managing. It was easy
for him to instill a feeling of confidence in
them, one that maintained that there was no
better team in baseball. He communicated
with them in a folksy manner, one in which
they could relate. And the players responded.
After two successive second-place finishes,
they were now in the World Series. Yet,
Tanner never lost touch of reality. He remembered the beginning as he sat in his
office while his players were leaving to
return to their hotel rooms and wait until the
next night to play. He remembered the year
1955 when he first arrived in the National
League as a player after bouncing around for
nine years in the minors.

"They gave me six dollars a day meal
money and they took my suitcase when we
went on a trip," the smiling Tanner said softly.
"But I didn't want to let my suitcase go. I
didn't believe them when they said it would
show up at the hotel. I had my only jacket in
there, but they told me not to worry and when
I arrived at the hotel, my suitcase was there. It
was like magic.

"Good things have happened to me. Look, I
ripped my Achilles tendon and I was still 32
games short of my pension. I was back down
in Dallas-Fort Worth in 1962 trying to play my
way back when I ran into Fred Haney of the
Angels. He asked me how it was coming and I
told him I couldn't get a jump on the ball any
more and that I would never be the same.
Haney said, 'You sound the same to me. The

4

way you play you never could get a jump on the ball. You sound healthy as hell.'

"About a month later, Haney called me and said that the Angels had bought my contract and they would make sure I got the pension time I needed. The following year they sent me down so they could play their youngsters. At the end of the season, Haney called me again and said that I could come up and make the club next year as a fourth or fifth outfielder, that he'd guarantee it. Then he said if you'd rather, we have an opening for a manager at Quad Cities (Illinois) and to take my time and think about it. I told them that I don't need any time, I'll take the manager's job."

It was a job Tanner always had wanted. He liked the action, the challenge. He worked at it, too. He spent eight years in the minors before getting his shot at the majors with the Chicago White Sox in 1971. He stayed with the White Sox for five years, then landed in Oakland in 1976. Working for A's owner Charlie Finley, anything could happen . . . and it did. In an unprecedented move, Tanner was traded to the Pirates for catcher Manny Sanguillen and $100,000 in 1977. It was the happiest day in Tanner's 35 years in organized baseball. He was returning home, to New Castle, Pennsylvania to manage his nearby hometown team.

At first, he was a stranger. There was a great deal of skepticism about Tanner's managing philosophy. While he was comfortable with it, it was strange to his players. However, it didn't take long for his optimism and college-style enthusiasm to rub off on the players. Once it did, the rest was up to the players. Tanner let them play and have fun.

"People thought his positive nature was a put-on," explained Willie Stargell, the elder statesman on the club.

"We thought we were coming out in pom-poms and tassles on our shoes," said Ed Ott, the hard-nosed catcher.

Tanner wanted a relaxed clubhouse and he got it. It grew over the years into a family-type hostel. Tanner welcomed the atmosphere, even participated in it. He treated his players as men, yet at the same time he wanted them to have fun while playing. He let the players be themselves without mentioning the word curfew. Some outside the club couldn't understand his carefree approach. He had a simple explanation for it.

"Well, Paul Waner used to wander into the lobby at 1 A.M. and Babe Ruth always managed to find a little spot to have some fun and I think if somebody had slapped a curfew on them, there might be two empty spaces in the Hall of Fame today," said Tanner. "The thing is you have to handle people like they are men. You try to be nice."

In Tanner's first year, the Pirates finished with a 96-66 record, their most victories since 1972. In 1978, they were 88-73, yet it was a dramatic late-season finish that excited everyone. On August 12, the Pirates were in fourth place, 11½ games behind the first-place Philadelphia Phillies. Tanner's optimism never waned. He insisted that the Pirates would catch the Phillies. By September 19, they had climbed into second place, one game behind. However, on the next-to-last day of the season, they were eliminated by the Phils. But they didn't die easy. They scored four runs in the bottom of the ninth inning before losing 10-8. That strong finish carried over into spring training of 1979. Tanner used it as an impetus for the new season.

"I'm going to say this," said Tanner. "Everybody picks Philadelphia (to finish first) but we can win it. We're contenders everytime. This is the most relaxed team in baseball. It's not worried about yesterday or tomorrow, just right now."

It was evident that the Pirates had hitting, but their pitching was suspect. Yet Tanner never hedged. He felt it was going to be the Pirates' year. He felt even more confident when the players reported in good shape.

"I'm not surprised that almost all our guys came down here in great condition," Tanner said on a hot, sunny day in Bradenton, Florida. "What else do they have to do after the baseball season? Most of them don't have to work during the off-season. When I played ball, the day after the season, I was either out

Tanner and pitcher Jim Bibby argue a point.

looking for work or already had a job to go to. Most of us had to go to work on other jobs just to keep up our families. Oh, there were a few players who made big money, but most had to scratch around to find work once the summer ended.

"Today, a player makes enough money in baseball so he can take it easy during the winter. His family is well taken care of. All a guy has to do with his time if he wants to keep in shape is to visit a gym every day, get into a program, or belong to a health club. When we had to work, it wasn't usually a cushy job. We'd come home tired, not even thinking about exercising. Really, there's no excuse for today's athlete not to stay in top condition all

year. Especially the veterans who've been around for awhile.

"All we did was send a letter to all our players telling each what we expected down here. From then on, it was strictly up to the individual. They're in much better condition than last spring. There are so many programs available to them. Most can go to facilities near their home. If a guy wants to stay in condition, there's every opportunity to do that."

When Dave Parker walked onto the field his first day, Tanner looked him over carefully. He noticed that Parker was a few pounds overweight.

"It looks like Dave had a great off-season

around the banquet circuit," said Tanner. "Dave'll get down, though. He's never in bad condition."

Tony Bartirome, the team's trainer, shook his head in agreement.

"Parker has a lot of water weight," observed the popular trainer. "He'll get rid of that in a couple of weeks once the weather gets warmer."

Tanner wasn't upset. He realized Parker wasn't just sitting around getting fat in the off season. In 1978, Parker had led the National League in hitting for the second straight season.

"Personalities go hand-in-hand with money in this case," explained Tanner. "A guy can be making a ton of money, but he has to be able to fit into a routine. Over the winter, Parker was in constant demand, both as a speaker and a participant. Dave wasn't able to get into any program like most of the others. A lot of players could become country club types, but not all of them care for that life. Most are family men. Staying in condition means taking care of the family a lot longer than the guy who doesn't."

Tanner looked across the diamond. He spotted Bill Robinson leisurely playing catch with Phil Garner. He illustrated another point.

"Look at Robby," said Tanner. "Bill's going to be 35 in June, but you'd never know it by looking at him. Robinson is an example of a player who's still playing because he worked and sacrificed to keep his body in condition. Robinson has outlasted plenty of players who are considered better than him. Robby's still around because he put his family first. Bill knows what he's doing is for them. It's called dedication."

Despite his calm exterior, Tanner is aggressive once a game begins. Although he has almost a laissez-faire approach to running a team, he has a vivid imagination in conducting the strategy of a game. He isn't afraid to replace a pitcher or pinch hit for a player who might possibly have been enjoying a perfect day at bat if he felt a change would be better. He makes liberal use of all 25 players on his squad. In fact, as the 1979 season wore on,

Tanner made extensive use of his bullpen. It wasn't unusual for him to call on three for four pitchers a game.

"All I know is that I got 25 guys out there and I'll use them," said Tanner. "Do I make more mistakes when I make so many changes? No, but I get second-guessed more."

Tanner heard it from the fans when the 1979 season was only three days old. The Pirates were playing the Montreal Expos in a three-game series in Pittsburgh's Three Rivers Stadium. Bruce Kison was pitching a strong game for the Pirates. Pittsburgh was ahead, 2-1, as the seventh inning began. Through the first six innings, Kison, making use of an excellent slider, had struck out ten batters. After Kison threw a couple of pitches. Tanner replaced him with Enrique Romo. A short while later, Tanner took out Romo. When he did, the Pirates' fans booed him. Three of them were so vocal that they jumped on top of the Pirates' dugout to vent their emotions It didn't upset Tanner.

"I didn't hear what they said and all that booing didn't bother me," commented Tanner. "I don't pay attention to stuff like that. They don't know the reasoning behind the moves I make. Kison's elbow tightened up and the weather had something to do with it. He had great stuff, but this was the most he has thrown since spring training. He did his job, but I could see the difference in his delivery in the seventh inning."

Later in the season, he made a much bolder move in a game against Philadelphia. Catcher Steve Nicosia, who was 4-for-4, was due up with the bases loaded. But Tanner lifted him for a pinch hitter late in the game. With a right-handed pitcher on the mound, Tanner wanted left-handed hitting John Milner to bat in a percentage move. Naturally, it was not popular with the fans.

"Boy, did I get second-guessed, people saying that I should have let him go for 5-and 5," said Tanner. "Then Milner hit a grand-slam home run and I was a genius."

Still later in the season, Tanner made perhaps his most unorthodox move as a manager. It was a move that gave him his

biggest thrill. Tanner enjoys describing it.

"We're playing the Giants in San Francisco," said Tanner. "They have the tying run on base and Kent Tekulve is pitching, but the hitter is Darrell Evans and he's a lefty. Now I want Grant Jackson to pitch to him but I want Tekulve to come back to the next guy if I need him. So I turn to my coach, Joe Lonnett, and ask him if he ever saw Tekulve catch a fungo. He says, 'Sure, all the pitchers do.'

"So I go to the mound and tell Tekulve to go play left field and he just stares at me. Then he goes out there and six guys run out from the dugout and give him a two-minute cram course in how to play the outfield. One guy is eavesdropping with a blade of grass and checking the wind.

"Now I give the ball to Jackson and I say, 'Pitch him away.' And Jackson looks at me and he says, 'Skip, you crazy? I pitch him away, he hits to left. You know who you just sent out there?'

"I tell him I know but that's the way I want this guy pitched. Evans hits the ball and it goes right to left field. There's Tekulve and he's flapping his arms like a duck and circling under the ball and damned if he don't catch it. Did you know what Tekulve told me later? He said, 'You're lucky I caught the ball. I was thinking of dropping it so I could come back in to get the save.'

"Look, managing is just an opinion, that's all. So are trades. In my opinion, the Pirates made a nice trade when they sent Sanguillen to Oakland."

Relief pitching was the area in which Tanner had to build fast. The departures of Rich Gossage and Terry Forster after the 1977 season left the Pirates short of capable relievers. In order to compensate for the lack of help in the bullpen, Tanner tried to get more innings out of his starters during the 1978 campaign. But that wasn't the answer. A stronger bullpen would make the starters that much more stronger. That thinking enabled the Pirates to hang tough at the end of the 1979 season and eventually win the World

11

Series. Tanner made frequent use of his relief pitchers to preserve victories throughout the season.

"That was a black day when we lost Gossage and Forster," recalled Tanner, "but what could we do about it? The next year they were the stars of the World Series, Forster for the Dodgers and Gossage for the Yankees. We decided to stick with our starting pitchers longer and not go to the bullpen so fast. So I began to manage with my arms folded. Then we went out and looked for the best guys in the minor leagues who could pitch three innings."

By changing pitching assignments and making a couple of wise trades, the Pirates replaced their two bullpen stars within two years. In 1979, three of their bullpen workhorses led the National League in appearances. Tekulve was high with 94, followed by Romo with 84 and Jackson with 72. That was how Tanner spelled relief, 250 appearances from three relief pitchers.

"We added eight or nine players in 1979," pointed out Tanner, "guys like Romo, Tim Foli and Bill Madlock. We had lost the division title in 1978 on the next-to-last day of the season. If we had Romo, we would have won it."

Tanner has no prescribed method for managing. His formula is to shake well and use freely. Rather than making a team edgy, Tanner keeps the players loose with his instinctive moves. They know that they will get to play often. Tanner gives them all a feeling of importance for what they contribute to the team. He has confidence in what each can do. Madlock learned Tanner's methods shortly after joining the club.

"He let me be the kind of player I feel I can be," said Madlock. "He placed no restrictions on me. I didn't have to look down for the bunt sign, and I could steal in any situation I wanted. That took a lot of pressure off me and helped me relax."

Garner, who has known Tanner longer than any of the Pirates' players, having played for him while both were in Oakland, never played better than he did in 1979.

"Aggressive is the best way to describe him," Garner said of Tanner. "He lets hitters swing away in situations where other managers don't. He let's the runners run, and he goes to the bullpen fast."

Yet, Lonnett, who has coached for Tanner for nine years, still can't figure him out during a game.

"You'd think I'd know what he's going to do, but I don't," said Lonnett. "He has no pattern."

Perhaps he doesn't need one. All he needs are 25 cooperative players. But in that mix of 25 personalities, there has to be a camaraderie, similar to a happy family.

"It used to be a lot of guys were working for more personal statistics," explained Tanner. "That's the way they got paid. Now with the long-term contracts, the personal stats don't mean as much. Everybody wants to be with a winner. Everybody wants to be known as a winner. When you put together a club, you don't get guys with certain stats, you get guys who are winners. I'm not saying they don't have personal goals, but they know that it's better to be with guys who win games. They receive more recognition that way."

Tanner did, too. When the Pirates won the World Series in a thrilling seven-game series against the Baltimore Orioles, Tanner emerged in the spotlight. It was a spotlight that had been given to his adversary, Earl Weaver, before the Series. Weaver was lauded as a genius, the bantam rooster who would scratch and fight his way to a victory with mostly a non-descript cast of players. Before the Series, Tanner was best remembered as the only major league manager who had gotten along with tempermental slugger Richie Allen when both were with the White Sox.

Certainly no man managed a Series under greater duress than Tanner. His mother died the morning of the fifth game with his club on the verge of extinction, trailing 3-1 in games. Yet, no man stood taller than Tanner that somber day. His inner strength was a beacon in the dark hours that surrounded him and his team. He was alone when he found out that his mother had died in a hospital in nearby Greenville, Pennsylvania, two weeks after she had suffered a stroke. When Tanner got to the stadium early that Sunday morning, he phoned the hospital to inquire about his mother.

"This is Chuck Tanner," he said to the operator. "How's my mother doing?"

"I'm sorry, Mr. Tanner," she answered. "Your mother died at 7:40."

He immediately called home. His family had been trying to reach him to tell him the sad news. He spoke with his wife, Barbara, and with his father, Charles Sr.

"I'll come home right away," Tanner said.

"No, your mother wouldn't want that," said his father. "Stay there and go get 'em."

The players knew the pain Tanner masked. In the quiet of the clubhouse, they went to him, embraced him, then went out and began to turn the Series around with a 7-1 victory. Somehow one got the feeling that the fun-loving Pirates won one for "Grandma" as they had fondly called Anne Tanner. After the game, Tanner softly talked about his mother.

"The last time I talked to her," he remembered, "she knew we were in the World Series, and I was kidding her that she better watch every game on TV or I wouldn't go. She told me, 'I'll watch 'em all.' And last Sunday, she was in the hospital watching the Steelers on TV, and I heard later that all of a sudden the nurses heard her yell, 'C'mon Bradshaw.' She loved sports. All her kids loved sports, me and my two brothers, and she and my dad loved sports, too. It was our life, so it was her life and my dad's life.

"When I was a kid I never wanted to do any work around the house. I never wanted to wash the dishes like I was supposed to. One day I remember she poked me in the shoulder and said, 'You don't like to work, all you want to do is play ball.' And that's all I ever did whenever I could. There was a playground over the hill from our house in New Castle. She still lived there, in a different house, and I live there now. And when we played baseball at the playground, the first 18 guys who

showed up every morning got to play in the game. So I made sure I got there early, and I'd stay all day. I was only 8 or 9, and the other kids were 14 or 15, but they stuck me in right field and I played. And at lunchtime, my mother would make a sandwich and bring it down to the playground for me."

Tanner continued, "I thought about her today when Dave Parker was up in the seventh. I remembered how he had phoned her on her 70th birthday in May and how she was so happy about that. He was her favorite player, and she told everybody how she had talked to 'Superman.' And when he was up in the seventh I said to myself, 'Hit one for Grandma,' and he lined that double to left field that put us ahead, 4-1.

"I remember when my grandmother died. I was a kid outfielder with the Atlanta Crackers in the Southern League at the time. But when my grandmother died, my mother and my dad told me that I didn't have to come home for the funeral, that my grandmother would understand. That's the way my mother and father always were. When I left home to play in the minors at 17, my mother told me, 'Do what you want to do, it's your life.' Later on I was playing in Owensboro, Kentucky, when I had to go to the hospital with bleeding ulcers. They came down to see me then, and another time they came out to Denver. She was great, just like my father's great, just like everybody's mother and father are great.

"My mother and father didn't have many rules for my two brothers and me. We just had to do what was right when we were kids, that's all. I'm sad now. I'm sad as I ever have been in my life. But I'm strong, too. I know everybody is supposed to hit the deck sooner or later. It's not hard for me to accept that because I have faith in God. I know my mother's in heaven now. You're supposed to cry when you're born and be happy when you die, but most people do just the the opposite. But you've got to be strong. I can be strong because the people around me are strong."

They certainly were. They not only won the fifth game, but the sixth game and the seventh. Grandma would have wanted it that way.

15

Tanner and coach Bob Skinner pensively watch the action from the dugout.

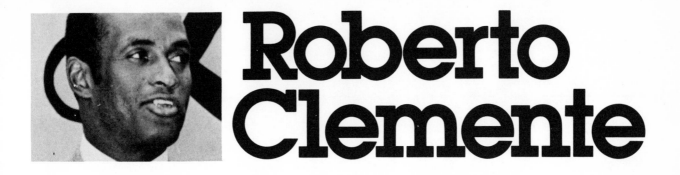

Roberto Clemente

He meant so much to the Pirates. He could do it all and did so better than most with the smoothness of a ballet dancer. In the 18 years he played for them, he was special. Roberto Clemente was regarded as one of the greatest players in the history of the game. He won four batting titles, hit over .300 eight straight years, ranked in the top ten in the National League in games played, times at bat and in hits (3,000), won the Gold Glove Award 12 times, was named to the All-Star team 11 times, was voted the National League's Most Valuable Player Award in 1966, and the Outstanding Player Award in the 1971 World Series. Not many players have matched his lifetime career batting average of .317. Indeed, Clemente was one of a kind the way he could hit, field, throw and run.

Yet, his career was never smooth. He had numerous injuries that reduced his effectiveness. More often than not, he played in pain. It was a constant pain that some of his managers never believed existed and a great many writers never did, either. As a result, his rela-

tionship with the press was not exceptionally good. The doubts of writers made Clemente suspicious and at times lonely. But the pain in his back was there and Clemente lived with it daily. The suspicions of the writers prevented Clemente from getting the recognition he deserved in his many years with Pittsburgh.

His teammates appreciated his efforts. Manny Sanguillen, for one, Willie Stargell for another. They are the two remaining Pirates from the 1971 World Series in which Clemente hit .414, leading Pittsburgh to a thrilling 4-3 come-from-behind victory over Baltimore. Eight years later, against Baltimore in the 1979 World Series, there were ghost-like undertones of Clemente. Sanguillen dedicated his game-winning hit in the second game to Clemente, and Stargell, without whose heroics the Pirates wouldn't have won, said the triumph was an extension of what Clemente started. It was the highest form of respect from two teammates who really knew the character of Clemente.

The brilliant right fielder's various ailments

17

during his productive career resembled a hospital chart. He had a tendon in his left heel that constantly rubbed against a bone, causing great discomfort. Often the heel became inflamed and created a great amount of pain when he ran. He had bone chips in his elbow that at times hampered his throwing and batting. Clemente also had a painfully sore shoulder, from a fall off a cliff near his home, that troubled him during an entire season. He suffered from constant headaches and even a nervous stomach. One season he was weak from the effects of malaria.

The most severe injury of all, however, was from spinal discs that had moved in his lower back and began to create a curvature of the spine. It forced him to play with a back brace when the pain was intense. That was the pain which Clemente endured every day that the writers doubted. Some even went as far as to label him a chronic complainer. It hurt Clemente because he had a deep inner pride that drove him to perfection. That pride was evident in his final season with the Pirates.

None of the 13,117 fans who were in Three Rivers Stadium on September 30, 1972, the final day of the baseball season, realized that they were seeing Clemente play for the last time. The Pirates had clinched the Eastern Division championship and were closing the regular season with a two-game series against the New York Mets. Still, it was a momentous occasion. Clemente had collected 2,999 hits and needed only one more to reach the 3,000 plateau in his last game of the year. Only ten other players in baseball's long history had reached that figure.

The previous day, Clemente came close. Some 24,000 fans had turned out to see Clemente perform the feat. Each time Clemente got up to hit against Tom Seaver, the fans cheered him encouragingly. They realized that Clemente, who was so near his goal, had experienced a hard season physically. He missed more than 50 games because of illness or injury. Even as the season was ending, he was troubled by the tendon problem in his heel.

In his first at bat against Seaver in the first inning, Clemente swung hard. He topped a high bouncer over Seaver's outstretched glove and it bounced toward second base. Ken Boswell raced in to field the softly hit ball. As he did, the ball glanced off his glove as Clemente streaked across first base. There was tension throughout the stands as the fans looked up at the scoreboard to see if the play would be scored a hit or an error. There was even confusion in the press box. The official scorer ruled the play an error, but he had trouble transmitting his decision to the operator of the big electric scoreboard because of a technical malfunction.

Minutes later, the hit sign flashed on. The crowd stood and applauded. The fans began to litter the field with paper in some spots. Time was called. The first base umpire gave the ball to Clemente, who immediately flipped it to first base coach Don Leppert to hold. With the ball in one hand, Leppert patted Clemente on the backside with the other. Clemente tipped his hat to the cheering crowd.

The press box was in an uproar. Finally, the official scorer got through to the scoreboard operator informing him to change the hit to an error. Suddenly, an "E" flashed on the scoreboard. The fans were stunned. They began to boo the scorer's decision. The celebration stopped. The crowd and Clemente had to wait. He figured to come to bat two or possibly three more times against Seaver. However, the next two times up, Seaver easily retired Clemente.

Clemente had one more chance. With the Pirates trailing, Clemente came to bat in the bottom of the ninth inning. As the crowd cheered him on, Clemente again faced Seaver. He leaned into an outside pitch and drove it on a line toward the right field corner. It appeared to be a hit. At the last second, Rusty Staub reached out and caught the ball in the webbing of his glove. The fans moaned. Clemente, in four at-bats, had failed to get a hit.

Clemente was asked about the scorer's decision on his first-inning ground ball that was ruled an error.

"I would not have wanted the official scorer to call it a hit if he wasn't sure of it," Clemente said without bitterness. "I don't want my 3,000th hit to be a cheap one or a gift, to leave doubt in the fans' minds."

There still was one more game for Clemente to collect his 3,000th hit. It wouldn't be easy. The Mets' pitcher on the final day of the season was Jon Matlack, a hard-throwing left-hander. The 13,117 fans who were in the stands on that final Sunday were there for only one reason, to see Clemente get his coveted hit. If he did, he would join two other Pirates' stars, Honus Wagner and Paul Waner, in the charmed 3,000-hit circle.

Again the cheers were there for Clemente when he came to bat the first time. Matlack stopped him. When Clemente batted again in the fourth inning, the Pirates' fans were getting anxious. Clemente calmly got set in the batter's box, turning his head in a circular motion to loosen his neck muscles. It was a familiar Clemente trait. Matlack threw him a curve ball. Clemente swung and drilled the ball deep into the left field corner. It hit the ground on one bounce and richocheted off the wall as Clemente trotted into second base with a double amidst loud cheers of the crowd. The lights on the scoreboard lit up a huge 3,000!

The fans stood and clapped. Clemente took off his cap and thanked them. Umpire Doug Harvey walked over to Clemente, handed him the ball and shook his hand in congratulations. The crowd continued cheering. It was indeed an historic moment. Matlack fully realized the impact and what it meant to Clemente. He held the new ball for a full minute, keeping Stargell waiting in the batter's box and further delaying the game in order to allow Clemente to absorb the adulation that he deserved.

Everyone who walked into the Pittsburgh clubhouse after the game did so for one thing, to congratulate Clemente on his historic hit.

"I give this hit to the fans of Pittsburgh and to the people of Puerto Rico," the happy Clemente exclaimed with tears of joy in his eyes.

While that hit seemed difficult to get, most hits came easily for Clemente. He was a great hitter. He had many big days throughout his career. Twice he hit three homers in one game. Another time, he drove in all seven of his team's runs. Twice he scored five runs in one game, and once he smacked three triples in a game. Yet, the game that gave him most satisfaction was against the Cincinnati Reds early in his career. Clemente clubbed three home runs, a double and a single and knocked in seven runs in that memorable game against Cincinnati. It was satisfying to him because he wanted to prove to some of his critics that he could hit home runs if that's all he wanted to do. However, in his next game, he returned to his normal style of hitting, which was an art in itself, being able to hit the ball anywhere it was pitched.

On August 22 and August 23, 1970, Clemente demonstrated what hitting is all about. No player in modern day baseball has ever had two consecutive hitting days that Clemente enjoyed. Pittsburgh was playing in Los Angeles. The Saturday night game went into extra innings. The teams were tied, 1-1, as Bob Moose of Pittsburgh and Don Sutton of Los Angeles were locked in a tight pitching duel. The Dodgers had scored in the first inning and Clemente drove in Bill Mazeroski with the tying run in the third.

By the time the 16th inning started, both Moose and Sutton had departed. Vern Mikkelsen was pitching for the Dodgers and Bruce Dal Canton had taken over for the Pirates. Pittsburgh had collected only nine hits off Los Angeles pitching and Clemente had four of them. Mikkelsen had retired the first two Pirates' batters before Clemente came up. He smashed his fifth hit, a single to right field, then surprisingly stole second base. The daring paid off when Milt May singled, driving in Clemente with the run that gave the Pirates a hard-fought 2-1 victory. The game lasted four hours, 21 minutes.

By the time the Pirates returned to their hotel, it was two o'clock in the morning. They had an early wake-up call because Sunday's game was set for one o'clock. The players were lucky to get seven hours sleep. Clemente had reached his 36th birthday earlier in the week. Normally, especially after such a long night game, Clemente would rest for a day game. But he couldn't that day. Stargell was bothered by an injured leg and couldn't play. Pittsburgh Manager Danny Murtaugh needed Clemente's important bat in the lineup, since the Pirates were battling for first place.

In his first at-bat against Alan Foster, Clemente picked up where he left off the previous night. He singled and then scored. When he came up to hit in the second inning, he knocked in a run with another single. The third time Clemente came to bat, in the fourth inning, he faced a new pitcher, Fred Norman. It didn't matter. Clemente doubled home another run. In he seventh inning, he singled again and scored on Al Oliver's home run. Clemente wasn't finished yet. He got up again in the eighth inning and walloped a home run off Charlie Hough. It was his second consecutive five-hit game. Unquestionably, the Dodgers were glad to see Clemente leave town.

Among Clemente's ten hits were two doubles, seven singles and his 10th home run of the year. He also knocked in four runs and scored five. His batting average zoomed to .363 as he took over the batting lead from Rico Carty of the Atlanta Braves.

One person who looked on with mixed emotions at Clemente's hitting fireworks was Al Campanis, vice president of the Dodgers. Back in 1953, when he was farm director of the Dodgers, Campanis went to Puerto Rico to scout the 18-year-old Clemente.

"He looked like the best young prospect I had ever seen," recalled Campanis. "I think we signed him for $10,000. I hated to see anybody beat the Dodgers these last two games, but if it was going to happen, it was kind of nice to see Clemente do it. He was the most complete ballplayer I ever saw and I'll always be proud of the fact that I signed him."

Campanis had to wait a year to sign him. Clemente's father refused to let his son play professional baseball until he finished high school. He told Campanis to come back the following year. Campanis came back, but by then other major league scouts had heard of

Clemente. Although Campanis reached him first and offered him a $10,000 bonus to sign, about a dozen other teams had hoped to sign Clemente. One team, the Milwaukee Braves, promised Clemente a $30,000 bonus. It was a tempting offer.

Clemente discussed it with his parents. The Milwaukee bid excited Clemente. His father realized his son's feeling.

"Yes, it is much more than the man from the Dodgers said he would give you," his father said. "It's a fortune. But you have given your word to the Dodgers. Your word is worth more than the money."

So, on February 19, 1954, Campanis signed Clemente to a Dodgers' contract. Clemente was happy. The Dodgers were the first team in modern major league history to employ a black player, Jackie Robinson. And Robinson was one of Clemente's heroes. The Dodgers thought so highly of Clemente that they assigned him to their top farm club, the Montreal Royals of the Class AAA International League. It was quite a beginning for a 19-year-old. But it didn't go smoothly.

Clemente reported to Montreal with a bad back. He had injured his back that winter playing with Santurce in the Puerto Rican League. Clemente switched to a lighter bat and the first time he used it in a game, he whipped it around so fast that he hurt his spine. It was the start of back trouble that was to plague Clemente throughout his long career. Besides the back ailment, Clemente encountered other problems not related to baseball. He spoke little English. Luckily, there were several Spanish-speaking players on the team, alleviating the problem to a degree.

However, the thing that troubled him most, was the fact that he was black. When the Royals traveled south to play in Richmond, Virginia, Clemente and the other black players could not stay in the same hotel as the rest of the team. They couldn't even eat in the same restaurants as the white players. It was very perplexing to Clemente. As a 19-year-old away from his native Puerto Rico for the first time in his life, he had trouble adjusting to the mores of society.

He also found it difficult to understand baseball. He knew he was the best outfielder on the Montreal team. Yet, he didn't play regularly. One day he blasted three triples in a game. It buoyed his spirits. But the next day, instead of starting, he was benched. He couldn't understand why. However, it was all designed. The Dodgers were trying to keep Clemente under wraps. At that time, if a player was signed to a bonus of $4,000 or more, he was obligated to play an entire season in the minors. But at the end of the first year, he had to be brought up to the parent club or else be placed on the market for sale to another club. The Dodgers didn't need any outfield help in 1954. By not playing regularly with Montreal, they felt Clemente would not attract the interest of any other major league team. If the Dodgers succeeded in their ploy, Clemente then would be eligible to return to Montreal for another year.

Ironically, it was in Richmond where Clemente caught the attention of the Pirates. Branch Rickey, the former Dodgers' sage who then was running the Pirates, dispatched his pitching coach, Clyde Sukeforth, to Richmond. He wanted Sukeforth to look over a pitcher named Joe Black. While he observed Black, Sukeforth was excited about the play of Clemente. He told Rickey that Clemente was a super prospect who could hit and field. The normally conservative Sukeforth never before had appeared so enthusiastic about a prospect.

"He could catch a fly ball in his hip pocket," Sukeforth told Rickey. "And he has an arm that could throw a baseball through a concrete wall."

The Pirates finished in last place in 1954 for the third straight year. Rickey, a shrewd baseball man, had remained silent about his interest in Clemente. He was waiting until the end of the year when the major leagues held their annual minor league draft meeting. Pittsburgh had first choice of any available minor leaguer. When the Dodgers' list of players was submitted, Clemente's name was listed. Rickey didn't hesitate. He picked Clemente, much to the chagrin of Dodgers' officials.

Over the winter, Clemente re-injured his back in an automobile accident. When he reported to the Pirates' spring training base at Fort Myers, Florida in 1955, he wasn't in top shape. But he hustled and made the team. However, Clemente couldn't prevent the Pirates from finishing in last place again. In his rookie season, he batted .255 despite the back problem that limited him to 124 games.

In 1956, Bobby Bragan replaced Fred Haney as manager of the Pirates. Clemente, working with batting coach Dick Sisler, overcame a weakness that opposing pitchers had detected during his rookie year. Clemente had a bad habit of bobbing his head and taking his eye off the ball when he swung. Opposing pitchers repeatedly made Clemente look bad by fooling him with a change of pace. Clemente swung at too many bad pitches. Sisler corrected the flaw and Clemente finished the season with a .311 average. He also thrilled fans with his outfield play. He had 20 assists in right field, often throwing out runners who had wandered too far off first base after a hit.

Back miseries again reduced Clemente's effectiveness in 1957. His back hurt so much that he often wore a brace when he played. His batting average slipped to .253. The next season he bounced back and hit .289 as the Pirates rose from last place to second with an 84-65 record. Pittsburgh fans had something to cheer about after the many years of losing.

They looked forward with anticipation to 1959. However, early in the season, Clemente was hit on the elbow with a pitch. He was sidelined for two months. The Pirates tumbled to fourth place. Clemente came under the jaundiced eyes of the press. They couldn't believe how one player could be injured so often. Even his manager, Danny Murtaugh, was growing weary of Clemente's ailments. He intimated that Clemente was dogging it. That cut Clemente deeply. It wounded his pride.

Clemente returned to Puerto Rico unhappy. He played winter ball but didn't go out much with his friends. He would leave the ballpark after a game and go straight home. He kept pretty much to himself, occupying his time by making wood carvings. The hobby brought him some inner peace. But at times, Clemente would sulk. He kept wondering why others didn't believe in him, didn't understand him. He was more determined than ever to have a big year in 1960.

The Pirates were the most exciting club in the major leagues that season. More than 20 times, they won games in the last inning. In 12 of those games, they scored the winning run after two were out. In addition to his hitting, Clemente won and saved games with his play in the outfield. But there still were the injuries.

One injury occurred for everyone to see, even his critics. In a game against the San Francisco Giants, Willie Mays hit a drive toward the right field wall. Clemente sped back, made the catch and crashed into the concrete. He held onto the ball as blood began to stream down his face. Dazed after the play, Clemente was taken to a hospital where he remained for five days. When he returned to action, he continued to hit and field well, sparking the Pirates to their first pennant in 33 years. Pittsburgh beat the New York Yankees, 10-9, on Bill Mazeroski's dramatic ninth-inning home run in the seventh game. Clemente hit safely in every game, leading the Pirates with nine hits and batting .320.

Although the Pirates slumped to sixth place in 1961, Clemente led the league in hitting with .351. When he hit .312 the following year, some called it a disappointing season. Clemente was puzzled by the criticism.

"I don't understand it," he said angrily. "They say I am not a team player, that I do not give my best. But I have won four batting titles. I kill myself in the outfield. I try to catch any ball hit in the park. I throw my arm out for the Pirates and I play when I am hurt. Mickey Mantle is like a god. But if a black or a Latin American is hurting, they say he is imagining things."

Clemente was indeed a team player. On a day when Mazeroski was being honored, Clemente was about to leave the clubhouse and head for the dugout. He looked over at three players who were playing cards.

Clemente was upset. He didn't mince his words as he yelled at them.

"They are honoring a great player and teammate out there on the field," shouted Clemente. "I will give you three minutes to get outside to see it, or you will have to fight me."

In 1966, Clemente enjoyed one of his greatest seasons. He played for a manager who believed in him, Harry Walker. Clemente was appreciative.

"I will leave it up to you whether or not you should play," Walker told Clemente. "I will believe you if you say you are hurt. I trust you."

Clemente returned the trust. He batted .317 and hit a career-high 29 home runs. In a span of less than two weeks, he hit six homers. Two of the homers went over the exit gate in right center field in old Forbes Field. The balls were estimated to have traveled over 500 feet and nobody remembers any player ever smashing two homers over that mark. Clemente also knocked in 119 runs and scored 105. He accounted for 342 total bases, second only to Felipe Alou's league-leading 355. Clemente was hoping that he finally would be recognized as the league's most valuable player. It was between him and Sandy Koufax of the Dodgers. When the votes were counted, Clemente had won. He was the first Latin American player to win the award.

Yet, it wasn't until 1971 when Clemente, at the age of 37, was fully recognized for his consummate ability. The Pirates won the pennant and met Baltimore in the World Series. Again Clemente hit safely in all seven games as the Pirates overcame a two-game deficit and won the Series. Clemente performed brilliantly. He hit .414 with 12 hits in 29 at-bats, including two homers, a triple and two doubles. His second home run enabled the Pirates to win the dramatic final game, 2-1. Clemente was unanimously voted the Series' most valuable player.

"Clemente was ashamed," said Sanguillen who batted .379 in the Series. "He was 37 years old, and they said that he had to have a great World Series or else people would not know how great he was. He was so ashamed. He'd tell me, 'Oh, when I was younger, I was so much better.'"

Once during the Series, Clemente cried after a game. Merv Rettenmund of Baltimore was on second base when Boog Powell hit a long fly ball that Clemente one-handed in deep right field. Rettenmund alertly tagged up and sped to third base, barely beating Clemente's remarkable 300-foot throw. Later in the clubhouse, Clemente's teammates congratulated him on such a magnificent throw, saying anyone but the speedy Rettenmund would have been thrown out.

"Ten years ago," Clemente said weeping, "I throw anybody out."

Perhaps more than anyone, Clemente realized that he was nearing the end of a long career with the Pirates. Yet, nobody realized when he reached the 3,000 hit milestone at the close of the 1972 season, that it would be his final significant accomplishment on a baseball field. As always, Clemente returned to Puerto Rico after the season. He didn't play much baseball that winter, but rested and looked forward to joining the Pirates for his 19th season.

It was New Year's Eve, a day that holds a special meaning for the Puerto Rican people. Not only is it a day for merriment, but it is one of prayer.

It still was too early in the day to celebrate the awakening of 1973. The heat of the mid-morning sun was beginning to make the day uncomfortable. At the San Juan Airport, some workers were busy loading cargo into a shopworn DC-7. They were off at a far end of the airport, almost unnoticed. The approaching flight was not a regular commercial plane. Instead, it was a special charter flight that was scheduled to take off as soon as the cargo was loaded and secured. The flight already had been delayed a day because of mechanical problems. And under that hot sun, Clemente was giving orders to the laborers, hurrying them on.

A week earlier, a massive earthquake had shaken the Central American country of Nicaragua. Not only was the damage extensive, but thousands of people were killed and thousands more were injured. A concerned world sent food and supplies to the little country. Clemente spearheaded Puerto Rico's aid. As chairman of the Puerto Rican Relief Committee, he telephoned hundreds of friends on the island to solicit money in order to buy much-needed supplies for the homeless victims accross the ocean. He was determined that the food, medicine and clothing would get to Nicaragua.

Clemente getting his 3,000th hit in game against the New York Mets on September 30, 1972.

An electric sign on a hill in Pittsburgh says it all the night Clemente died in a plane crash.

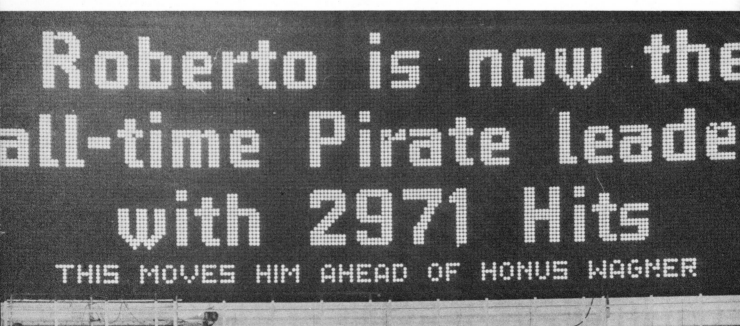

Roberto is now the all-time Pirate leader with 2971 Hits

THIS MOVES HIM AHEAD OF HONUS WAGNER

Originally, Clemente didn't intend to go on the flight. But a few days earlier, he had received a phone call from the president of Nicaragua. The president explained to Clemente that he was worried because a great deal of the supplies sent by other countries were being intercepted by black market profiteers. Clemente also was upset and promised the Nicaraguan president that he would see that the supplies he was sending would arrive safely to government officials.

The Pirates' superstar had certain ties to Nicaragua. In 1971, Clemente was manager of the Puerto Rican team that played in the amateur baseball championship in Managua. At the time, Clemente paid a hospital visit to one of his fans, a young boy who had lost both of his legs in an accident a month earlier. Clemente was moved by the youngster's spirit.

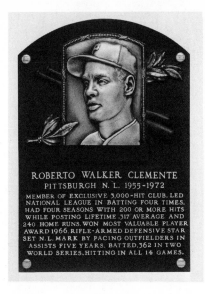

ROBERTO WALKER CLEMENTE
PITTSBURGH N. L. 1955-1972
MEMBER OF EXCLUSIVE 3,000-HIT CLUB. LED
NATIONAL LEAGUE IN BATTING FOUR TIMES.
HAD FOUR SEASONS WITH 200 OR MORE HITS
WHILE POSTING LIFETIME .317 AVERAGE AND
240 HOME RUNS. WON MOST VALUABLE PLAYER
AWARD 1966. RIFLE-ARMED DEFENSIVE STAR
SET N.L. MARK BY PACING OUTFIELDERS IN
ASSISTS FIVE YEARS. BATTED .362 IN TWO
WORLD SERIES, HITTING IN ALL 14 GAMES.

Clemente with his wife, Vera, and their three sons.

While he still was in Managua, he made arrangements for the boy to be fitted with artificial limbs. The upcoming flight had an extra meaning for him. Besides his mission of mercy to the quake victims, Clemente would also get an opportunity to check on the progress of his little friend.

Sanguillen, who was playing winter ball in Puerto Rico at the time, was with Clemente at the airport. While Clemente's eyes sparkled with anticipation, Sanguillen had a worried look. He didn't like the condition of the plane or the way the cargo was being loaded. He begged Clemente not to make the trip.

"Roberto," pleaded Sanguillen, "I don't like the way these things are being placed in the plane. Nobody knows if all the weight is balanced."

There was cause for Sanguillen's concern. The cargo was being placed all over the plane, into any open space found by the workers. The boxes were piled high on top of each other. Nobody even thought about weighing the cargo. Clemente's main concern was delivering it.

"We will have to take the chance," he told Sanguillen. "We must get these supplies to Nicaragua by tonight."

Still, Sanguillen insisted that Clemente not go.

"I wish you were not going," said Sanguillen. "I do not trust this plane."

Clemente just smiled.

"When your time comes and it is your turn to die, there is nothing you can do," said Clemente.

In addition to Sanguillen, several others on the island were concerned about the plane. The old four-engine craft had been involved in an earlier accident. Yet, it was the only plane Clemente could charter at the time. Two of the plane's engines had been repaired and the craft was fitted with two new propellers. The plane's crew was unconcerned and told Clemente that everything was fine.

Clemente went home and said goodbye to his wife, Vera, and his three little boys. His wife was preparing to take the children to her mother's house and accompany Clemente back to the airport. Within an hour, Clemente kissed his wife goodbye as the plane was about to depart.

"Don't wait for us to take off," he instructed his wife. "We still have some things to do. Go back and take care of the children."

While his parents were gone, Clemente's son Robertito had cried to his grandmother.

"Daddy has gone to Nicaragua, but he's not coming back," he sobbed.

"Nonsense, Robertito," assured the grandmother. "He will be back in three days."

Meanwhile, there was another strange occurrence on the other side of the island. In Carolina, Clemente's hometown, his father, Melchor, was troubled. He was disturbed about a terrible dream he had, and told his wife, Luisa, about it when he awoke.

"I had a very bad dream," he said. "I dreamt I saw an airplane crash into the sea."

His wife tried to dismiss it.

"It was not our Roberto's plane," she replied. "God will not do such a thing to our son."

Melchor wasn't satisfied with her answer.

"But Roberto shouldn't be making this trip on New Year's Eve," he insisted. "He should be home with his family."

Later that afternoon, Clemente climbed aboard his old plane. He was ready for the 1,200-mile trip to Nicaragua, knowing that in less than four hours he would deliver his cargo. The pilot warmed up the engines and a few minutes later got clearance for takeoff. Slowly, the plane headed down the runway with Clemente and three crew members aboard. It lifted off slowly and began to head west over the Atlantic in the face of a strong wind. As the plane circled, one of the engines exploded. The pilot immediately radioed the control tower and informed the operator that he was returning. Seconds after his broadcast, there were a couple of more explosions, and then another. The plane was out of control. It crashed into the ocean which was being whipped by the winds. In a few minutes, the plane sunk. At the age of 38, Roberto Clemente was dead!

The news of the plane crash shocked the entire island. Rescue squads were quickly dispatched to the area where the plane went down. The rescuers couldn't find anything. Divers attempted to probe the waters but couldn't see anything. Sanguillen, who was going to play a game that night, rushed to the crash site. Distraught, he made several dives into the water. He wanted to continue, hoping against all odds that he would find Clemente. He finally had to be restrained by others who convinced him that sharks might be in the area. Helpless, Sanguillen cried. He had lost his best friend. Church bells tolled throughout the entire island. And in Pittsburgh, high on a hill, an advertiser's sign changed its electric message to read, "Adios Amigo Roberto."

Clemente's spirit never really left the Pirates. The nation's baseball writers met in the spring of 1973 and were unanimous in their agreement to waive the mandatory five-year period required before a player could be eligible for voting into the Hall of Fame. They changed the rule for Clemente and voted him in at a special election. The Pirates retired his number "21." Suddenly, there weren't enough honors that could be bestowed upon Clemente, a superstar who was never fully appreciated until the end.

"He was the most decent man I ever met." said Pirates' pitcher Steve Blass. "And yet, no one seemed to understand him."

Maybe now they will.

Dave Parker

For the third straight year, the Pittsburgh Pirates had finished second in the Eastern Division of the National League. There wouldn't be any playoffs or World Series for them. Yet, on the final day of the 1978 season, the fans in Three Rivers Stadium were on their feet applauding the Pirates as members of the division-winning Philadelphia Phillies watched in amazement.

Manager Chuck Tanner created a dramatic moment in a meaningless game to show his appreciation for Dave Parker. He also wanted the fans in Pittsburgh to display their admiration and they responded enthusiastically. Replacing a player in the field is a unique occurrence in baseball. It is a gesture that is characteristic of basketball or football, occurring during a time out when a star player is replaced with the total attention of the fans fixed at that moment. Yet, Tanner had a feeling for the dramatics. As Parker trotted in from right field, the fans gave him a standing ovation all the way to the dugout where the big outfielder received the congratulations of his teammates.

Parker had concluded another great season. He had batted .334 to lead the league in hitting for the second straight year. The fans acknowledged that with their applause. But they also were wondering whether they had seen the last of Parker in a Pirates' uniform. Although Parker had one year remaining on his $200,000-a-year contract, he and his agent, Tom Reich, wanted to renegotiate for a longer and more lucrative deal. Parker had expressed his desire to remain in Pittsburgh. He was happy with his teammates. He had a good rapport with Tanner and Willie Stargell, and at the still youthful age of 27, he had not reached his peak. However, Parker had an explicit demand. He insisted that his contract dealings with the club be concluded before the beginning of spring training in 1979. He did not want to begin the new season with an overhanging distraction that would affect his concentration on the field.

The Pirates had to sign Parker or risk losing him to the free agent market at the end of the 1979 season. Then, they wouldn't get any compensation for Parker. They had one other

option. If they failed to satisfy Parker's contract demands, they could trade him. The team's president, Dan Galbreath, wanted Parker to remain a member of the Pirates. So did Harding Peterson, the general manager. He looked upon Parker as the backbone of the Pirates for the next 10 years and said he hoped to sign the big slugger by Thanksgiving Day of 1978.

A week before Thanksgiving, the phone rang in Parker's home. He had just finished dinner and was relaxing in front of the fireplace with his dog lying next to him. The telephone call brought a large measure of joy to Parker. He was informed that he had been voted the most valuable player in the National League.

"Oh! Wow!" exclaimed Parker. "This is something else. I'm going to celebrate. Oh! Wow! This is the greatest. When you win the MVP in the major leagues, it's the greatest thing that can ever happen to you.

"I said last season, 'When the leaves turn brown, I'll be wearing my second batting crown.' At this time, I'll say that when the leaves turn green, I'll be playing for the same team."

Tanner smiled. So did Peterson. Tanner thinks that Parker is the greatest player in the game today. Peterson knew he would have to pay Parker a high sum to sign him. During the summer of 1978, a newspaper poll of baseball's general managers revealed that Parker was the player they most coveted. It didn't go past Peterson. He also realized that the evaluation by others placed Parker in the million dollar bracket. Two months later, Parker signed a five-year contract worth $7 million. The amount made Parker the highest paid athlete in a team sport. It wasn't an inflated dollar, either. The league's other general managers would have gladly paid him the same amount because they also recognized his value.

"Well, basically I think those general managers are right," Parker said with a chuckle. "I didn't vote me the best. The general managers did. It's better for them to say it than for me to say it. I shouldn't be poppin' my bib like that.

"I just feel like I'm the Rolls Royce of baseball players, the best, the finest tuned. I always knew I had the ability to reach that goal. My salary only proves that my team recognizes that. I have a responsibility to give the people who come to the park their money's worth. Once I cross those lines, I play as hard as I can. I will play as hard as I can if there are ten people in the park or 40,000. I take pride in my ability as an athlete. I have no control over how I play. That's just the way I'm built. When I cross those white lines I go into automatic pilot. I can't play the game any other way. I want to show the public a player can get lifetime security and still play the game aggressively. I've seen other guys get secure in this game and their interests change. They get sidetracked in business fields. I got a lot of baseball to play yet."

Parker is aggressive in everything he does, hitting, running, throwing and fielding. He plays the game with a consummate passion, as if every game was his last. There were times when Parker was injured seriously because of his all-out play. The most serious injury occurred during the 1978 season on a play that Parker never will forget.

The Pirates were playing the New York Mets on June 30 in Three Rivers Stadium. Parker was at second base when he broke for third on a hit. He was intent on scoring and turned toward home at full speed. John Stearns, the ruggedly-built Mets' catcher, positioned himself for the throw. Just as Stearns caught the ball and swept his arm to tag Parker, the two collided with a sickening thud. Players from both dugouts ran to home plate as Parker and Stearns lay motionless on the ground. Stearns got up with bruised ribs and sore legs. Parker had to be helped from the field. He was a frightening sight. Blood was oozing from his mouth and left eye.

Parker's left cheekbone was depressed. Three of his bones were cracked. Surgery was necessary to repair the damage. Five days later, Dr. Eugene Myers operated on Parker. The doctor placed a permanent wire in Parker's jaw. Miraculously, Parker returned to

the lineup ten days after the operation wearing a specially constructed helmet with a football mask to protect his injured cheek.

Parker had been elected to the All-Star game, but his injury prevented him from playing. He returned to action on July 16 after having missed eleven games. The first week he didn't experience any great difficulty in hitting with the cumbersome mask. But then he went into a batting slump, the first of his career. His average, which was .315 at the time, slipped to .288. His weight also dropped. Parker lost 17 pounds from his 235-pound frame.

"I never experienced anything like it," Parker said about the slump. "Not in the Knothole League, American Legion, or the majors."

But Parker never quit. Despite the pain in his cheek, which throbbed at times like a dull ache, Parker did not complain or make excuses for his hitting woes. He wanted to play

every day. He wanted desperately to win his second straight batting title. Parker sparked the Pirates' strong September run at the pennant. During the month, he was the club's hottest hitter, with a .415 average. He fell just short of collecting 200 hits, finishing with 196. Still, he had a career high 30 home runs, 12 triples and 117 runs batted in.

Prior to the collision with Stearns, Parker had left some other catchers in pain. One who felt Parker's aggressiveness was Steve Yeager of the Los Angeles Dodgers. Yeager was knocked unconscious in a collision with Parker. Another was John Oates, who was with the Philadelphia Phillies in 1976. His crash with Parker left Oates with a broken collarbone. Since he was wearing a chest protector at the time of impact, it only accented the force with which Parker crashed into Oates. The catcher vividly remembers the incident.

"I thought I could hit Parker low," explained Oates, "then tag him as he went over me. Instead, he went right through me."

Although aggressive on the field, Parker is the opposite off it. He is a blithe spirit. He is expressive. He is quick-witted. He is flamboyant. Since he also is big and colorful, he immediately draws attention when he enters a clubhouse. In fact, he creates attention. Parker is quick to greet his teammates, often with jibes almost as soon as he sets foot in the door. They expect the kidding. His chief adversary is Phil Garner, who takes delight in chiding Parker. Most of the other players look on with amusement.

Parker was a few days late in reporting to training camp in 1979. Garner rode him verbally about how he had signed for that huge sum of money and didn't care any longer about playing ball. Parker just smiled and waited to get back at Garner. Despite all his clubhouse bantering, Parker had serious goals for the 1979 season. He wanted to play in the World Series for the first time and he wanted to win the Triple Crown. Only 11 players have led the league in batting, home runs and runs-batted-in during a single season. The last time

a National League player did it was in 1937.

"I've never worried about my batting average." said Parker. "Now I'm developing a home run swing and the RBI's will come. I'd like to win the Triple Crown like Frank Robinson did (with Baltimore) in 1966 because he was my idol. I want to get into the area of Willie Mays or Roberto Clemente. I'm going to push this God-given ability. I'm pursuing the ultimate.

"I wanted to make sure I received the highest salary in baseball, become the first million-dollar player. I'm the highest paid athlete in team sports, but I can live up to it. The public needs to see a player who's gotten security and then still goes out and applies himself. What I feel for the game makes me give 110 percent everytime I go out there, not the money. The highlight of the game to me is scoring from first on a double in such a way that people look at me in amazement, as if they are saying, 'My, how fast that big man can move.'

"Some of my satisfaction comes from people. I like to feel like a dominant source. I do everything well, so I get satisfaction from all phases of the game. Like when I make a good throw. If there's a runner on second and a fly ball is hit to right, the crowd anticipates my throw. They're all on their feet now. I make a good throw, and they're all saying 'ooh' and 'wow.' That's my salary. I try to give them their money's worth. They see me running hard to first, and they say: 'Hey, that big guy can run.' I like to hit a triple and show my speed, hit a home run and show my power."

Television viewers received an exciting look at Parker's all-out play during the 1979 All-Star game. Although he only produced an infield single and a sacrifice fly at bat, it was Parker's outstanding outfield play that earned him the Most Valuable Player Award, a tribute indeed to his fielding. In fact, one play came after an embarrassing moment for Parker.

Jim Rice of the Boston Red Sox had hit a fly ball to Parker. Parker should have caught the ball easily, but he lost it in the lights at the

Seattle Kingdome. Rice tried to stretch the hit into a triple. As he raced for third, Parker fired a strike to third baseman Ron Cey of the Los Angeles Dodgers. Cey tagged out the sliding Rice.

An inning later, Parker was challenged again. The score was tied 6-6 when the American League mounted a threat. On a single to right field, Brian Downing of the California Angels tried to score from second base with the tie-breaking run. But Parker's strong, accurate throw to catcher Gary Carter of the Montreal Expos nailed Downing. Parker received extensive praise in the winning National League dressing room.

"You have to admire him, that he makes all that money, that he has all that security and still goes out and plays so hard," said Carter. "He goes out there and works and hustles. He has personal pride, and he wants to go out and do well."

Parker's strong and accurate throws helped make Tom Lasorda of the Dodgers the winning manager. Lasorda relishes winning games that command a great deal of attention, and always has been known to praise his players.

"I told Parker after he made the throw on Rice's hit that he had all the instinctive moves of a great outfielder," said Lasorda. "When he turned and threw the ball to third without even looking, it came in like a shot out of a cannon. He's just a tremendous player."

Parker was moved by the praise because it had come from rival players and managers.

"I never thought about X amount of dollars when I was playing tonight," said Parker. "Pride takes over. It's a pleasure and an honor to be here. Anybody who is not here is missing something. Maybe some people will forget now that I'm not hitting .330 but they have a right to expect me to hit .330. I expect it myself.

"I guess it's hard for some people to relate to a person making the kind of money I am making. It's hard for them to imagine a guy making that much money just for playing baseball. They don't understand that we're the top 500 or 600 men in a profession that

43

millions aspire to and millions watch as entertainment. It has nothing to do with money. You play for pride."

Because he's big and brash and outspoken, Parker occasionally is misunderstood. Some look upon him as a showboat. It's a misconception. He just does things with flair whether it is swinging a bat, catching a ball, running the bases or wearing a gold Star of David chain around his neck. For those who ask about the chain, Parker has a ready answer. He shrugs his shoulders and replies that he is a star and his name is David. His answer is honest and yet some are offended by it. That's where the misunderstanding occurs. Much like Joe Namath, Parker has charisma. Only the great ones have it. There is a thin line between greatness and ego. It is one thing to boast and not deliver. But Parker delivers.

"I'm kind of a flashy player," admits Parker. "I've popped off, and then I've backed it up. I've predicted two batting titles, and I've won them. In 1978 I hit only .310, and people said that I had an off year. You know what? They're right. A lot of things were involved. I twisted my left knee and that forced me to play cautiously at times, not to take the extra base or steal a base when we were five runs ahead.

"I never said I was the greatest player in the game, initially. The experts did. Sure, I'm verbal. I verbalize to get up for the game. I got to get in there and air it out. The reason the great (Muhammad) Ali said he talked a lot was that he put himself on the line and then had to go out and back it up. I push myself in that regard. Without a doubt, I can do all the things I've said I can."

Maybe even more. Tanner, who has been around baseball for 34 years, thinks so. He is Parker's biggest booster.

"He's the best player in the game today," said Tanner. "Nobody can touch him. He'll be even greater when he's between 30 and 35 years old. It's frightening how good he can become. The reason is simple. Parker is intelligent, and he'll never stop improving. If he has three great years in a row, he won't look

44

back. He will look ahead. He will say to himself, 'I got to do something to top last season.'"

Parker has hit over .300 each of the last five years. He might have hit that high in his first full season with the club in 1974. Parker finished with a .282 average but missed ten weeks of the season with a painfully pulled hamstring muscle. Yet, the consistency he has displayed the past five years has drawn comparisons between Parker and Clemente. Parker already has statistical advantages over the Pirates' Hall of Famer in several categories, including batting average, runs batted in, home runs, doubles, runs scored and stolen bases.

When Parker was named the league's most valuable player in 1978, the comparisons to Clemente became more prominent. Clemente was the last Pirates' player to win the MVP Award in 1966. Only one other Pittsburgh player won the award, shortstop Dick Groat in 1960. Yet, with all the talk about Clemente and himself, Parker did not lose his perspective.

"If I just get close to what Clemente did for the Pirates, I'll be proud," said Parker. "I idolized Clemente in some ways. In spring training in 1972, I worked out with him in the outfield. He would say, 'Wooo, I used to be able to throw like that.' I found that to be a relaxing thing. Then Stargell took me under his wing. He is a soft-spoken, very kind individual, 24-karat gold. In '71, when I was playing A ball and he was hitting 48 home runs for Pittsburgh, I read where people would tell him that he was going great. And he would say that there was a guy in the minor leagues who was going to rewrite the record books."

Parker and Stargell are close. Parker looks upon Stargell as a father image. Whenever Parker has any personal problems, he discusses them with Stargell. After Parker won a Gold Glove Award for his fielding in 1978, he walked over to Stargell during spring training one day in 1979, hugged him and wished him happy birthday. He then handed a golden baseball that he ripped off his trophy to the 38-year-old veteran. Stargell looked at it in amazement. Parker wanted Stargell to share in the award because he was appreciative of the fact that Willie had helped him with his fielding.

Stargell admires greatness. He has been with the Pirates since 1962 and admiringly watched Clemente win four batting titles. Now Stargell is admiring Parker.

"He's one of those rare individuals who come along every 15 or 20 years," claimed Stargell. "Rare and unique and strong. There's no telling what he can accomplish. No pitcher can intimidate him. And if they get him out, he forgets it. He understands it's a matter of saying, 'Okay, he's tough, but so am I.' He has a drive which makes him devastating.

"If you appreciate art, you look at the whole picture. That's how you have to see him, the way he backs up the bases, how he gets off so fast in the first three steps going after a ball but always gets control of his body, the way he plays the outfield like a madman when he's not hitting. He's like the tenth man in softball out there. On a ground ball he's backing up first before I'm there to take the throw. We were both after a foul ball one time with our arms outstretched, and we came together face to face like two big pairs of scissors. It was the only time that I ever kissed him. We hit and flew apart by yards and yards. He talks a lot to keep people loose, but he doesn't mean any of it. Just stick around and watch him for the next 15 years."

It is inconceivable that Parker will play for another 15 years, but that's how special he appears in Stargell's eyes. No matter how many years he plays, Parker never will stop trying to be the best. His strong inner sense of pride drives him, makes him want to excel far more than any player in the game.

Since his young days, Parker has had a fierce desire to succeed. He has done it quickly. It has been only ten years since Parker came out of a rough neighborhood in Cincinnati. He grew up, or perhaps survived, in the South Cummingsville ghetto near Crosley Field because of his athletic prowess

and his ability to fight. Parker was an accomplished street fighter. He knew pain and sorrow, but he never lost the perspective of wanting to get out for a place in the sun. When a knee injury in high school jeopardized his football career, he concentrated on baseball. Even then it was a struggle. He had to use his fists to stay on top.

"I was a young bully who got respect by treating everyone the way I wanted to be treated, sort of a neighborhood equalizer," recalled Parker. "I was the leader of a club called the 'Mod Spot.' It's a competitive thing to live in a ghetto. You're always thinking, 'I'm going to get out, some way.' My dad struggled. He and I had some misunderstandings. I moved in with some relatives for a while, but there was a lot of love, still is."

The love was extended by his oldest sister, Dorothy. She pleaded with Parker to come home during his junior year in high school because their mother missed him. Dorothy also emphasized that he had a career in baseball to pursue. Parker returned home. He began playing baseball again and made it to the Connie Mack World Series where a number of major league scouts saw him play. Parker seemed happy again.

"I always loved baseball," said Parker. "I lived at Crosley Field, even worked there. I was the worst vendor in history. I kept watching Frank Robinson and Vada Pinson and never really sold any hot dogs. I'd go home and fantasize about being them, having cars like they did—matching white Thunderbirds with red upholstery. I was always telling my mother, 'I'm going to be a baseball star and buy you a new home.'"

There must have been some doubts, not on Parker's part but in the minds of baseball scouts. In the 1970 free agent draft, Parker was not chosen during the early rounds. In fact, it wasn't until the 14th round before the Pirates finally selected him. Parker was far from discouraged. He felt the reasons he was picked so late were that the scouts were worried about his knee injury and that he was looked upon as a militant because of stories about how he always argued with his coaches. He signed a $6,500 contract with Pittsburgh and went to play for Bradenton in the Florida Rookie League. Now, only ten years after signing his first professional baseball contract, Parker is making a million dollars a year. Nobody in baseball made it so quickly. Who would have imagined that a 14th-round pick would someday be worth a million dollars?

49

At left, Parker is helped off the field after 1978 home plate mishap.

When Parker joined the other Pirates' rookies, he was listed as a slow-footed catcher. However, when Parker was clocked in 6.8 seconds for the 60-yard dash, the Pirates changed their minds. Parker was told to discard his catcher's mitt. The Pirates' thinking then was to make Parker an outfielder. Parker smiles when he recalls the decision.

"That 6.8 time was slow for me," confessed Parker. "My knee still wasn't strong. Besides, I almost got killed in the outfield a few times. Some of those fly balls almost hit me in the head."

Despite his fielding woes, Parker showed that he could hit. He was having a fine rookie season, batting .318. Then misfortune struck. Parker wasn't ready for it emotionally. His sister, Dorothy, died during childbirth. It hit Parker hard. He felt his world had come to an end. It was his first experience with death. A troubled Parker had bad dreams about his sister and couldn't concentrate on playing. He quit baseball and returned to Cincinnati, sad and heartbroken. But his mother convinced him that his place was in baseball, that he should go back to the game that made him happy. He listened and returned to Bradenton. He finished the season hitting .314.

In 1971 Parker was moved up to Class AA. He was assigned to the Pirates' Waterbury team, but had trouble getting started. After 30 games, he was batting only .228. The Pirates dropped him to Class A, and he finished the year with the Monroe team, hitting .358. It didn't go unnoticed by the Pirates. They invited Parker to join them for spring training in 1972.

Parker was thrilled. That was the year he met Clemente and Stargell. He has seen them both play while he was a youngster growing up in Cincinnati. Clemente was one of his heroes along with Robinson and Willie Mays. Now he was standing in right-field right next to Clemente. Parker felt awed and his hitting was awesome. His batting average in spring training was .400 and Parker was convinced that he had made the team. However, when the Pirates trimmed their roster, Parker was shocked when he was told that he was being sent to Salem in the Class A Carolina League. Peterson, the team's minor league director at the time, informed Parker about the decision near the batting cage during a morning workout. Angered, Parker threw his bat across the grass toward first base. Peterson became incensed at Parker's outburst and stomped over to the big outfielder.

"Go get that bat," ordered Peterson.

Parker looked at him without saying a word. Then he slowly began to retrieve the bat.

"You've been around here two years and you think you know everything," shouted Peterson.

Parker remained silent.

"Run!" screamed Peterson.

Parker turned toward the enraged Peterson.

Tanner adjusts cap on Parker after the big outfielder signed new contract in 1978.

"You talk to me like a man," said Parker. "I'm a man first. There's other things I could be doing."

Peterson was seething now. He ran up to Parker and started to grab him. Parker remained cool.

"Yeah, grab me," he said, challenging Peterson. "Give me a reason to punch you."

Peterson back off. The next day Parker left to join the Salem club. It was as if Parker played the entire year with a vengeance. He led the league with a .310 batting average, and led in at-bats, hits, runs scored, runs-batted-in, doubles and stolen bases. Parker answered back the best way he could, with his bat.

In 1973, Parker was elevated to Class AAA ball. He was assigned to Charleston, West Virginia. He hit .317, but he was unhappy. The Pirates weren't a serious pennant threat that season. They were struggling. It was obvious by August that they wouldn't finish in first place. Parker felt that he should be called up by Pittsburgh. He made his feelings known. When it didn't happen, Parker jumped the team.

"Pittsburgh was in fourth place, going nowhere in the second half of the season," said Parker. "I'd hit .300 everywhere I'd been. They had nothing to lose by bringing me up. I'd already given baseball three and a half years."

Parker returned home to Cincinnati. His mother and his father weren't pleased with his decision. They convinced him that he still was

53

young and would get his chance to play in the major leagues. Within a week, Parker smoothed over his differences with the Pirates and they told him to report to Pittsburgh. Parker couldn't have been happier. What he did was take his destiny into his own hands. He forced the Pirates to make a move.

"It was a power play," admitted Parker, "but I was ready."

He also was ready for the majors. The remainder of the 1973 season, Parker batted .288. There wouldn't be any more minor league towns for him. Parker was a major leaguer. He was with the Pirates the entire 1974 season, his first full year in the majors. By 1975, Parker stood on the threshold of stardom. He hit .308 that year and .313 in 1976, and has been hitting .300 ever since.

Yet, despite all that he has done, Parker gives the impression that he is ready to accomplish even better things. He still is young and has the God-given talents that he pushes to the hilt. He doesn't worry about how many home runs he will hit because he knows they will come. Parker has an unquenchable zest for the game because he has a genuine love affair with baseball. He is loud and he is brash, but baseball is his stage and there is perhaps no more colorful player in the game. Away from the arena, he is a quiet, private person. It is a unique contrast of Parker the baseball player and Parker the man. They are separate and yet they are one.

A couple of years ago, the Pirates were in Houston playing the Astros. After the game, two youngsters gained access to the Pirates' clubhouse. Innocently enough, they wanted Parker's autograph. One boy had a baseball. The other had a small piece of paper. Parker looked at both. He took the ball and signed it. However, he didn't sign the paper. Instead, Parker reached into his locker and picked up one of his gloves. He autographed it and gave it to the surprised youngster.

"I saw it happen," recalled Tanner. "Dave didn't make any noise about it. He did it quietly, and it was just one instance that shows the type of individual Dave Parker is."

In the years ahead, maybe everyone will get to know the real Dave Parker.

Willie Stargell

In 1975, he had batted .295, hit 22 home runs and knocked in 90 runs. At the age of 34, Willie Stargell appeared to have found the fountain of youth. Although he was approaching the autumn of his years, Stargell was anxiously awaiting the 1976 season. He was confident that he could continue his fine hitting and hoping to lead the Pirates to their first pennant in five years. Ever since the death of Roberto Clemente in 1972, Stargell had become the new leader of the Pirates. It was a role he had quietly assumed while the noise of his productive bat had led the Pirates to consecutive first-place finishes in the Eastern Division in 1974 and 1975.

The 1976 season was less than a month old when Stargell's life was suddenly interrupted. The intrusion came unexpectedly. It hit Stargell hard. The crisis didn't happen on the ball field. It happened far away from it. But it affected his life so dramatically. The trauma came so quickly that it scared him. Although he had come from a ghetto, he never was as frightened as this particular night. He felt powerless. That was the hardest part, being

there and not being able to do anything. In the early morning hours of May 24, when his wife Dolores was stricken with a blood clot on the brain, Willie Stargell wondered what life was all about. He'll never forget that night the rest of his life.

Earlier in the day, Stargell had played in a doubleheader. After dinner, he was relaxing at home with his wife, mostly sitting around watching television. Dolores complained about having a terrible headache. Then she began regurgitating. Stargell decided to take his wife to the hospital. But before he could get her there, she had a seizure. Stargell had not seen anything like it. After he finally reached the hospital, the doctors gave him the bad news: His wife had a blood clot in the lower part of her brain. It severely threatened her life. The doctors had to operate immediately. If the operation failed, Dolores would die. Even if it was successful, she faced the possible loss of her vitality. She would be a wheelchair victim.

"The doctors gave it to me straight," remembered Stargell. "They said I might lose her. They started operating at one o'clock in the morning and it took two-and-a-half hours to finish. Two-and-a-half hours! That's about the time it takes to play a baseball game. Those two-and-a-half hours seemed like a year. I sat there waiting and thinking of all the things we'd done and hadn't done. The mind plays all kinds of tricks on you at a time like that. You start thinking what if she pulls through the operation and she isn't going to be all right, you know, crippled or. . . ."

It was the longest night of Stargell's life. He waited at the hospital, alone with his thoughts. There wasn't anyone to comfort him. As he sat there in the early light of dawn, he prayed and he wondered. Miraculously, his wife survived the delicate operation. Now there was the waiting. It was agonizing. Every night, while she hung between life and death, Stargell maintained a vigil at her bedside. Only when she started to improve did Stargell return to the world of baseball. It wasn't easy. His concentration was practically destroyed.

"I had trouble keeping my mind on the game," admitted Stargell. "It was almost totally impossible to concentrate on baseball. I'd be out there physically, but mentally I was back in the hospital with her. She had tubes and needles sticking out of her when I saw her and it scared the hell out of me. I really couldn't concentrate. I could only see Dolores with all this equipment strapped on her. For days they said she could die at any moment."

This was a new kind of pressure for Stargell. After each game he would leave the ball park and drive to the hospital to be with his wife. The strain took a lot out of him. Thankfully, Dolores survived. She not only survived, but she regained her health. But for the rest of the season, Stargell was not able to blot out of his mind the pictures of the tubes, the needles, the pumps. It clearly was reflected in his play. He didn't produce in the manner that had made him the key to Pittsburgh's success since Clemente had died.

Stargell's average dropped to .257. He managed to hit 20 home runs, but his runs-batted-in total was only 65, his lowest figure since his first full year with the Pirates back in 1963. Stargell admitted that he was tired, that

the long ordeal of his wife's illness had taken its toll on him mentally, physically and emotionally. After the season, Stargell did a lot of thinking about his career. He felt the harrowing experience had made him psychologically stronger. Although he would draw from the past, he would look ahead to the 1977 season.

"When Dolores' blood clot happened, I just couldn't let myself hit rock bottom," explained Stargell. "That's the easy way out. Throw up your hands and quit. That's not what my life has been. That's not what it's going to be."

It was perhaps during that crisis that Stargell the man appeared bigger than Stargell the player. He developed inner strength, strength that transcended to his teammates. He became the Pirates' spiritual leader. He tied it all together in a knot which later became the team's family syndrome. It grew stronger with the years.

It wasn't easy. Despite his new outlook, which he openly shared with others, Stargell suffered a setback. It began during spring training, when he suffered an inner-ear ailment which sidelined him for the early weeks of the 1977 season. He constantly suffered from headaches and dizzy spells. Stargell couldn't play regularly, couldn't get into a groove. His physical ailments kept him out of action for days at a time.

In July, Stargell experienced another setback. He was in the dugout when a fight broke out during a game against the Philadelphia Phillies. Powerful Mike Schmidt didn't like a high, tight pitch that skinny Pittsburgh pitcher Bruce Kison had thrown at him. Schmidt ran to the mound and wrestled Kison to the ground. Stargell raced out toward the mound to act as a peacemaker. Somehow, in that tangled mess of bodies around the mound, Stargell injured his elbow.

"Schmidt had a neck-lock on Kison," explained Stargell. "I wanted to separate them. Schmidt is not your average neck-locker. I got bumped but I didn't feel any pain in my elbow. Later, my arm just stiffened up. The doctor asked me if I had bumped it. I said I might have during that little thing we had

with Philly the other day."

Then Stargell got the bad news. The doctors told him that he had a pinched nerve in his elbow that could only be alleviated by surgery. Stargell's season was over. He played in only 63 games, the fewest in his 15 years with the club. His batting average was a respectable .274, but he hit only 13 homers and drove in only 35 runs.

For the second straight winter Stargell did a great deal of thinking. He fully realized that he was at the crossroads of his long career. He didn't dismiss the prospect that his career might be over. After all, the injury plus his age made him think that baseball was for players younger than himself. He realized that he would have to work harder than ever during the off-season, exercising and pushing his body to great lengths. He faced the grim reality of having to make a comeback in 1978, at the age of 36. He was driven by pride to play the way he knew he still could perform. Not many players make it back at that age. But Stargell is special.

"I felt I should have hit .300 with about 30 homers and 100 RBI's last season, so for me it wasn't a good year," Stargell said while preparing for the 1978 campaign. "I know there were some people saying I was through, but nobody remembered to ask me about my feelings on the subject. They just summed things up in their own words. People don't realize that there are a lot of emotions in baseball or how much pride and deep feelings are worth. I still get butterflies before a game. That still means I give a damn.

"You know, any time you're hurt, you have to really fight for your credibility again. But I know everything is going to be all right. I'll be back hitting. Never mind what the doctors say. I just know I have the capability to have a good year. I have the desire to compete and be out there.

"I can't wait to get up there again. Not everybody graduated from the same school of psychology. Different guys handle this situation different ways. I probably would have retired long ago if we hadn't been contenders all

these years. It helps to have a cause to shoot for, to have everything on the line. I run my best race down the stretch."

Indeed the Pirates again were contenders in the 1978 Eastern Division race. And Stargell euphorically responded to the challenge of another championship, another stretch run. He hit .295, belted 28 home runs and knocked in 97 runs in 122 games. They were his highest totals since 1973 when he led the league with 44 home runs and 119 runs-batted-in. His performance earned him the Comeback Player of the Year Award.

Stargell was back. Affectionately called "Pops" by the other Pirates, he was the spiritual and inspirational force of the team. Pittsburgh made a strong stretch run at the Phillies that season. The Pirates closed fast the final weeks of the season but fell two games short of catching the first-place Phils. Despite the late-season excitement, the Pirates dropped below the one million mark in attendance for the first time since 1969.

More important to the players, however, Stargell brought a certain calmness to the club. He created a family-type atmosphere that had a wholesome effect on the players. The players were loose and happy. There was no room for tension amidst the blaring disco tapes in the clubhouse. These were a relaxed bunch of Pirates, and Pops was their leader.

Stargell promulgated the harmony. He comforted himself after a game with a cold bottle of white wine while others drank beer. He spent $1,500 to purchase about 6,000 little gold stars which he bestowed on players who earned them through their performances on the field. He wanted to make the players visible after a notable accomplishment. They became known as "Stargell's Stars." They were effective in harmonizing the family atmosphere promoted by Stargell.

"We're only playing out there," maintained Stargell. "If we had to concentrate so damned hard that we can't have any fun, we may as well put a suit on, sit in an office and give dictation to some secretary—that's how a business should be run.

"It wasn't always this way. But you must sit

back and evaluate what are the important things. Do you dwell on things that tear you down? Baseball is a helluva challenge and it damn sure ain't easy. But everybody has a choice. You decide what kind of life you want to live. A miserable life, or a happy life? I don't want to go to bed disliking anyone, or walk around grumpy as hell. What I try to do is adopt an attitude when I'm getting ready for the game.

"I tell myself, 'This is going to be the best day I've ever had in baseball . . . and the most enjoyable.' I try to put nothing but positive thoughts in my mind. We do want to have fun. We only have a few years in the game. There's so much to learn, so much to enjoy. You can't be tied up in knots and play baseball. When the umpire hollers 'Play Ball,' he says 'PLAY Ball.' That means fun, relaxation. He doesn't say 'Work Ball.'

"It's talent that gets a player here and mentality that keeps him here. You come into the game without ulcers. It's important to leave the game without ulcers. Each game should be cherished as a highlight of one's life. When I first got to the big leagues, I struck out seven times in a doubleheader in St. Louis. The eighth time I fouled out to the catcher. People clapped. The rest booed. It really hurt. I went home and cried. I kept asking myself, 'Is this what I want to do with my life?' I decided that I would have to put up with the action and the reaction. I was okay the next day."

And he was okay for nearly every one of his 18 years with the Pirates. The 1979 season was perhaps the most satisfying of his long career. He seemed to do it all for the Pirates, spiritually, emotionally and physically. He hit .281 with 32 home runs and 82 runs-batted-in. He sparked the club during the playoffs and during the World Series. But throughout the season, he provided the Pirates with inner strength. Dave Parker kidded about it.

"Pops Stargell? He can't hit, can't run, can't throw, but I love him anyway," said Parker. "He means a tremendous amount to everyone on this ball club. He's our leader, our stabilizer, and for me, my baseball father."

Parker wasn't the only one to appreciate

Stargell. Phil Garner was another.

"I have never seen him get mad," said the scrappy second baseman. "I know I can't do that. But it helps, because I find myself trying to emulate him. I know things eat at him but he's able to control them. He has great ability and a great love for the game. He's not a motivator in the sense that he's going to give great speeches."

Stargell's presence didn't go unnoticed by opposing players, either. Before Tim Foli joined the Pirates during the 1979 season, he had viewed Stargell from opposing dugouts for many years.

"I realized from playing against him that he was a dominating player," said Foli. "However, I didn't realize how dominating he is as an individual. He radiates respect. He always gives 110 percent."

Stargell's extra effort was magnified in a showcase like the World Series. But Stargell also had sparked the Pirates in their late-season pennant drive and into the championship playoffs against the Cincinnati Reds.

One hot, muggy night in August, Stargell had managed only a single in four at bats against the smoking fastballs of J.R. Richard of the Houston Astros. The modest performance didn't go unnoticed by Parker.

"Hey, Pops," needled Parker, "maybe you should start taking it easy. You're not getting around on the fastball anymore."

Stargell just smiled. He is different than most hitters. While today's hitters are obsessed with gimmicks like batting gloves and sponges, Stargell disdains such aids. He never wears a batting glove, even during the cold weather early and late in the season. Even routine pre-game batting practice is significant to him.

A great many hitters take batting practice with the idea of trying to hit the ball as far as they can. Stargell methodically goes through a designed ritual. In his first turn in the batting cage, he uses the time to loosen and stretch his massive back and shoulder muscles. He carries that practice into a game when he uses a series of windmill motions with his bat while waiting for the pitcher to deliver the ball. During his second turn of batting practice, Stargell tries

to hit the ball to all fields. Finally, when he engages in his final practice swings, Stargell concentrates on his home run stroke.

While some hitters switch to a lighter bat against a pitcher like Richard, whose fastball has been timed at well over 90 miles an hour, Stargell does the opposite. His theory on hitting a pitcher with the velocity of Richard is to use a bat that is one ounce heavier than normal. In that way, Stargell feels he avoids committing himself too early on the fastball.

"It's an old trick I picked up from a pretty good player, Roberto Clemente," revealed Stargell.

He picked up more from Clemente. On a day long before the 1973 season. Stargell became the new leader of the Pirates. It was the Pirates' first spring in 18 years without Clemente. Only two months earlier, he had died in a plane crash. Stargell was discussing Clemente's death with a writer. The two sat talking in empty, sun-splashed bleachers in Bradenton, Florida. There was a certain stillness in the air, and the realization that Clemente wouldn't be there anymore after what seemed like a lifetime with the Pirates.

"I don't think you could say that I will be the team leader because Clemente is gone now," said Stargell. "He was my friend but he was a different man than me. But I learned a lot from him. I guess, yes, if there has to be a new leader right now, it might be me but I can't tell people how. I just have to try and do it."

That spring, more out of necessity than outward desire, Stargell emerged as the new leader of the Pirates. That spring, Stargell turned 33 years old. He met the new challenge as team leader. He batted .299 and led the National League in homers with 44, in runs-batted-in with 119 and in doubles with 43. Only once before, in 1971, did Stargell hit more homers, 48, or drive in more runs, 125.

And, like Clemente, Stargell never received the national acclaim he truly deserved until the dramatic 1979 World Series against the Baltimore Orioles. The 38-year-old patriarch continued the clutch hitting he had provided during the final pennant push and in the playoffs with a memorable performance that

Stargell in spring training in 1977.

reached its crescendo in the seventh game. Stargell was easily voted the Series' most valuable player.

In the excitement of the Pirates' clubhouse, champagne corks exploded wildly, and the bubbly stuff freely splashed around the crowded room. The players happily doused each other. It was an age-old ritual. Occasionally, the players took a drink from the bottles.

Everyone who was admitted into the locker room was looking for Stargell. It wasn't easy to reach him. The floor was strewn with uniforms, socks, caps and towels. Players hugged, and raised their fists and index fingers to signify the Pirates were No. 1. The noise was loud but nobody cared. And above the din was the music. It reverberated off the walls in a high pitch and reached every part of the room just as it had reached the hearts and minds of millions of baseball fans. It was Sister Sledge's well-worn rendition of "We Are Family."

It was Stargell's song. The players' song, the Pirates' song. It was this song that perhaps crystallized the Pittsburgh Pirates, that tied them together in some mystical way and made them winners, world champions.

The room was hot with the mass of humanity and the intense heat of the television camera lights. Stargell wasn't on camera now. Instead, he was off to one side of the room, a bottle of Chardonnay white California wine vintage 1977, in his hand. Pops, head of the family, savored the moment. It reflected on his face. He looked serene and happy, and behind the soft eyes one could almost detect the years of memories flashing by.

"We are family," someone shouted. Stargell smiled back softly. He had just completed his greatest season, greatest playoff and greatest World Series at an age when most athletes already had begun a second career somewhere away from the noise of the crowd. And more

Willie takes his cuts in 1972 in Bradenton.   Stargell tries Three Rivers batting cage in 1977.

than anything else at this particular moment, Stargell remembered his own family.

As he stood tall in the maelstrom of noise and people in the bedlam that was the Pirates' clubhouse, he spotted his sister, Sandra, among the crowd. He called for her to come close to him. She made her way through the crowd and Stargell waited for her before saying anything else. When Sandra reached him, they embraced. It was a display of true love and happiness. There also were tears. Stargell sniffed, then turned to the mob in front of him with his sister by his side.

"My sister, she knows what this night means to me," began Stargell. "She was with me when I signed with the Pittsburgh Pirates in 1959. She was with me when I broke in. I got a fifteen hundred dollar bonus and one-seventy five a month and you talk about an excited individual. That was the biggest thrill of my life . . . until now.

"When I was 17, I broke my pelvis playing football. The doctor put a pin in it and said, 'That's it, Willie. Forget about playing sports.' My sister will tell you, I told the family, 'I'll be damned if I'm gonna let one man tell me I can't play ball.' The next year I signed with the Pirates.

"At that time, my dream was just making it to the major leagues. Once I got to the majors, I wanted to win a World Series. We did that in 1971 and I thought, 'Okay, that's my fulfillment.' But then I knew I wouldn't be satisfied until we won again. This team is too much. I love these guys. I'll go to war with them any time.

"I'll never get to the point where I'll forget what it used to be like. Both my parents worked two jobs to make it better for me. My mother was a hairdresser and also worked in a cannery. My father worked there, too, and also at the Naval Air Station in Oakland. I had

69

to do most of the work in the house. I cooked, ironed, washed, cleaned up and had to take care of my younger sister. The other kids in the neighborhood were out playing and I had to stick around the crib and take care of the house."

It was amazing. This was Stargell's shining hour and he wasn't thinking of where he was, at the top of the baseball world, but rather from where he had come. It was quite revealing. It poignantly displayed why he was so genuine, so human. As he stood there, it was obvious why he was revered by teammates and rival players, as well as others with whom he had come in contact.

Born in Earlsboro, Oklahoma, Stargell and his parents moved to Alameda, California while he still was a youngster. Alameda was a lot different than Earlsboro. Stargell had to grow up and survive in a ghetto.

So, every year, Stargell returns to the ghetto. He goes back to his roots and extends his hand. He also asks other athletes, both black and white, to join him in helping the unfortunate kids in the ghetto. It's an important trip for Stargell. He gives his time and his money through the Black Athletes Foundation which he organized. Stargell concentrates a great deal of his time in fighting sickle cell anemia, a disease which has crippled or killed thousands of blacks. Among those who have joined Stargell in the fight to find a cure for the deadly disease have been Tom Seaver, Hank Aaron, Ernie Banks and Steve Carlton.

"We have raised money and received federal funds but we have found that we are most successful in our direct contact with ghetto kids," said Stargell. "The athletes donate money that they make from speaking engagements to the Foundation and they go directly into the ghetto and try to encourage the kids to get out. They know that we lead the good life and they want to do something about helping less fortunate people.

"It is just a question of doing something worthwhile. It is a matter of making others aware. The athlete's prominence places him at the top of the pyramid of our society. He can use that prominence to find a shortcut to get-

ting results. We find that often an athlete will walk into a company president's office at the same time as a salesman and that more often than not the executive will see the athlete first. People have always been saying, 'If you need help, ask.' Well, we walk into the executive's office and we ask.

"I've been in the ghetto and I know there is a way out. Now I want to go back into the ghetto and help lead others out. I've even asked people who ask me for my autograph to give me a dollar. I'm so involved with the fight against sickle cell. That way I'm doing something for them and they can do something for me. Autographs are so impersonal anyway. I feel kind of funny autographing something personal to someone I don't know. If a guy comes up and says, 'Can I have your autograph for my son Jim?' My feeling is, 'I don't know Jim. I'd rather sit down and talk to Jim.' At the same time, if there are 200 kids and they all want your autograph, you can't sit and talk to just one."

It was a long way from the ghetto to stardom for Stargell. But Stargell never forgot.

Last October, the manager across the way in the Baltimore clubhouse, Earl Weaver, never forgot the first time he saw Stargell. Even on the night, when Stargell destroyed his Orioles with his booming bat, Weaver remembered.

"I saw Willie in the Arizona Instructional League back around 1961," recalled Weaver. "I had a kid right-hander named Johnny Ellen pitching and he started out pitching Willie low. Willie hit that pitch over the right field fence. I told the kid to get the ball up, and the next time, he did, but Willie hit that one off the left field fence. 'Up more,' I told him the next time, and the pitch was across the letters and Willie drilled it into centerfield. The next time up, the kid threw one around Willie's cap. Willie almost took his head off with a liner and the kid yelled to me, 'That high enough?'"

Throughout his long, storied career with Pittsburgh, Stargell has experienced highs and lows. Through it all, he always has displayed an even temperament. No one can recall Stargell ever losing his temper.

"My father taught me one thing," said

Stargell. "He said that when things are going good for you, don't get too excited about it. And when things go bad, don't get down on yourself, either."

In the first month of the 1970 season, Stargell had a reason to get excited. But he didn't. During the abbreviated month of April, Stargell set a record for home runs for the month with 11. Naturally, the rest of the baseball world was excited. Some observers speculated that Stargell would break former New York Yankee outfielder Roger Maris' record of 61 homers. Stargell wasn't affected by the pressure put upon him by others or the excitement generated by his home run spree.

"I keep trying to tell people that this is not pressure," said Stargell. "Pressure is being raised in a government project, the way I was in Alameda. Pressure is thinking about whether something will turn up for dinner that night. Pressure is having to worry about paying your bills. Everyone confuses pressure with excitement. What I'm doing now is exciting. But pressure? Nah! Pressure to me is living from one day to another."

Perhaps Stargell felt pressure in 1976 and 1977. In 1976, he played most of the season under the severe emotional strain after his wife was struck by a clot on the brain. The following year he had to overcome the test of coming back from an injury at the age of 36 when many felt he was washed up. His leadership qualities came through in both experiences.

"The first time I knew Willie Stargell was a leader was when I first took over the club and told him that I was going to bat him fifth behind some of the speedsters I had on the club," disclosed Manager Chuck Tanner. "Here's a guy who had been batting fourth all of his life, and when I dropped him to fifth, he came in and told me that he thought it was a great idea.

"It was a big thing on his part to move from fourth to fifth and I knew right there what kind of leader he was. He has continued to prove it every day since I've been here. His attitude in the clubhouse inspires everyone. In his quiet way he is a leader. What a great

72

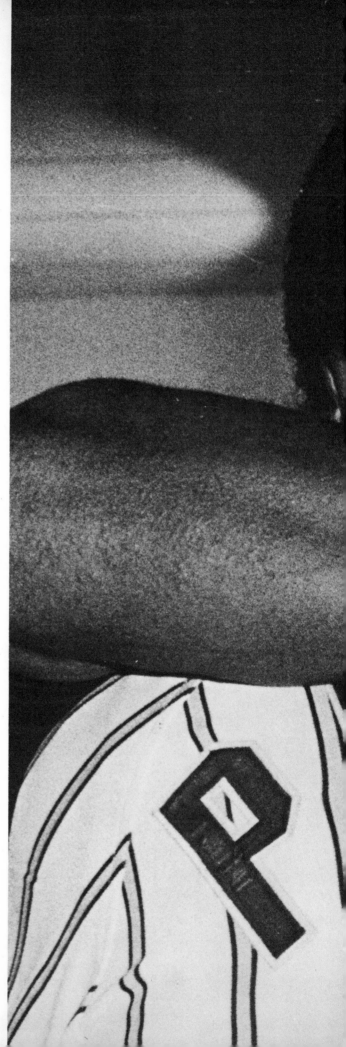

honor it is for me to manage a player like Willie Stargell.

"What can you say about a man who's so great that he's going to the Hall of Fame some day? When we were down, 1-0, in the last game of the Series, the guys on the bench said to him, 'Come on Pops, hit one and get us out of here.'"

Pops delivered. His two-run homer carried the Pirates to their fifth championship in seven appearances in the World Series. Stargell, who usually leaves quickly after a game, didn't that night. The night belonged to him.

"This is a touching moment," reflected Stargell. "After tomorrow, we disperse. We'll stay in touch, but we're all going back to our real families and the good living. I've made a lot of money. I have a lot to be thankful for. I have nothing to complain about."

He could have complained nearly a month later. When the vote for the National League's Most Valuable Player Award was announced, Stargell and Keith Hernandez of the St. Louis Cardinals finished in a first-place tie. It was the first time in the 49-year history of the prestigious award that it was shared by two players.

What created the deadlock was that Stargell was ignored by four of the writers who did the voting. If only one of them had given Stargell even a tenth-place vote, he would have been the winner. The amazing thing was that no player ever had won the award with as few first-place votes as received by Hernandez. Stargell collected ten first-place votes to only four for Hernandez. It was another milestone for Stargell, who twice had finished second in the MVP balloting, in 1971 to Joe Torre and in 1973 to Pete Rose.

"I'll take it," said Stargell. "What are we going to do, break it in half? I thought it would go to the guys who play every day. I don't play for awards, I play for rewards. But I'm happy for myself and I'm happy for Hernandez. I know what kind of player he is."

Stargell looks at awards differently than most athletes. While he was in New York to pick up an award for his World Series heroics, he didn't look upon the honor as possibly a

75

tool to get a bigger salary during his remaining years with the Pirates.

"I don't even like to talk about money," claimed Stargell. "What is important to me about the award is the fact that I'll be able to meet an awful lot of people I didn't know before. You learn something from meeting new people. I've always felt you are only going to be here a short length of time. Let's enjoy it. We're fortunate to be chosen to be out on that field, and we're responsible for our jobs."

He appeared completely relaxed. It still was early in the day and he was dressed in western garb. He had a felt cowboy hat next to him on the couch of a posh New York hotel.

"I'm part Seminole," revealed Stargell. "They're farmers and they've been trying to get me to wear this stuff for years. These hats and boots are so comfortable I don't know if I'll ever wear shoes again."

One thing is certain: he doesn't ever want to leave Pittsburgh. He has a love affair with the city and its people. If he had wanted to leave, he could have done so after the 1976 season when he would have become a free agent. But Stargell rejected higher financial offers from several clubs and remained with the Pirates.

"Why should I leave?" asked Stargell. "I love this city and I love this team."

It is a mutual love affair. Pittsburgh fans love Stargell, as do his teammates. He is the most popular Pirates' player.

"We all have a great deal of love and respect for Willie," said Garner. "Whatever he wants to do or say, it's law on our ballclub."

The family feeling was started and nurtured by Stargell. It is only natural for the players to call him Pops. It's a symbol of the love and affection they have for the veteran first baseman. It is perhaps the elixir that keeps him going, wanting to play a game generally reserved for those much younger.

"When I lose the desire to go out there every day, then I'll let some other excited youngster enjoy it," said Stargell. "Until then, someone will have to take it away. When I think of old, I think of 300-year-old sheep. It's a shame people dwell on age, because they give in to it. People said that I was washed up, but if I think I'm qualified to do something, nothing is going to hold me back. If I quit because I let someone influence me it would eat my heart out."

With a heart as big as Stargell's, that will not happen. He is "Family" . . . the leader of the Pittsburgh Pirates' close-knit family.

The Family

It was a different kind of spring, far different than any other. It took Lee Lacy only a couple of days to realize it. He had been signed by the Pirates as a free agent only a month earlier, after having played out his option with the Los Angeles Dodgers. In just a few days in Bradenton, he knew the Pirates' training camp was unlike any other that he had spent in six springs with the Dodgers and one year with the Atlanta Braves. Quite frankly, Lacy didn't know what to expect. He never had been exposed to the unabashed frivolity and candidness practiced by the Pirates' players. It didn't take him long to comprehend that it was a normal atmosphere for this team.

One day, Lacy was getting a rubdown. Suddenly, a grotesquely masked person jumped up at him from underneath the training table. Stunned, Lacy pulled back and clenched his fist, ready to defend himself. Ater a moment, Lacy recognized that his antagonist was pitcher Jim Rooker, the self-anointed clown of the clubhouse.

It was only the beginning. A short time later, the unsuspecting Lacy was asked if he ever had seen trainer Tony Bartirome display his strength, picking up three people at once. Lacy said no. Unknowingly, Lacy was being set up. He was about to fall prey to an old Pirates' ruse that Bartirome learned many years earlier from a Pittsburgh character called Socko McCarey. The trick didn't originate with McCarey. He in turn, had learned it from someone else, back in the 1920s. More than 50 years later, it still worked, for those innocent enough to want to see it.

The other players moved in for the kill. They knew they had a live subject in Lacy. Two players were picked. The third was Lacy, who was instructed to lie down between the other two. That was as far as Bartirome got to ever lifting anybody. Lacy was a dead duck at this point. He still didn't know what was going on, still anticipating to see Bartirome show his strength. Instead, Lacy's pants were unzipped and filled with any number of things such as shaving cream, chocolate milk, soda pop, baby oil, toothpaste, liniment or whatever item was handy. The fun over, Lacy got up shaking his head with laughter.

"All right, I love that spirit," he yelled.

Omar Moreno

79

We Are Family!

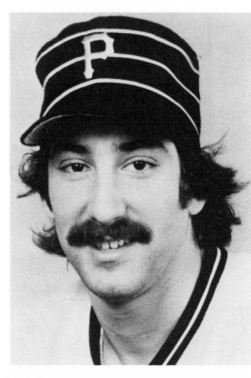

80   *Matt Alexander*   *Dale Berra*   *Jim Bibby*

Bert Blyleven

John Candelaria

Mike Easler

Tim Foli

Grant Jackson

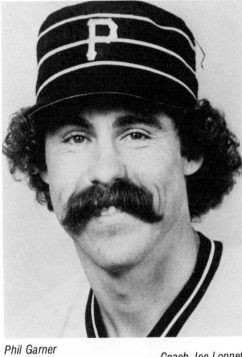
Phil Garner

Coach Joe Lonnett

Coach Harvey Haddix

Bill Madlock

Lee Lacy

John Milner

Coach Al Monchak

Omar Moreno Dave Parker

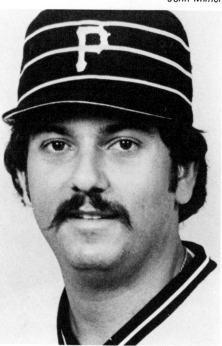
Steve Nicosia Dave Roberts

Ed Ott Bill Robinson

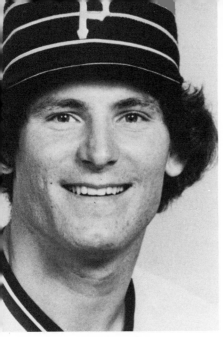

Don Robinson

Enrique Romo

Jim Rooker

Manny Sanguillen   Rennie Stennett   Willie Stargell   Manager Chuck Tanner

Coach Bob Skinner

Kent Tekulve

Lacy was formally initiated into the Pirates' family with a playful incident. No other team in baseball is as homogenous as the Pirates. It started years ago when Joe L. Brown was general manager, but it has not flourished as well as in recent years. Brown always told the veteran players to make the new ones feel at home.

"I think Lacy is rejoicing over getting out of that white-collar thing in L.A. and seeing some fun," noted Parker.

"I hear that when you get too loud in the Dodgers' clubhouse, they call you aside and say, 'We don't do that,'" said Phil Garner, the scrappy second baseman.

"We're different. Brotherly love is so much bull. You get 25 guys together, some from Puerto Rico and some from the ghetto and some from rich white neighborhoods, and a lot of them are bitter the way they grew up. Are you going to tell me they will all love each other? But this team gets it out in the open and brings everybody into it."

Only the previous day, Parker and Garner were enjoying the light attitude. Parker had reported to training camp two days late, leaving him wide open to Garner's barbs. Garner began needling Parker the minute he walked into the clubhouse.

"Yeah, that's it, get all that money and come down late," hollered Garner. "Prima donna! All you sportswriters put that in the newspapers. I've been down here busting my butt and he gets here when he pleases."

Parker was ready for Garner.

"If I hit like you do, I'd have been down here at Christmas," snapped Parker. "You think that perm you got makes you look like a brother, and that you'll hit like one."

As Parker went to his locker to dress, Garner explained the good-natured bantering to those who weren't accustomed to hearing it.

"Our needling has a purpose," explained Garner. "It's the way he gets up for a game, and it gets everyone else up. If you feel down, sorry for yourself, he gets the spark going in you. Dave's found that by picking on someone, mostly me, makes guys rally around, laugh. Suddenly, they're ready. It's group therapy."

Parker and Garner set the tone for the clubhouse atmosphere.

"Garner has great mental toughness," pointed out Parker. "I know he'll just shrug at most of what I say. He knows his strong points, so I pick on his weak ones and it helps him think about them."

It was time to hit. Garner, already dressed and waiting for the order to take batting practice, got up from his stool. Parker, still finishing dressing, came out from his locker looking for him.

"Where is that little bugger?" asked Parker.

He knew it was Garner who had taped a bubble-gum card of Mets' catcher John Stearns on his locker. Written on the card was "My hero."

"If I hit third this year, we'll win the pennant instead of finishing second again," chided Garner. "I'm leading the club in everything down here."

The Pirates were dedicated to being World Champions in 1979. For three straight years they had finished second. Being so close every time was becoming frustrating. In 1976, they had won 92 games. In 1977, they had won 96, and 1978, they had won 88, just falling short of catching the Philadelphia Phillies with a late stretch run.

Actually, the halcyon clubhouse ways of the Pirates had developed during the closing months of the 1978 season. Their strong finish had left them only 1½ games short. The memory of the race carried over to the spring.

"We came from 14 games back," pointed out Stargell, the patriarch of the Pirates. "We were extending our hands to everyone. When we just fell short, we wished we had another week to play. When we came to spring training this time, we were not prepared to lose."

The feeling was infectious. The entire team appeared loose and confident. Tanner felt that it was the best 25-man squad he had ever been given to manage. Of course, there were questions. Every team has them early in the spring. Specifically, the Pirates were concerned about whether Omar Moreno could hit better, whether Frank Taveras would acquire

Don Robinson

Bert Blyleven

Willie Stargell

John Candelaria

Kent Tekulve

Chuck Tanner

← Dave Parker

more range at shortstop, and with Garner playing permanently at second base, whether young Dale Berra could provide solid third base play. Also, would young, hard-throwing right-hander Don Robinson improve on his rookie record of 14-6 and, would John Candelaria come closer to the 20-victory season he had in 1977 than the 12-11 mark he had produced in 1978?

They weren't huge problems, but Tanner had to keep a sharp eye in those areas which could prove troublesome. After their close finish the previous year, the Pirates felt they had all the ingredients of a championship team. Others in Pittsburgh thought so, too. A young Pittsburgh announcer made some promotional spots with Parker after practice one afternoon. Parker was given the script and he did the "promo" about a half-dozen times,

"This is Dave Parker. I am glad I'm in Pittsburgh, I like the city, I like the Pirates and I like the fans. All of us together can bring the pennant back to Pittsburgh."

Yet, things didn't go smoothly the early weeks of the regular season. Harding Peterson, the Pirates' general manager, wasn't pleased by Taveras' play at shortstop. He felt that Taveras' erratic fielding was hurting the club. In a bold move during the third week of April, Peterson traded Taveras to the Mets for Tim Foli, who was languishing on the New York bench. The trade was a surprise because Pittsburgh had dealt a regular for a reserve. If Foli couldn't cut it with the Mets, how could he be expected to make it with the Pirates? It was a gamble.

The Mets had returned from a bus trip to nearby West Point, where they had played an exhibition game against Army. Joe McDonald, the Mets' general manager, walked up to Foli in the clubhouse at Shea Stadium. He quietly told Foli that he had been traded.

"Where?" asked Foli.

"Pittsburgh," answered McDonald. "For Frank Taveras."

"Fantastic!" exclaimed Foli.

That's all there was to it. There wasn't any need for any long conversation. Foli had been unhappy with the Mets. He had been to bat only seven times with New York during the 1979 season. He packed his bags quickly. He was happy to be heading for Pittsburgh.

"I felt great, just great," said Foli. "Pittsburgh was a team that had been on top, dominating, for ten years. The best team I ever played on in the majors was my first year with the Mets in 1971. They finished two games over .500."

This was Foli's second time with the Mets. He had lasted two years the first time. In 1972, the Mets traded Foli to the Montreal Expos. He played five years with Montreal before being sent to the San Francisco Giants early in the 1977 season. The Mets reacquired Foli in 1978.

Foli never really distinguished himself. He earned the reputation of having a bigger temper than anything else. The highest he ever hit was .264 for the Expos in 1976. His lifetime average was an unimpressive .244. If it wasn't for Foli's temper, few people would have heard of him. He was the chief combatant in several fights over the years, suffering a broken jaw, a broken wrist and a broken nose.

It was no wonder he was called "Crazy Horse." Once while playing in the minors, he slept on second base after an extremely depressing game. One time he punched Mets coach Joe Pignatano. Another time he tried to fight first baseman Ed Kranepool in the New York dugout. It was the frustration of playing and losing year after year that triggered Foli's temper.

"I hated to lose, hated not being good enough to turn things around for a team," admitted Foli. "I knew all the time I couldn't ever be a superstar, but I wanted to play for a winner. I played for Gene Mauch (at Montreal) for five years and I've just begun to realize the things he taught me about not going outside myself were right. I was plenty hard-headed then.

"I like to think that in the field I can play shortstop with anyone. People always talk about range. I've got as much range as anyone if I know the hitters and where to play them, and I do. I was a .240 hitter, I had to know the game. Mauch made me study it. I had to learn

86

Kent Tekulve

the pitchers, everything I could. Gene told me, 'You're never going to be a Hall of Famer. You have a chance to be a great shortstop and play on a winning club. But don't try to be perfect.' "

It didn't take long for Foli to fit in with the Pirates. The team was made for him. It was a winning team and Foli easily made the transition. He was told what was expected of him and he went out and did it. He stabilized the infield and he hit better than at any time in his career. He not only hit a solid .291 for Pittsburgh, but he knocked in 65 runs from his second spot in the batting order, a high RBI figure from that position. Foli was more relaxed and knew what was expected of him.

"We altered his outlook basically by telling him that we didn't believe that here, that we take the good with the bad," said Parker. "It didn't take long for him to settle in the groove."

Foli managed to control his pent-up fury. The relaxed, open clubhouse of the Pirates and their family image gave Foli a feeling of belonging. He didn't have to lash out and display his emotions. Winning helped.

"I was a wild person," said Foli. "I'd make an error and want to tear up the clubhouse. I'd take it out on others, players, myself. I was high-strung. I've always been high-strung. My theory was that nobody ever died from a bloody nose and I wanted to be around the action. But this team taught me that you can't get too excited when you win or too down when you lose. I realized that I wasn't a superstar and wouldn't be one. I couldn't carry a club but I could fit in. That was the secret. I fit in.

"One thing Chuck Tanner has done for me is give me the confidence to do what I can do. I was always playing on teams that were behind. I was dying more than I was living. I have to play the way I do because I'm not a finesse player. My job is to advance a runner to second or third. Second is the minimum."

His steady play was well appreciated by the other Pirates. He was like a bull terrier, who scratched and fought for any edge. He hustled and he inspired his teammates. He was a most valuable player.

"He was the gear that put it all together," said Garner. "Foli solidified our infield. He was a take-charge guy. He knows how to play the game. He helped us to put more pride in our defensive game. Foli has been a catalyst. Frankly, we got him as more of a defensive player and he turned out to be a heck of an offensive guy, too."

In the World Series, Foli hit even better than during the regular season. He was 10-for-30, a .333 average, with a double, a triple and three runs-batted-in. He also scored six times, one less time than Stargell. He was greatly satisfied. Foli had become part of a winner.

Joe Brown, the former Pirates' general manager who retired after the 1976 season, admired Foli's play after seeing all of the play-off games and the World Series. Brown made a confession.

"I wouldn't have made that trade," revealed Brown. "But Pete is his own man. He spotted something no one else did. He recognized that Foli was the type player who could fit in with this Pirate team."

Nobody had to convince Foli.

"I'm born again," he exclaimed.

Even with the addition of Foli, Peterson wasn't satisfied. Third base worried him. He knew the Pirates would have to further solidify the left side of the infield. By June, it was apparent that Berra would not hit enough. There wasn't anyone in the minors who could make the club a bonafide pennant winner. Peterson began talking trade with the San Francisco Giants for another unhappy player, Bill Madlock. Peterson got him on June 28.

Unlike Foli, Madlock had strong credentials. He was a two-time National League batting champion when he played with the Chicago Cubs. He was a lifetime .313 hitter, but like Foli, he never had played on a winner. He had led the league in batting in 1975 with a .354 average and in 1976 with a .339 mark. Yet, the Cubs traded him to the Giants in 1977 for Bobby Murcer. Despite his outstanding hitting ability, Madlock had been an All-Star only once.

"The Cubs didn't treat me with respect," claimed Madlock. "I asked for one million dol-

lars over five years, which was nothing. But (owner Phil) Wrigley said, 'He's not a good ballplayer. He's injury-prone. He won't last two years.' I never even met Wrigley. I felt bad.

"Chicago is a very conservative city. It's a very conservative organization. The Cubs are like the Dodgers; they want to mold you into a Dodger. Wrigley tore up contracts for Ernie Banks, Rick Monday and Jose Cardenal. I was there three years and he didn't come around.

"You know what makes me sick? Looking at Larry Bittner and seeing him wearing Billy Williams' number. I'm not knocking Bittner, but he's no Williams. They didn't even retire Williams' number.

"I was the first one to challenge them. They used me as an example. I didn't even get the team MVP award. It went to Monday. They made up an award for me at the team dinner. It was 'The Guy Who Made Things Happen' award or something like that. Then they went out and paid Murcer a half-million more than I got and he was five years older than me. What does that tell you?

"I don't know what you have to do. Not being with a winner until now has hurt me. But what they can't take away from me is my talent. I don't understand why a Bobby Bonds, one of the five best hitters in the majors, keeps getting traded. You can look at it two ways. You can say somebody else wants you or you can wonder why you keep moving."

Madlock thought he would find things better in San Francisco. He was happy with his new multi-year contract and went along with the Giants' plans. They switched him to second base so that Darrell Evans could play third. The new position didn't affect Madlock's hitting much. He batted .302 in 1977 and .309 in 1978. But Madlock was growing unhappy with the Giants.

First, there was a misunderstanding with Manager Joe Altobelli. It was festered by the players' attitude more than anything else. Madlock felt that John Montefusco and other pitchers ran the club.

"When Montefusco won, he said 'I won,'" disclosed Madlock. "When he lost, he said 'we

lost.' The trade to the Pirates was like waking up from a bad dream. All the clubs I've been on expected me to carry them. I was the main thing. Now I'm batting sixth and I've got the highest lifetime batting average of anybody. That speaks for itself. Here one monkey don't stop the show.

"I was so happy to get away from San Francisco. I can't tell you how much. This is like night and day. I'm just glad I got out of there in time. The balloon busted after I left, didn't it?"

It certainly did. With the team in near-revolt, Altobelli was fired in September. By then, Madlock was helping the Pirates make a September run for the flag.

"I'm just glad I wasn't there," said Madlock. "They look for people to blame. Well, they can't blame me."

Still, the trade that brought Madlock to Pittsburgh surprised him.

"I could have understood it better if they had gotten a regular for me," explained Madlock. "But a pitcher (Ed Whitson), a guy you can use only once every four days. Well, I was surprised. They got what they wanted, I guess. And Pittsburgh got what it wanted. But a lot of people wouldn't make that trade."

It was another coup by Peterson. In 85 games with the Pirates, Madlock batted .328 and lifted his season's average to .298. He also tightened the left side of the infield. The Pirates were solid enough to win it all.

During the championship against Cincinnati, Madlock's fielding attracted praise from Reds' scout Ray Shore.

"He has soft hands," pointed out Shore. "He makes the plays."

Madlock laughed at the evaluation.

"I'm no Brooks Robinson," he admitted. "But I'm not going to hurt you. At third base, I'm comfortable. At second base, I was scared. But this is my first time in the playoffs. I haven't slept much, no more than four hours a night. I've learned that you have to let your ability take over. You can't try to do too much."

Madlock had a big World Series. He was 9-for-24, a .375 batting average. He came close to tying a Series record for consecutive hits. Going into Game Six, Madlock had five straight hits and had been on base seven straight times. However, in his first time up in the second inning, he grounded out, falling short of the consecutive hit record by one.

In the 7-1 rout of the Orioles in the fifth game, Madlock had four singles and was intentionally walked once. He scored one run and knocked in another. After the game, he was asked if he considered himself the best hitter in the National League.

"Not really," answered Madlock. "There are 10 or 15 very capable guys. I consider myself one of them."

As far as Baltimore Manager Earl Weaver was concerned, Madlock was the best. Someone wanted to know how the Orioles were going to pitch to Madlock in Game Six.

"I can't discuss it," replied Weaver, "because we haven't been able to do it. Some of the scouts said he was a high-ball hitter. Some said he was a low-ball hitter. I'll tell you what: He hits the hell out of both of them!"

When Madlock joined the Pirates after his San Francisco ordeal, the scrappy Garner was switched to second base. Although Garner was adequate at third, it was felt that he was a better second baseman and would strengthen the middle of the infield. He was a lot like Foli, pugnacious and spirited. He admits to not having the natural skills of a Parker or a Stargell. That is why he has battled hard all his career. In fact, it took him quite a while to convince people that he had any baseball skills at all.

Garner started battling before he ever made it to the majors. He was originally drafted by the Montreal Expos in 1970. However, he never played for them or any of their minor league teams. Garner wouldn't sign with Montreal. The Expos made it clear they were not going to pay Garner much money because he didn't have any power. Garner simply told them to forget it and joined a fast semi-pro team in Liberal, Kansas. One night Garner was playing a game in Boulder, Colorado. The opposing pitcher was Burt Hooton. Garner reached him for two hits. An Expos' scout, who was in the stands, talked to Garner after the game.

"You still don't have any power," said the scout. "You won't change our opinion."

"I told him to come back the next night," said Garner. "I hit a 400-foot homer. He comes to me and says one home run means nothing. The next night I hit two homers. You know what? I never saw him again!"

Making it on his own was nothing new to Garner. He had been doing it as a child growing up in Rutledge, Tennessee. His father was a minister and the church was directly behind the Granger County Jail.

"When I was six or seven years old," said Garner, "my brother and I used to go down to the grocery store and buy cookies for three cents each. Then we'd sell them through the bars to the prisoners for a nickel."

His early experience in the free enterprise system helped Garner cope with the system. After the year of semi-pro ball, the Oakland Athletics made Garner their No. 1 selection in the 1971 free agent draft. After four years in the minors, Garner was brought up to Oakland in 1975. A year later he was an All-Star.

"In Oakland I learned about people," disclosed Garner. "These were high-paid guys. I was making a big 16 grand. I couldn't dress with them and I couldn't drive their kind of cars but I learned what people like Sal Bando are all about. He is about the same thing as Willie Stargell."

In his first two years with the Pirates, Garner did not hit for a high average. He batted .260 in 1977 and .261 in 1978. But he was a plugger. He played both second and third and even some shortstop. In 1979, Garner raised his batting average to an impressive .293. It wasn't a fluke, either. Garner continued his hot hitting in the playoffs and through the World Series. He batted .417 against the Cincinnati Reds and .500 against the Orioles, leading all Pittsburgh hitters.

Yet, Garner had to overcome adversity to remain tough and lead the Pirates in hitting. In the first inning of the first game, Garner threw away a routine double play ball. The miscue helped the Orioles score five runs in the inning. Baltimore won the game, 5-4. But in the fifth game, Garner made a sparkling play behind second base that started a rally-ending double play, helping preserve Pittsburgh's 7-1 triumph.

Still, the error that Garner had made in the first game stayed with him. He took the loss as a personal insult. He is a hard loser.

"Fifty years from now," he said, "I'll be sitting on the front porch telling my grandchildren about all this. I'll be rocking in the rocking chair, smoking on a corn cob pipe, and I'll say, 'Damn, I made that error on my first play in the World Series.'"

Asked if it was the pressure of his first Series game that caused him to make the error, Garner replied, "The pressure came right after that play. Like, what the hell was I going to do with the second ground ball?"

What he did was overcome any lasting effects. He's too much of a fighter to let it hurt his play. The error simply motivated him to deal better with future pressure sitiations. He has too much of the old Gashouse Gang spirit in him to quit.

"Sometimes you think, 'My God, I got to dive for that one . . . I got to go in there, knock the shortstop down to kill the double play,'" said Garner. "But you think of the people in the steel mills or at the office who work every day and never get to feel that excitement. Who never have been as lucky as me. How do you handle a situation you've always wanted? Some guys walk away from it. Some guys mouth off about it. Me? I just can't wait for the games to start."

He really couldn't. By the time the Pirates reached the seventh game, Garner had hit safely in 23 consecutive games, starting during the pennant drive and carrying through into the playoffs and World Series. All the games were big. The pressure was on in each one. But Garner met the challenge. He was outhitting everyone. After the first six games of the Series, Garner had 11 hits and a gaudy .524 average. Even Stargell realized how important Garner was throughout the Series. Before the deciding seventh game, he emphasized Garner's play to some writers.

"If you guys don't make Garner MVP, I'm going to have to slap some heads," warned Stargell.

Before the sixth game in Baltimore, Garner was doing some slapping of his own. One writer started to ask him a question, prefacing it with, "If you guys lose tomorrow night . . ." Garner waved him away before he could finish.

"Don't ask me about losing," he exclaimed. "If it happens we'll talk about it later. I can't comprehend losing before a game. After coming this far, to lose tomorrow night won't be any consolation. Sure, we played great to come back, but it won't be enough."

Garner wasn't in any mood to talk about losing, or even facing that possibility. The Pirates' traveling secretary, Charles Muse, found that out on Monday afternoon. Since Garner was the Pirates' player representative, he was discussing with him the travel schedule if the Pirates lost on Tuesday night. He suggested that it might be better if the players packed at the hotel and brought their bags to the stadium so they would be ready to fly home immediately after the game. Garner looked him straight in the eye and snapped, "Hell no!" Still, Muse was determined to press his point and Garner reluctantly agreed.

"But I didn't like it," he emphasized. "I didn't like packing that bag and lugging it to the ball park. I never think about losing."

That night Garner did his best to make sure the Pirates wouldn't lose. Against Jim Palmer, he cracked two hits and assisted in a double play in the Pirates' 4-1 victory. He finished the Series with 12 hits, the same as Stargell. It was a long way from semi-pro ball.

"You make good plays during the regular season," Garner said. "You make a lot of them. You hit well. But you do it here and it's just brought to light more by the fact that everything is on television. It just seems like everything is bigger than anything you've done before."

Catcher Ed Ott might not agree. Every day was a big one for him during the 1979 season. While third base presented a problem for the Pirates at the beginning of the season, there

also was a question mark behind the plate long before the start of the season. The club had tripped over its defensive flaws in 1978 and one of the stumbling blocks was in the catching area.

It was such a problem that the Pirates used two, and at times three, catchers during the course of the season. Most of the time was split by Ott and Duffy Dyer, who had been obtained from the New York Mets in 1977. The third catcher was veteran Manny Sanguillen, who had been reacquired from the Oakland A's.

The problem was that opposing baserunners didn't encounter too many problems stealing bases against the Pirates. Dyer's arm wasn't accurate enough and Ott's wasn't strong enough because he had a sore arm during the first half of the season. Ott had cost the Pirates several games with bad throws. Not only did Ott experience problems behind the plate, but he got off to a slow start with his bat and hit far below expectations.

Ott really didn't have much experience as a catcher. He began his career with the Pirates in 1970 as an outfielder. He was a good one, too. In 1974, he led the International League in assists with 21. When the chunky Ott joined the Pirates in spring training in 1975, he was converted into a catcher and sent back to Charleston to learn his new position. He learned quickly. He led the league in putouts and total chances for a catcher and was named to the All-Star team. The Pirates brought him up in 1976, but his first full season wasn't until 1977 when he shared the catching duties with Dyer.

Ott batted .264 that year, playing in 104 games. After his slow start in 1978, Ott finished strong. He had overcome his arm miseries and during the last two months of the season, he hit .326, enabling him to finish with a .269 average. It buoyed his confidence. His outlook was even brighter when Dyer played out his option after the season and signed with the Montreal Expos. When Ott reported for spring training in 1979, he was the club's No. 1 catcher. He relished the role.

"I don't have any doubt that the job is

94

mine," said Ott. "And I don't think they do either. It makes a big difference when you know the job is yours. Now I don't have to worry. I can work on my defense and other things will come around. I can relax a little more and still play my game.

"My arm bothered me last year and it really hurt my defense. And I let my defense bother my offense. That's a cardinal sin in baseball. But my arm hurt so bad it finally got to me. Then towards the end of the season, it felt better and everything came around. The way I finished gives me a lot of satisfaction. I know I can do the job."

Looking at Ott objectively, he has been a catcher for only four years. That's not very long for a major league catcher. In fact, they were four short years. The most games Ott ever caught in a single season was 121, and that was in the minors. Before the 1979 season, Ott had caught only a total of 255 major league games in his first two full years with the club, and not all of them were complete games.

What Ott had to primarily concern himself with was refining his technique in handling balls thrown into the dirt. He also had to improve on catching the ball in the proper position to give his pitchers the most favorable area to the umpire. Then, too, he had to learn what hitters like and don't like, and utilize that knowledge with what his pitcher was capable of doing in certain situations. Not only was Ott still learning, but he took it upon himself to do so quickly since he now was the No. 1 catcher. That's why spring training was so important to him.

"Some pitchers can get the ball over in a 3-2 situation," noted Ott. "Some can't. You have to learn to go with the pitcher's strength against the batter's weakness. Out there the other day, I felt completely comfortable. I think I made the pitchers relax, too. It's great when the pitchers have confidence in you because it gives me confidence."

Ott was confident that he would have a good year, both behind the plate and at bat. After spring training began, Ott set some personal goals. He taped them on his locker as a daily reminder. His batting line read, average .295; runs batted in, 58; runs scored, 69; homers, 16; and stolen bases, 13. He also wanted to make sure he had a quicker release in throwing the ball when the season started.

"I know I said .300 last spring," said Ott, laughing. "It's down to .295 this time. That's a little more realistic. I'm also working on a quicker release, trying to get rid of the ball faster. When I'm catching, sometimes I think too much. I want to be able to come up and throw boom-boom. That's something I have to do."

Ott didn't quite reach the batting goals he had set for himself. He finished with a .273 average. But he did improve behind the plate. He got to know opposing batters better; became more knowledgeable about his own pitchers and they, in turn, developed more confidence in Ott; and he kept opposing baserunners from taking too much liberty on the base paths.

Still, Ott also had some anxious moments. One occurred with a member of his pitching staff. When reliever Enrique Romo joined the club, Ott couldn't seem to call the right pitches for him. Romo repeatedly shook off his signs. Ott was getting frustrated. He didn't know what to do. At first he tried talking to Romo privately. But Romo didn't speak fluent English and Ott could see that he wasn't getting his points across. Ott then approached Rennie Stennett for help. Stennett suggested that all three players should have a meeting and he offered to translate. Ott was relieved.

"Romo was shaking off so many pitches, I said, "How long has this guy been pitching?" said Ott. "He doesn't speak English too well, and all I can do in Spanish is swear at him. So, Rennie translated and we got it worked out.

"My pitchers have to trust me to call the game. You see the relievers more often and keep your timing with them. It's like hitting. You have to keep your eye sharp and your rhythm right. That's what it's like with a pitcher and a catcher. You can lose that rhythm. Tekulve and I have been playing together for a long time. I joined the Pittsburgh organization 10 years ago, and I've known

Teek for eight. In a way, I can help him more than the pitching coaches. I know him better."

All the pitchers got to know Ott, too.

While the infield was finally solidified with the acquisitions of Foli and Madlock, there remained one problem in the outfield. Parker was a fixture in right field and Omar Moreno was set in centerfield, leaving left field as a question mark. Making it that way was the condition of Bill Robinson's thumb. At first his thumb injury didn't seem serious. But Robinson was hampered by the injury and it affected him mentally.

On opening day of the 1978 season, Robinson had suffered a thumb fracture. In a game against the Chicago Cubs, Robinson slid into second base and his thumb hit Ivan DeJesus' knee. Robinson got up in pain, shaking his thumb. At first, he didn't think it was anything more than a sprain. He played several more games but the thumb didn't feel right. He discussed the injury with Manager Chuck Tanner. Tanner suggested that Robinson have the thumb checked by a doctor. When the Pirates arrived in Los Angeles, Robinson went to see a specialist. The doctor diagnosed Robinson's injury as a bone chip fracture. Robinson spent the next 11 days on the disabled list.

Robinson returned to action on May 30. However, he still didn't feel right. He began to press. He wanted to duplicate his 1977 season when he had batted .304, hit 26 home runs and knocked in 104 runs. It was the best season of his nine-year major league career, which began with the New York Yankees, continued with the Philadelphia Phillies and reached Pittsburgh in 1975. Only a strong finish, the month of September when he batted .290, enabled Robinson to lift his average to .246 at season's end. Still, he drove in 80 runs.

It was a disappointing season for the veteran outfielder. In 1977, he had attained full-time status for the first time. Still, he had to play five positions to do it, shuffling from the outfield to the infield. Robinson demonstrated his versatility by playing first base, third base and all three outfield positions. He was the

first to admit that his thumb contributed to his batting woes.

"I was taking baby swings at the ball," revealed Robinson. "I was afraid to extend my bat on my hands. I didn't pop the bat. Hey, the hitter uses his hands. When something is wrong, it affects your mind and your game.

96

Omar Moreno

My thinking wasn't the same. I let my head get away."

When the season ended, Robinson didn't wait long to begin his winter workouts. He always has made it an obligation to keep in shape during the off-season. He is admired as one of the best conditioned athletes in the game. Although he was traded by Philadelphia to the Pirates in 1975, Robinson still works out daily during the off-season with the Phillies in Veterans Stadium, which is not far from his Turnersville, New Jersey home. He uses the weight equipment, the Nautilus machine and even manages to get in some batting practice.

This time it was different. When Robinson started to hit the ball in November, his thumb began hurting again. Robinson contacted the Pirates. He talked about surgery. He felt if it was needed, he wanted it performed right away so that he would be ready when spring training began. Robinson went to Pittsburgh for consultation with the team doctors. Robinson had prepared himself for an operation.

"The doctor said we were in a 'damned if we do and damned if we don't situation,'" said Robinson. "He could have operated but he didn't really want to."

Instead, Robinson didn't participate in any more batting drills. He just continued his exercising. Yet, he couldn't wait until the spring to find out about his thumb. He took some swings in January and happily discovered that his thumb didn't hurt. As usual, Robinson reported to training camp early. With his thumb miseries gone, Robinson was in a good frame of mind.

"This will be the year of the Pirates and the year of Bill Robinson," he said. "I feel good weight-wise, attitude-wise and, if there is such a word, physical-wise."

He was determined to make up for 1978. Yet, he did derive some satisfaction from the fact that he had driven in 80 runs in 1978 and he didn't want that to go unnoticed.

"Only 11 men in the National League drove in more runs than me," pointed out Robinson. "Sure, I should have driven in more, but I did have an injury problem. I drove in more runs than Joe Morgan, but he had an injury, too. And I drove in more than Mike Schmidt."

However, when the 1979 comapign opened, Robinson found himself alternating with John Milner in left field. Milner had gotten off to a good start and Tanner decided to play him ahead of Robinson. Although Robinson understood, he felt uncomfortable with his new role of super sub. He had a talk with Tanner and accepted the manager's thinking. Tanner wanted to alternate the two, playing Milner against right-handed pitching and Robinson against left-handers. Regardless, Tanner would employ Robinson in the outfield during the late innings for defensive purposes. It was an adjustment that Robinson had to make and he did without any negative results.

After 12 years in the majors, Robinson had learned patience. In his earlier years, he used to sulk when he wasn't playing regularly. Now he was a mature individual, who was approaching his 36th birthday. Robinson kept ready. On days off, he took extra batting practice. He knew he would get his chances to play because over the previous three years, Robinson was the Pirates' most productive right-handed hitter. By the first week in June, Robinson was getting playing time and helping the Pirates win.

In a night game against the Los Angeles Dodgers in Pittsburgh, Robinson whacked two home runs leading the Pirates to a 5-4 victory. The home runs were his 13th and 14th of the season, and were as many as he had hit in 1978. Despite being platooned, he not only was leading the club in homers but in runs-batted-in, with 34. After his second homer, Robinson jumped high and came down with both feet on home plate.

"It wasn't to show off, believe me," he explained after the game. "It was just utter excitement and jubilation and a lot of faith in the Man Above. I thank the Good Lord for tonight. And since I let the Lord into my life a couple of years ago, I've learned to accept things. You just ask him for help and he'll help you. Of course, everything won't be perfect, but it has helped me to be at peace with myself. I've learned to relax. My best year in baseball was 1977 and it was the year I found the Lord.

"My attitude is fine now. But I can honestly say it wasn't a couple of weeks ago when I was only playing against left-handers and when I lost my job. But I kept the faith, kept myself in shape and here I am. Hey, I'm not thinking about home runs. I'm strong enough to hit them. But the main thing is to relax and have fun. The home runs will come."

When the season ended, Robinson had 24 homers. He also drove in 64 runs. He had indeed adjusted to his role as a platoon player.

What made Tanner platoon Robinson was the slugging of John Milner. The left-handed power-hitter was secured in a late 1977 deal with the Texas Rangers. Most baseball fans remember it as the deal that sent Pirates' slugger Al Oliver to Texas for right-hander Bert Blyleven. But Milner also was in the deal.

The Pirates had coveted Milner during his first six years in the National League when he played with the New York Mets. Milner also was a versatile performer. He could play either the outfield or first base. The Pirates felt he would be very valuable as a replacement at either position, giving Robinson or Willie Stargell a day of rest.

"We gave up a good hitter and we had to get a hitter in return," Tanner said about the trade that brought Milner to Pittsburgh. "Milner can come off the bench and hit. It's good to have a guy like that around. We can put him in a game and not lose anything."

Actually, Milner arrived in Pittsburgh with a cloud hanging over his head. The word was that Milner lacked motivation, that the slightest injury would cause him to ask out of the lineup. After being touted as the Mets' new hitting hope his rookie season of 1972, Milner fell out of favor with management despite smashing 23 home runs in 1973 and 20 in 1974. In 1976, he produced his best batting average, .271.

Yet, when Joe Torre took over as manager of the Mets in 1977, he voiced his respect for Milner's abilities. Torre had a long talk with

Bill Robinson

Milner and simply explained to him how much he needed his bat in the lineup. Torre said that if he expected to turn around the lowly Mets, he couldn't do it without Milner's help. Torre told him that the first base job was his and that he wanted him to play every game. Milner responded positively. He played, even at times with a bad knee. It didn't go unnoticed by Torre. He noticed the time Milner dove for a ball with his ailing knee, then went from first to third on a hit. He also was delighted when Milner stole four bases in his first five attempts after not having stolen a base for two years. Torre said all he did was to try and relax Milner.

The first day Milner reported to his first Pirates' training camp in 1978, he asked for a private meeting with Tanner. Milner wanted to clear the air, to convince Tanner that any derogatory remarks he heard about him in New York were not true, that he wanted to play ball and that he was happy to be with the Pirates. After the session, Tanner appeared convinced.

"I treat a new player like nothing has ever happened to him before," said Tanner. "I wasn't worried about Milner's attitude. I wasn't worried about his desire. He had been in the big leagues for six years and he must have been doing something right."

Early in the season, Milner didn't get a chance to start many games. However, injuries to other players gave him a chance to play more. One day he was in left field. The next day he was on first base. Wherever he was needed, he played. And he played, hurt at times, once with a sprained ankle, another time with a sore shoulder.

"If I feel I can run just enough and swing the bat just enough, I want to be in there," said Milner. "In New York, I kept hearing about nagging injuries keeping me out of the lineup. Nagging injuries! Once the bone was torn from the muscle in my leg. Is that a nagging injury?"

In his first season with Pittsburgh, Milner batted .271. But he also hit two grand slam home runs, off left-handed pitchers, no less. It

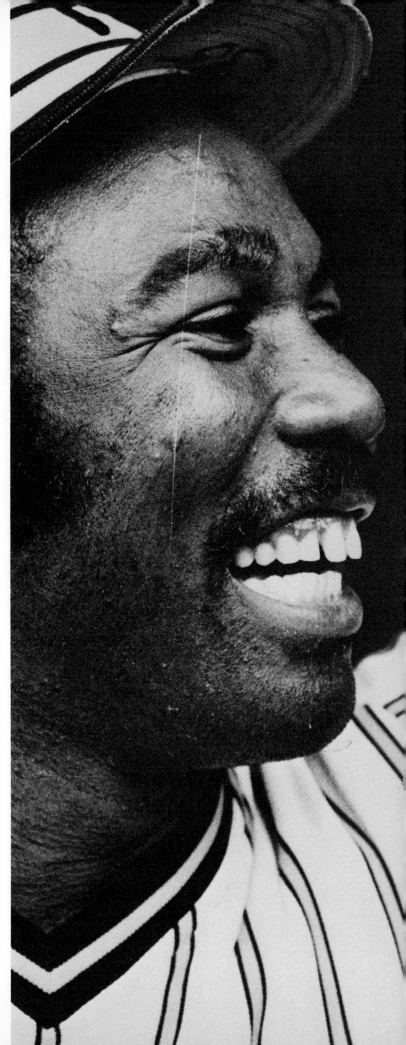

Manny Sanguillen

John Milner slides across home plate against St. Louis.

was a very satisfying year for Milner.

"I'm happy to be here," said Milner. "Pittsburgh is a contending team while the Mets were a rebuilding team. New York was good to me for six years and I have no regrets. But you spend X number of years in one town and then maybe it's time to move on to somewhere else. You start all over again.

"You're going along good in a season and then you get hurt and can't play. I was leading the league in home runs and runs batted in in 1973 and then went down to Atlanta for a game and pulled my hamstring. I think I was leading the league for a while in 1975, too, and then I pulled a muscle stretching for a ball at Shea Stadium. It's frustrating. You find yourself asking, Why me?

"Once you pull a muscle and you're out of the lineup for two weeks, it's just like spring training again. You have to start all over. I have my mind together mentally now. I knew everything was set when I first came here. I want to be ready when they call on me. I figure I'll be able to give Stargell a rest once in a while, and maybe Robinson will need a day off now and then in the outfield."

Milner didn't get much chance to have a day off once the 1979 season began. He swung a hot bat at the beginning and Tanner couldn't take him out of the lineup. After the first 18 games of the season, Milner was hitting a phenomenal .464. At first, he took over at first base when Stargell injured his hip sliding during a game against the Phillies. The first game

Milner went 3-for-4 and the second game he was 2-for-3, the hits being a pair of two-run homers that helped beat the St. Louis Cardinals, 7-6.

After the game, most of the reporters gathered around Milner as he sat on a table with Parker and Stargell. Yet, Milner had the spotlight to himself. One writer was skeptical about Milner's current batting boom.

"I can hit, man," said Milner.

Parker and Stargell were ready to offer support.

"The man can play, damn it," said Parker.

"The reporters have now discovered John Milner," said Stargell.

"If he can't play first base, put him in right field," said Parker.

Stargell was expected back in the lineup in a couple of days. Milner faced that reality.

"If Willie is ready to play, he's ready to play," remarked Milner. That's all there is to it. I can't be looking to see if I'm gonna play here or play there. All I want to do is be an asset to the ballclub."

He was an asset. Tanner was able to make good use of Milner. He spotted him at first base and played him in left field against right-handed pitching. Milner finished the season with the highest batting average of his career, .276. He also hit 16 home runs and drove in 60 runs. Combined with Robinson, left field gave the Pirates 40 homers and 134 runs batted in. Everyone was happy.

The Pirates were set in the remaining two

outfield positions. Parker was irreplaceable in right field. Omar Moreno was set in center-field. There was no outfielder faster than Moreno on the Pirates or in the league. Moreno had played two full seasons for Pittsburgh and led the major leagues in stolen bases in 1978 with 71. Moreno is modest about his running but if anyone challenges him, he is willing to demonstrate his speed.

Several seasons back, Miguel Dilone, who now is with the Chicago Cubs, was a member of the Pirates. Everyone marveled at Dilone's speed. From third to home he looked faster than anyone. Naturally, there always was dis-cussion about who was faster, Dilone or Moreno. One day; Dilone proposed to Moreno that they compete against each other in a 60-yard race. Moreno agreed. While many of the Pirates watched in anticipation, Moreno settled the argument by finishing first.

"I beat him," Moreno said softly. "Now he stay quiet the rest of his life."

Speed never was a question with Moreno. Neither was his fielding. In the outfield, he was a gazelle. His fluid motion enabled him to get a quick jump on a ball coming toward him. He also could turn and outrun a baseball that was hit to either side of him. His glove was a weapon.

It was his bat that created concern. Playing only part time in 1976, Moreno batted .270, which was acceptable. However, in his first full season, in 1977, Moreno hit only .240. Then in 1978, he hit .235. Now the Pirates' worry was big. They contacted Harry Walker, the team's manager from 1965-1967. Walker, a great student of hitting, now was the baseball coach at the University of South Alabama. The Pi-rates explained the problem to Walker and the former batting champion told them to send Moreno to him.

The Pirates were hoping for another cure-all from Walker. A few years back, Walker aided Matty Alou with his hitting. The results were extraordinary. Alou led the league in batting in 1966 with a .342 average. After the 1978 season, Moreno was instructed to report to Walker in Alabama. Walker worked with Moreno every day for three weeks. It was only

Bert Blyleven

John Candelaria

Bruce Kison

Jim Bibby

Jim Rooker

Grant Jackson

Don Robinson

after Walker felt convinced that Moreno had corrected some flaws in his swing did he allow his student to leave and return to his home in Panama. Moreno was brimming with confidence when he reported to training camp before the start of the 1979 season.

"I'm a better hitter now," exclaimed Moreno. "Harry Walker worked with me about keeping my right shoulder level when I swing. Before, I was lifting it up and that's why I was popping up to left field so much. Walker wants me to hit the ball on the ground more between shortstop and third base so I can use my speed. If I had hit .270 or .280 last year, I know we win the pennant. If I hit .270, I can score 100 runs and steal 100 bases."

Tanner agreed. With Moreno batting at the top of the order, he had to hit and he had to get on base to maximize his speed. Tanner was exploring several options in the eventuality Moreno failed to hit consistently. He could insert Robinson in centerfield or he could use Lee Lacy, who had joined the club as a free agent from the Dodgers. Either move would weaken the Pirates defensively.

The key to the Pirates' hitting attack was Moreno. Tanner wanted him on base as often as possible. He was confident that the young centerfielder had benefitted from Walker's instructions. But to insure that he did and did not revert to a faulty swing, Tanner instructed Bob Skinner, his batting coach, to keep a close eye on Moreno. Whenever Moreno made a mistake, Skinner immediately corrected it. The rest was up to Moreno.

He didn't fail. Once the season began, Moreno looked like an entirely different hitter. In fact, he was hitting better than anyone anticipated. After the first month, Moreno was batting .343. No one would have expected that he would have more hits or more runs batted in that Parker. Because of Moreno's early season burst, the Pirates weren't timid in trading shortstop Frank Taveras to the New York Mets. Although they felt that Taveras was inadequate in the field, he had been effective at bat as the team's leadoff hitter. Now, that was the spot assigned to Moreno, who was moved up from second position in the batting order.

For the first time in Moreno's three years with the club, he felt content. He was confident that he would hit now. Moreno appeared more relaxed and wasn't as withdrawn as in the past. He would openly talk about his hitting, about how he had shortened his swing and was concentrating on getting base hits rather than swinging for home runs.

"I'm not trying to hit home runs like I did last year," disclosed Moreno. "I hit a lot of fly balls to the outfield then. I'm trying to hit more balls between short and third where I have a chance to use my speed. Now, I feel relaxed. I don't worry any more."

Parker noticed the change in Moreno. He felt all along that Moreno would hit. He pointed out that Moreno had a few years of experience and that made a difference.

"I've said all along that Moreno had the tools to be a phenomenal superstar in this game," said Parker.

Even Tim Foli, who was new to the club, realized how much Moreno had changed as a hitter. Batting second behind Moreno, Foli had an excellent opportunity to observe him game after game from his close up vantage point in the on-deck circle.

"There's no comparison between Omar of the past and Omar of this year," said Foli. "If he hits .300, there's no telling what he can do because of his great speed. Even when he hits the ball on the ground, it's tough to get him out. Last year, he had a big swing. But this year, he's really compacted it. He's hitting the ball well."

Moreno hit well all season. He finished with his highest batting average, .282. He just missed collecting 200 hits, finishing with 196. But he did manage to score 110 runs, which he had said he could do if he hit .270 or .280. However, it was his runs-batted-in total that attracted a lot of attention. Moreno knocked in 69 runs, a high figure for a leadoff batter.

Not only did Moreno hit, he ran. He was a potent force on the bases. Moreno stole 77 bases in 98 attempts, giving him a total of 148 in two years.

"I'd say the key to our club is Omar," said catcher Steve Nicosia. "If Omar gets on base and Foli moves him over, we've got three shots. Then you've got Parker, Stargell and Robinson."

The Pirates' attack began with Moreno.

Actually, hitting was not the Pirates worry. The biggest concern was ptiching. The biggest anxiety revolved around John Candelaria, the ace of the staff. The concern centered around Candelaria's nagging back and forearm miseries that had limited his effectiveness in 1978. In 1978, Candelaria had only a 12-11 record although his earned run average was a respectable 3.24. However, in 1977, Candelaria was the best pitcher in the National League, and perhaps in all of baseball. He finished with a 20-5 record, a 2.34 earned run average and a winning percentage of .800. He led the league in the latter two categories.

Despite his ailments, Candelaria hung tough. Because of his tenacity, he was a favorite of Tanner. Tanner always looked to Candelaria to pitch the important games. Four of the 12 games that Candelaria won in 1978 were 2-1 decisions.

"If I had to pick a pitcher to win a game if it meant my life, of all the pitchers in baseball, I'd pick Candelaria," maintained Tanner.

The Pirates were hoping that 1979 would be better for Candelaria. They were hoping that he would have a year free from pain so that he perhaps would win 20 games again. They needed Candelaria's sound arm to lead a pitching staff that was not strong with starters. He was definitely a key. Fortunately, Candelaria's forearm problem disappeared. However, as the season progressed, his recurring back trouble reappeared. Candelaria missed quite a few starts and couldn't throw with his normal velocity. Still, he finished with a 14-9 record and a fine 3.22 earned run average. He was the staff's biggest winner.

Yet, it was in the pressure games that Candelaria excelled. The first was the opening playoff game against the Cincinnati Reds, when he was matched against Tom Seaver. It was a performance that was accompanied by pain. The pain was there on the first pitch of the game. Ott detected it immediately and went to the mound to talk to Candelaria. The big left-hander chased him back behind the

plate. Between innings, Ott told Tanner about it. Pitching coach Harvey Haddix was made aware of it and alerted the bullpen. Candelaria continued to pitch, and he gave the Pirates seven strong innings before leaving with the score tied 2-2.

"My back hurts more than ever now," revealed Candelaria. "I don't remember what it's like to pitch without pain."

The pain did not end for Candelaria when the World Series began. The cold weather that gripped the Series didn't offer him any relief, either. Although Candelaria was knocked out in the fourth inning of the third game, Tanner named him to pitch in the sixth game when both teams returned to Baltimore with the Pirates trailing, 3-2. Candelaria was superb. He pitched six scoreless innings before the pain forced him out. Still, he was credited with the win in Pittsburgh's 4-0 victory.

Candelaria didn't always pitch in pain. He didn't know its meaning when he signed to play with the Pirates in 1972. He was chosen off the Brooklyn sandlots in the second round of the free agent draft. Despite the fact that he was big, 6-7, and could throw extremely hard, a lot of teams shied away from him. The main reason was that Candelaria had a basketball scholarship from the University of Utah. Another reason was that Candelaria was a tough kid because he had been raised in a rough element. Neither of the two reasons bothered the Pirates. Although Candelaria hadn't pitched in three years, devoting his time to basketball instead, Pirates scout Dutch Deutsch insisted upon drafting the big lefty. They did, but they still had to sign him.

That winter, Pirates' General Manager Joe Brown went to Puerto Rico to sign Candelaria. The 19-year-old Puerto Rican youngster was on the island to play basketball for the country's national team. Brown decided to enlist Roberto Clemente to help him sign Candelaria.

"While they were getting me to sign, Clemente talked to me in Spanish," recalled Candelaria. "He asked me how much of a bonus they were offering me and I told him $13,000. Clemente told me not to sign, that I could get much more later."

Clemente was right. A short time later, Candelaria signed for a $40,000 bonus, a large amount for a second-round selection. Candelaria paid off quickly on the Pirates' investment. After only 2½ years in the minors, he was brought up to Pittsburgh midway through the 1975 season. He finished with an 8-6 record and a 2.75 earned run average.

In his third major league start that year he won his first game. He outpitched Seaver, beating the New York Mets 4-1 with a four-hitter in Shea Stadium. He was a guest on former Pirates' slugger Ralph Kiner's TV show after the game. He admitted that was the only time he was nervous all day, confessing that it was the first time he ever was on television. What he was worried about was hurrying back to his mother's house on Staten Island for a lasagna dinner. Candelaria had purchased the house for his mother with his bonus money.

Candelaria saved his best for last. He faced the Cincinnati Reds in the third game of the National League playoffs in Three Rivers Stadium. The Reds had won the opening two games in Cincinnati and were ready to claim the pennant against the rookie. Candelaria pitched his heart out. He struck out the first four Reds' batters, and seven of the first nine. Candelaria had allowed only one hit, Dave Concepcion's second-inning home run, until Pete Rose reached him for a two-run homer in the eighth inning, giving the Reds a 3-2 lead in a game they eventually won in the 10th inning, 5-3. As Candelaria left in the eighth inning, the crowd extended him a standing ovation. He had struck out 14 batters, setting a National League playoff record.

"The kid showed me something," said Reds' Manager Sparky Anderson. "It's a shame he didn't win. It was the best performance by a left-hander I've seen all year."

Candelaria had more thrills waiting for Pirates' fans. In 1976, his first full season, Candelaria finished with a 16-7 record. But the game that Pittsburgh fans remember most occurred on August 9. Candelaria excited a small crowd of 9,860 by hurling a no-hitter against the Los Angeles Dodgers. In pitching his masterpiece, Candelaria struck out seven and walked only one while facing only 29 batters on a promotional night designated as "Candy Night." It was the first no-hitter tossed by a Pirates' hurler in Pittsburgh since Nicholas Maddox did it at Exposition Park in 1907.

Except for two fine plays by Al Oliver and one by Dave Parker, all the outs were routine. Oliver hauled down Dave Lopes' long drive to deep center in the second inning. Then Parker made a running catch immediately afterward on a shot to right by Ted Sizemore. The drama intensified with two out in the ninth inning. Bill Russell hit a shallow fly ball into centerfield that looked like it would drop in for a bloop hit. But Oliver, running at top speed, gloved the ball, preserving the no-hitter as the crowd roared.

While Candelaria was being interviewed after the game in the dugout, his teammates were busy. They laid a path of white towels from the clubhouse entrance to Candelaria's locker. Along the way, they piled up several rows of candy bars. Candelaria smiled as he walked by.

"This is something I dreamed about since I was a little boy," exclaimed the Candy Man. "It's something every kid dreams about. I feel fantastic, just great. I was very nervous in the last inning. I was just trying to keep the ball down, trying to get them out. It's just tremendous.

"When Russell hit the ball, my first thought was that it was going to drop in. Then I saw Oliver moving in and I knew he had it. I threw a lot of no-hitters on the sandlots but they don't mean much next to this. This is my greatest thrill and will be until we win a World Series. I'm positive my mother is drunk by now. I imagine all my friends in Brooklyn are going wild. I'm going to go home and drink beer all night. I don't think anyone could blame me. I don't know if I'll come down for a while. Not many people in baseball have done this."

Pirates' owner John Galbreath rewarded Candelaria. He telephoned Candelaria after the game to tell him and his catcher that both would receive a "little gift" for their efforts.

Most assuredly, it wasn't candy bars.

While Candelaria's recurring back problem was a genuine worry for the Pirates before the 1979 season, the condition of the middle finger of Bruce Kison's pitching hand also gave the team serious cause for concern. It didn't seem like much of a problem on the surface. After all, how much trouble could a blister really create? In Kison's case, plenty; so much so that for two years, he was a sub-par pitcher.

Kison's lingering ailment first. appeared during the 1977 season. It was unfortunate, to say the least. In 1976, Kison had enjoyed his finest season in six years with the Pirates, winning 14 games and losing nine. His earned run average was a solid 3.08 and he was realistically thinking of winning 20 games during the 1977 campaign. However, shortly after the season began, Kison developed a painful blister on his finger. It remained with him all season. Even extra rest and every known treatment of blisters that had been used over the years in baseball, didn't help Kison. Although he pitched 193 innings, the same amount he had worked in 1976 and in 1975 when he was 12-11, Kison was ineffective. For the first time in his career, Kison finished below .500, with a 9-10 record.

Kison felt confident that the long off-season rest would cure his blister ailment. He looked with great anticipation to spring training in 1978. Kison had a strong spring and threw without any trouble. He appeared convinced that the blister had finally disappeared. However, early in the season, in a relief assignment against the Chicago Cubs, the blister reappeared. Kison was dismayed.

"It's a chronic thing, a blood blister," disclosed Kison. "Last year, I continually threw and put a lot of stress on it. I had a great spring training, really popped the ball. I accomplished everything that I hoped to accomplish, and now this again. . . ."

The ailment forced Tanner to remove

111

Tim Foli

Kison from the starting rotation. He was sent to the bullpen as a long reliever until his finger was healed completely. Tanner and Kison were both hoping that when the warm weather arrived, the problem would be alleviated. Until then, Kison was content with his new role of relief pitcher.

However, Kison's finger didn't improve. At the end of May, he was placed on the 21-day disabled list. When he was activated, his finger hadn't improved noticeably. He still experienced difficulty gripping the ball. The only alternative left was surgery. It was performed on June 8, and on July 6, Kison was restored to the active roster. It wasn't until July 17 that Kison made his first start of the 1978 season. He finished the year with a 6-6 record. The biggest satisfaction was knowing that the blister problem finally was cured.

Yet, during spring training in 1979, Kison's name was rumored to be on the trading list. There were more pitchers on the roster than spots for them. Candelaria, Bert Blyleven and Don Robinson were being counted as definite starters. Kent Tekulve, Enrique Romo and Grant Jackson were set in the bullpen. There were four places open, to be filled among Kison, Jerry Reuss, Jim Rooker, Jim Bibby and Ed Whitson. Kison was well aware of the prospects of being traded.

"When I was younger, I might have felt that I wasn't wanted any more," reasoned Kison. "But a lot of clubs need pitching. A trade's not something I lose sleep over. If we need something on this team I'm sure we'll give up a pitcher, and I know I'm certainly not an untouchable."

But Kison stayed. And he experienced his finest season since 1976. Kison finished with a 13-7 record and an earned run average of 3.24. The tall, skinny right-hander flirted with immortality when he one-hit the San Diego Padres, 7-0, on June 3. It was the first one-hitter of his career and yet Kison was disappointed that it wasn't a no-hitter.

Amazingly, Kison had pitched one inning of relief the previous night. He wasn't expecting to pitch, much less start, when he arrived at Three Rivers Stadium early Sunday afternoon. Don Robinson was the scheduled start-

er. While Robinson was warming up in the bullpen, his right shoulder wouldn't loosen up. Ten minutes before the game, Tanner asked Kison if he could start. When Kison said he could, Tanner handed him the ball and told him to go as long as he could.

Kison threw easily. He threw strong. He was pitching as if nothing ever had happened to him. After seven innings, Kison was working on a no-hitter. The tension began to mount when the Padres came to bat in the eighth inning. Kison disposed of the first two batters. He was only four outs away from a no-hitter. The third batter of the inning was Barry Evans, the No. 8 hitter in the order. Kison threw him a slider that broke over the middle of the plate. Evans hit a hard ground ball toward the third base foul line. Phil Garner lunged for the ball and it barely tipped his glove as it rolled safely into left field. The official scorer ruled the ball a hit. Kison had lost his bid for a no-hitter.

After the game, Kison was angry. He stormed into the clubhouse, convinced that the play should have been ruled an error. His disappointment was understandable. But Garner agreed with the official scorer's decision.

"It was a hit," said Garner. "I had a bead on the ball and then it hit the dirt and took off towards the line. I made a lunge for it at the last second and it barely tipped my glove. I had been playing him closer to the line all day. On that pitch, it was supposed to be down and away. Right before the pitch, I took a step away from the line. That step was the difference."

There was only one other ball that came close to being a hit. In the seventh inning, Dan Briggs belted a long drive toward the right field wall. Parker raced back, leaped and pulled the ball down. The crowd of 18,329 then began to cheer louder with every out recorded by Kison. Kison heard the cheers.

"The crowd reaction gave me a big lift," admitted Kison. "You try to avoid thinking about a no-hitter but it's hard. I remember what it was like when Ken Brett almost threw one here and then when Candy got his. It had me laughing inside a little. It's nice to be in that situation. It was fun while it lasted."

After the season, Kison became a free agent and signed with the California Angels. After being a member of "The Family" for nine years, Kison was gone to another town in another league.

One of the newest members of "The Family" was right-hander Bert Blyleven. He joined the Pirates prior to the 1978 season along with outfielder John Milner in the deal that sent slugging outfielder Al Oliver to the Texas Rangers. Blyleven had the right personality to survive in the zany atmosphere of the Pirates' clubhouse. Like other members of the Pirates, he was loose and fun-loving, having played the part of a joker at times during his two-year tenure with the Rangers. Once during pregame warmups, Blyleven took the field with his uniform shirt and pants turned inside out. Another time he appeared properly dressed except for the fact that he neglected to put on his white socks. Willie Horton, a former teammate, remembers when the devilish right-hander scared him to death by placing a small firecracker in one of his cigarettes.

Yet, despite his seemingly happy mood, Blyleven has had somewhat of a frustrating career. When the Pirates obtained Blyleven, it was his third club in eight years. He began his major league career with the Minnesota Twins in 1970 before moving to Texas during the 1976 season. In 1973, he was 20-17 with a 2.52 earned run average. The previous year, he was 17-17 again with a 2.66 ERA.

Despite having won 54 games in three years, Blyleven became disenchanted with Minnesota. He didn't have a good relationship with Calvin Griffith, the club's owner, and asked to be traded. Blyleven forced the issue when he refused to sign his 1976 contract. Rather than lose Blyleven to the free agent market. Griffith traded him to Texas when the season was two months old.

Although he finished with a creditable 14-12 record with Texas in 1977, it was a disappointing year for Blyleven. In June, he pulled a groin muscle that gave him considerable pain. The pain was so severe that one doctor advised Blyleven not to pitch for at least six weeks. Determined to pitch, Blyleven re-

Phil Garner

turned to the mound ten days later, preferring to struggle with the pain. In September, he suffered another setback, aggravating the injury to the point that his leg was discolored from the hip to the knee. He was sent home to Anaheim, California to rest, figuring his season was over. Still, Blyleven was determined to pitch. He took some shots and carefully exercised the leg. When the Rangers arrived in Anaheim at the end of September to play the Angels, Blyleven reported to the ballpark. He asked Manager Billy Hunter to let him pitch. After watching Blyleven work out, Hunter was convinced he could pitch and gave him a starting assignment the night of September 22.

With a heavily taped leg, Blyleven made his final appearance of the season. It was a night he'll never forget. The pain quickly returned, but Blyleven wouldn't quit. After seven innings, he had a no-hitter. In the eighth inning, he suffered another muscle pull in the leg. Hunter went to the mound to replace him. Blyleven shook his head, refusing to come out.

"If I have to throw underhand I will," said Blyleven. "I'm not going to come out of here."

Courageously, Blyleven hung on. The tension reached a peak in the bottom of the ninth inning after Blyleven had retired the first two Angels' batter. Blyleven bore down against the next batter, Thad Bosley, and struck him out, painfully completing the no-hitter.

Surprisingly, Blyleven had a career record of only 122-113 when he joined the Pirates. It was surprising because Blyleven had one of the lowest earned run averages among active major league pitchers. But Blyleven had lost numerous low-run games. The Pirates discounted Blyleven's record.

"It's a matter of Bert putting it all together one of these years," said Pete Peterson, the club's general manager. "Hopefully, he'll start doing that in 1978."

Just as he always will remember the no-hitter in his last appearance in 1977, Blyleven won't soon forget his first outing with the Pirates in 1978. Showing no ill effects from his groin injury, Blyleven was pitching a shutout against the Chicago Cubs in Three Rivers Stadium. Blyleven entered the seventh inning, leading 3-0. However, after the first two Cubs' batters hit safely, Manager Chuck Tanner removed Blyleven. Blyleven was surprised.

"I can't recall the last time I was taken out of a game with a shutout going," said Blyleven. "I know I gave up a couple of base hits but I don't think I was in any real danger. I've been taken out of games many times, but I figured to be around at least until the Cubs scored. I thought I had a chance to go nine. But Chuck Tanner is the manager and whatever he does has to be okay with me. He knows the moves and when to make them. Chuck makes a guy feel important the way he does things. I guess I'll just have to get used to some things over here."

One thing was being ready to bat. In the American League, Blyleven didn't have to worry about taking his turn at the plate. He wasn't quite used to it in his first game with Pittsburgh.

"I came in, took a drink of water, sat down and somebody yelled to me that it was my turn to get on deck," recalled Blyleven. "That startled me, I said to myself, 'What's going on around here? I'm supposed to be resting.' I got used to it, though."

In his first year with the Pirates, Blyleven finished with a 14-10 record. He led the Pirates' pitching staff in several categories, including strikeouts, starts, complete games, ERA and shutouts. From June 4 through July 20, Blyleven didn't lose a game while winning six times.

Although his earned run average was higher in 1979, rising from 3.02 to 3.61, Blyleven had a better record, 12-5. He led the staff in starts and strikeouts for the second straight season. He reached a milestone on July 12 when he made Terry Puhl his 2,000th strikeout victim. Blyleven was strong from May 31 until July 31, posting an 8-1 record, and was strong again in the championship playoffs and the World Series.

Blyleven is the only player in the major leagues who was born in Holland. However, in 1953, when Blyleven was only two years old, his parents moved to Saskatchewan, Canada. Three years later, the family settled in Paramount, California. When Blyleven was 10 years old, his family moved again, this time to Garden Grove, California. It was there that Blyleven first started to play baseball even though he didn't know anything about the sport. When some neighborhood friends pressed him to try out for Little League, Blyleven admitted that he never had played baseball. He joined his friends and decided to be a catcher because the equipment appealed to him.

"I liked all that gear," revealed Blyleven. "But ignorant, that was me. I didn't know at the time what the game was all about. However, when I started to throw the ball back to the pitcher harder than he was throwing it to me, we changed positions. I wasn't gung-ho for the majors until I was 16. Then, in 1969, the Twins signed me out of high school."

Yet, when the Pirates signed him, there were some skeptics who felt that Pittsburgh didn't get equal value in return for Oliver. However, Blyleven, along with Milner, has made the trade an advantageous one for the Pirates. In fact, Tanner feels that the 29-year-old Blyleven hasn't reached his peak yet.

When the Pirates acquired Blyleven, they reaped another dividend by signing free agent Jim Bibby. In 1977, Bibby had played out his option with the Cleveland Indians. Ironically, the big right-hander was being pursued by the Pirates' closest rivals, the Philadelphia Phillies. The hard-throwing veteran was looking for security, and when the Phillies didn't offer it, he signed with the Pirates.

Bibby was by no means a stranger to the National League, although his exposure in the senior circuit was relatively short and inconspicuous. Bibby began his major league career with the St. Louis Cardinals in 1972. He didn't last long with the Cardinals. Early in the 1973 season, Bibby was traded to the Texas Rangers. In his only full season with the Rangers in 1974, Bibby won 19 games, but he also lost 19. Later, after pitching for Cleveland for 2½ seasons, the best he could do was a 13-7 mark in 1976.

Nevertheless, Bibby had strong credentials. He was a strong-armed hurler who could either start or relieve. Although he was only 9-10 in 1973, in many ways it was his best season from a standpoint of individual accomplishments. First, he no-hit the world champions, the Oakland A's. Then, he pitched a one-hitter and a two-hitter. In the same season, in a game against the Minnesota Twins, Bibby struck out a career-high 15 batters. Since the Pirates had lost Goose Gossage and Terry Forster after the 1977 season, Bibby was an attractive addition.

"When I singed here, I signed for security and because I wanted to play on a contending ballclub," said Bibby. "I want to get into the World Series or a championship series. If that means I work out of the bullpen, that's fine. If it means I start, that's fine, too."

Bibby waited 51 days to get his first start with the Pirates. He responded with a route-going, four-hit victory over the Montreal Expos, 5-2. Bibby had to survive a shaky first inning. Dave Cash opened the game with an infield single off Bibby's pitching hand. One pitch later, Cash stole second base. After Rennie Stennett misplayed Stan Papi's ground ball, the Expos had a threat going. Before Bibby could pitch to Ellis Valentine, Tanner yelled to him from the dugout.

"Close your eyes and throw the darn thing," shouted Tanner. "Don't worry about anything . . . just turn it loose."

Tanner obviously was trying to rattle Valentine. The Montreal outfielder realized it.

"Hell with that," Valentine snapped. "We're not afraid of him."

Maybe not. But after Bibby settled down on the way to the victory, Valentine certainly did not help his team's chances. He hit only one ball out of the infield during the game.

"They heard," admitted Tanner after the game. "Sure I was yelling at Bibby. It was his first start and he was a little bit nervous. But he pitched a terrific game. It's hard any time when you ask a guy to do two things at once. You ask a guy to start-relieve, relieve-start, it adds pressure."

In his first season with Pittsburgh, Bibby started 14 games and relieved in 20 while compiling an 8-7 record. He tossed two shutouts. It didn't seem to bother him whether he started or relieved. He felt strong all year.

"Pressure is something you put on yourself," said Bibby. "I don't do that, yet some players do."

At 6-5, 250 pounds, Bibby is physically more intimidating than anyone on the Pirates except Dave Parker. His huge hands make him appear even bigger and he can throw a fastball better than 90 miles an hour. His hands are so large that one Pirates' player said that " they block out the sun." A baseball looks more like a golf ball in Bibby's hands. Yet, it's not as much an advantage as one might think.

"Actually, it hurts you in a way, especially a fastball pitcher." admitted Bibby. "You throw the fastball with the tips of your fingers, and if the ball slips back, it hurts your speed. That's how they teach you to throw the changeup, use the same motion but put the ball closer to the palm where you can't put much speed on it."

No one was happier than Bibby when the

Lee Lacy

Pirates made Harvey Haddix the pitching coach for the 1979 season. Haddix was Bibby's pitching coach during his three years with Cleveland. A former pitcher, Haddix could detect mechanical flaws, such as not gripping the ball properly, easier than most.

Haddix' approach to pitching was different than other coaches. While some pitching coaches stress concentration on the batter, the plate, the catcher's glove and letting the pitcher's motion take care of itself, Haddix insists on concentrating on the grip, the windup, the motion, the follow-through and letting the strikes fall into place.

"Motion and delivery are very important not only to a big man, but to any fastball pitcher," believes Bibby. "A fastball pitcher has a tendency to lose his rhythm because of how hard he throws the ball. Harvey not only knows about pitching, but he explains it well. Harvey makes pitchers see what he is talking about.

"My job isn't easy. I don't think there's enough emphasis placed on it. Not every one can be the extra starter and the long relief pitcher. It takes some concentration. You don't know when you're going to pitch, but when you do, you have to come in and hold the other team to one or two runs for several innings. With a club like ours, that can explode for runs, that's important."

The presence of Haddix made Bibby a better pitcher in 1979. He appeared in the same number of games, 34, as in 1978. But he started 17 and finished with a 12-4 record. He also lowered his earned run average from 3.53 to 2.80. Bibby began the season in the bullpen. However, he was moved into the starting rotation on July 10 and he met the challenge by winning six consecutive games. He also fulfilled his hopes of pitching in a World Series.

Bibby's role as a starter was created by an injury to right-hander Don Robinson. At 6-4, 240 pounds, Robinson isn't quite as big as Bibby, but he throws just as hard. His fastball has been clocked at 94 miles an hour. He also throws a curveball with almost as much velocity, which is enough to frighten any batter. However, early in the season, Robinson de-

Omar Moreno

veloped shoulder problems that forced him out of the regular rotation.

It wasn't the first time Robinson had suffered an injury to his throwing arm. On August 26, 1977, Robinson, in his third year of minor league ball was wondering if he ever would pitch again, let alone make it to the major leagues. On that day, Robinson was operated on for bone spurs on his right elbow, an operation that sends fear through any pitcher. Robinson had a 13-inch scar on his elbow, and he was worried about his future as a baseball player.

"I really thought I was finished," admitted Robinson. "Even though the doctors told me it was a routine operation, I had seen too many pitchers never come back from surgery."

Facing a winter of uncertainty, Robinson began a rehabilitation program that he hoped would allow him to at least pitch winter ball in Puerto Rico. When his arm responded to the weight program, Robinson was sent to Puerto Rico to pitch for the Bayamon team, managed by Pirates' coach José Pagan. He made progress and was instructed to report to the Pirates' spring base at Bradenton.

117

"If it hadn't been for winter ball, I wouldn't have been invited to spring training," said Robinson. "They let me pitch one inning every five days in order to bring my arm back slowly. It isn't often that you can go to winter ball under those conditions. They told me if I did well in spring training I'd have a chance to make the club."

Robinson worked hard. Every time he pitched, he did well. During the exhibition season, Robinson yielded only three runs in 22 innings. He made the club.

"José did a good job with him," pointed out Peterson. "He brought him along slowly. Robinson has great poise. He's a lot like Candelaria. They don't scare."

Three weeks into the season, Robinson got his first victory, in his third appearance of the year. Previously, he had worked four innings of relief against the Cardinals and later was charged with the loss against the Cubs when he was victimized by three unearned runs. But

nine days later, the 20-year-old Robinson got his first major league triumph when he five-hit the Mets in New York, 2-1, just seven months after his frightening operation.

"This is the greatest feeling of my life," exclaimed Robinson. "I've always dreamed I'd be in the big leagues. I don't care who my first win was against, the Phillies, the Reds or the Mets. This is great."

When the season ended, the Pirates realized they had a pitcher with a bright future. Robinson had an outstanding rookie year, winning 14 games and losing only six. No other Pirates' pitcher won more games. His efforts earned him Rookie Pitcher of the Year honors.

Big things were expected of Robinson in 1979. Before the season, the Pirates listed him as a definite starter. However, unexpectedly, Robinson suffered a new ailment. This time it was his shoulder. It would stiffen up on him when he began to throw. At first, it was attributed to the cold, damp weather prevalent in

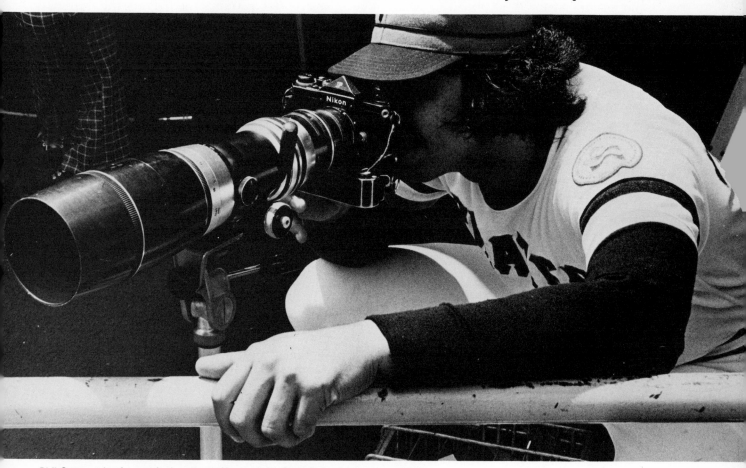

Phil Garner tries for acrobatic putout. Above, John Candelaria checks out camera.

119

the early months of the season. When the shoulder didn't loosen enough in the warm weather, Robinson was examined by a doctor.

"I don't think it's serious," said Robinson. "I don't think it's a sprain or anything like that. It just feels tight. I had the same tightness when I was in the rookie league in 1975. It lasted almost three months, but it went away the next spring. It hasn't bothered me until now."

Robinson's shoulder didn't come around all season, even after long periods of rest between starts. His unavailability left the Pirates' starting staff a bit thin. Even when he did start, Robinson experienced pain. He started 25 games, but he finished only one and his record was only 8-8. In the championship playoffs and in the World Series, Robinson worked out of the bullpen. He delivered in clutch situations, saving one playoff game and winning another. In the World Series, he pitched well and got some big outs.

When the Series ended, Robinson entered the hospital again. This time he was operated on for a torn muscle in his right shoulder. He had to undergo his second winter of rehabilitation in three years. But at 22 years of age, he has plenty of time remaining to earn Stargell stars.

With his starting pitchers ailing and injured, Tanner didn't hesitate in employing his strong relievers. Tanner told his starters to throw as hard and long as they could, then he replaced them with one of his talented bullpen aces. The top reliever was Kent Tekulve.

The 6-4 Tekulve is the most unlikely looking pitcher on the staff. At 160 pounds, he is so skinny that he gives the appearance of an ostrich on the mound. What frustrates most hitters is that he delivers his fastball or his slider in an unorthodox sidearm motion. Off the field, with his tinted wire-rimmed glasses and a pronounced Adam's Apple, Tekulve could easily be mistaken for the town librarian.

Even more unlikely is the fact that Tekulve even made it to the major leagues. He did not pitch professionally until he was 22 years old. Tekulve was drafted by the Pirates in 1969 after graduating from Marietta College, where he was studying to become a school

teacher. He never seriously thought about being a professional ballplayer.

Tekulve bounced around the minor leagues for 6½ years, never really distinguishing himself. He toiled in relative obscurity in such towns as Geneva, New York; Salem, Virginia; Waterbury, Connecticut; Sherbrooke, Canada; and Charleston, West Virginia. After shuttling between Charleston and Pittsburgh for two years, Tekulve finally earned a permanent spot on the Pirates' roster in 1976 at the age of 28. That year he appeared in 64 games, won five and lost three and compiled an earned run average of 2.45.

Still, the Pirates weren't impressed. Before the 1977 season, the Pirates obtained ace reliever Goose Gossage from the Chicago White Sox. It left Tekulve wondering what baseball was all about.

"The trade bothered me a little at first," admitted Tekulve. "Before it was made, I was going to be the short relief man, and I was ready. But as things turned out, the trade was for the betterment of the team. Goose and I sort of double-teamed our opponents. I'd hold them in the sixth, seventh and eighth innings, and he'd do it in the ninth. I feel I was kind of responsible for some of his saves. I think I did get overlooked somewhat. I felt I had a good year but everything was Goose. But he was the man on the spot who had to get the job done late in the game."

That season, Tekulve and Gossage each appeared in 72 games, setting a Pirates' record for appearances. Tekulve had a neat 10-1 record, yet Gossage received the most attention. When the season ended, Gossage's value on the free agent market was magnified even more. He was lured to the New York Yankees by a multi-year contract worth $2.5 million.

The departure of Gossage put Tekulve on the spot. He was counted upon to fill Gossage's spot as the short relief man. It was a tough act to follow. Mentally and physically, Tekulve was ready.

"I know I have a different job to do," Tekulve said prior to the 1978 season. "Last year I was the middle man. Sometimes I would pitch short relief and other times I would pitch long. But this year, I'll be the stopper.

120

Phil Garner avoids base runner.

For the first time since I've been in the major leagues, I'll be doing something I was trained for. I pitched 103 innings last year and that was as a middle man. The big difference between being that and a short reliever is the amount of time you spend warming up. As a long man, you're up and down, up and down before you ever get into the game. But as a short reliever, you usually just warm up one time and go into the game. The less time you throw in the bullpen, the stronger you are on the mound.

"I think I can be just as effective as Goose. I should be able to save 20 to 25 games, but I won't be as spectacular as he was. I'm not going into a game and strike out the side very often. I'll probably throw fewer pitches than he did to get the same job done. I'm probably in the best shape of my career and I don't know why. Usually when you get older, you're supposed to feel worse. But my arm feels good and my legs are strong. I'm hoping I'll be ready to go from day one."

He was ready. Tekulve became the new bullpen favorite of the Pirates' fans. He appeared in a club record 91 games, winning eight and losing seven while producing an earned run figure of 2.33. He worked 135 innings, 32 more than in 1977. Tekulve also set a club record with 31 saves, breaking the Pirates' record of 30 set by Dave Giusti in 1971.

It was no wonder that Tanner counted heavily on Tekulve in 1979. He didn't hesitate to motion for Tekulve whenever he required late-inning relief. Tekulve made 94 appearances. He toiled 134 ⅓ innings, was 10-8 and had an ERA of 2.82. Tekulve's cap became lined with two rows of Stargell's stars. Counting his work in the playoffs and the World Series, Tekulve appeared in 101 games for the Pirates.

"People never thought I would do much in this game," said Tekulve. "I didn't have the right build and had a funny, almost underhand motion. The scouts kept telling me that I'd never make it throwing the ball sidearm. They always wanted me to switch to overhand, but that was my natural motion. Nevertheless, they thought I was just a gimmick pitcher. When I got out of Class A, they said I'd have

122

Tim Foli slides into home plate against New York Mets.

trouble in Double-A. When I did well there, they said wait until Triple-A and so on. I'm just happy that I had the fortitude to stick with my natural motion. The scouts insisted that I throw overhand and if I had switched, I probably wouldn't be here today.

"Some people ask me if I have any limits on how many games I can pitch. I don't know because I haven't gotten there yet. So far, I feel I can pitch more. You know, I don't ice my arm or do anything special for it. I just take normal care of it. Besides, I don't have to

worry about straining any muscles there because everyone says I don't have any."

All he has is a rubber arm and a Superman T-shirt. What he really needs is a phone booth, and that's what he has in the bullpen.

Tekulve's right-handed counterpart in the bullpen is Enrique Romo. Romo was acquired by the Pirates in a winter deal with the Seattle Mariners in 1978. Obtaining Romo was a top priority with Tanner. Tanner needed another durable right-handed pitcher to combine with Tekulve for solid late-inning relief. It would

125

help the skinny Tekulve to remain fresh and strong, something he was not able to do in 1978 with his middle and late-inning appearances.

Although he was 31 years old, Romo had only two years of major league experience. Before being purchased by the Mariners in 1977, Romo had bounced around the Mexican League for 11 years. His best year there was his last, 1976. Romo was 20-4 with an earned run average of 1.89. In 233 innings, Romo struck out 239 batters. He almost had the same ratio in his first year with Seattle. In 114 innings, Romo fanned 105 batters. Despite the fact that he was 8-10, Romo led the Mariners in ERA (2.84), saves (16), appearances (58) and strikeouts.

In 1978, he pitched in 56 games for Seattle. He compiled an 11-7 record with a 3.70 ERA and again topped the staff with saves, 11. The fact that he could throw hard and was especially adept at throwing a screwball made him attractive to the Pirates as well as several other contending clubs.

Romo worked mostly as a middle-inning reliever for the Pirates, enabling Tanner to finish with Tekulve, or with Grant Jackson if the strategy dictated a left-hander. The durable Romo pitched well and enjoyed his best year in the majors. He finished with a 10-5 record and a 3.00 ERA, striking out 106 batters in 129⅓ innings.

Tanner never hesitated in using him. He appeared in 84 games, the second highest number on the staff. Between July 1 and August 24, Romo won seven straight games. In 12 appearances from July 27 to August 11, Romo hurled 19⅓ scoreless innings. He was the long reliever Tanner had needed.

The presence of Romo enabled Jackson, a veteran left-hander, to concentrate on late-inning relief in combination with Tekulve. Despite the fact that he was 36 years old, Jackson made more appearances, 72, than ever in his three years with the Pirates. He finished with an 8-5 mark and an earned run average of 2.96, his best totals with the club. His 14 saves were second to Tekulve and a personal high.

127

Sam Nicosia waits for throw.

It was quite a rewarding season for Jackson. In his 14-year major league career, Jackson's credentials resembled a travelogue. He pitched for seven clubs, including two periods with the Philadelphia Phillies. He began with the Phils, went to San Diego, came back to Philadelphia and put in time with Baltimore, the New York Yankees and Seattle before the Pirates obtained him in 1977.

When Tekulve got off to a slow start, Jackson provided steady early-season relief. It didn't go unappreciated by Tekulve, either.

"Jackson did a helluva job," pointed out Tekulve. "It's a good thing he did because I wasn't going that good. That's the secret to any bullpen. When one guy is having trouble, the other guy has to pick up the slack. It's hard to believe he is 36 years old. He just has everything together."

On a predominantly right-handed pitching staff, Jackson was the only left-handed relief hurler on the club. Jackson was not affected by any batter.

"Left-handed hitters, right-handed hitters, it doesn't make any difference to me," he said. "If I'm pitching well, I can get anybody out. Most people think a relief pitcher is supposed to come in and strike batters out. Listen, I don't care if a guy hits a rocket as long as somebody catches it. Outs are the main thing, not strikeouts. The older you get, the more you realize that."

Surprisingly, the secret to Jackson's late success has been his fastball. He contends that his arm is stronger now than it was 12 years ago.

"I don't know why it happened, but I'm faster now than I have been for a long while," said Jackson. "I've talked to other pitchers and some said the same thing happened to them. It wasn't anything I did, it just happened. You just have to know what you are doing out there on the mound. Anyone who comes up to the plate with a stick can hurt you. What you have to try and do is take the sting out of the bat. You learn how to pace yourself so you just don't throw and throw in the bullpen. I remember a 19-inning game with the Yankees. I threw 14 innings in the bullpen and the last five in the game. My favorite saying is 'give me the ball.' I've been going in the same gear all along, full throttle forward."

That's the way it was with the Pirates in 1979. From July 19, they never were more than three games out of first place. They were in first place for the first time on July 28. After August 5, they held the Eastern Division lead except for seven days. And by the time they had clinched the pennant, on the final day of the season, everyone had contributed. There was the veteran left-hander Jim Rooker, who twice came off the disabled list and won four games; left-hander Dave Roberts, who was acquired from San Francisco in July and won five games; outfielder Mike Easler, who hit .283, primarily as a pinch-hitter; reserve catcher Steve Nicosia, who batted .288; Matt Alexander, who stole 13 bases and scored 16 runs as a deluxe pinch-runner; Dale Berra, who filled in at third base and shortstop; Lee Lacy, who worked in left field and replaced Dave Parker in right field when he was injured; Rennie Stennet, who started the season at second base, and Manny Sanguillen, who provided some key hits and kept the team loose with his humor.

They were all part of "The Family."

Phil Garner avoids San Francisco's Derrell Evans' spikes.

The Playoffs

Grant Jackson was wrong. During the early days of spring, he had predicted that the Pirates would win the Eastern Division pennant on September 23. He was a week off. Pittsburgh didn't win the flag until the last day of the season, September 30. Appropriately, they clinched the title at home, beating the Chicago Cubs, 5-3. It was another typical Pirates' victory. Bruce Kison went six innings for the victory, Kent Tekulve picked up his 31st save and wonderful Willie Stargell crashed his 32nd home run before 42,176 wildly cheering fans. The two runs knocked in by Stargell gave him 1,476 for his career with the Pirates, moving him past the legendary Honus Wagner in the Pittsburgh record book.

Jackson sat on a trunk in the uproarious Pirates' clubhouse, and was not strenuously indulged in the merrymaking. Jackson had been to other pennant-clinching parties during his 14-year career. This was his fifth championship celebration. He had drank champagne with Baltimore and later with the New York Yankees. He was content to let the others do the celebrating. He remembered his spring forecast.

"I was only seven days off," Jackson said with a smile.

Certainly nobody faulted him. After all, the Pirates did win the battle of the East. The exact date wasn't important. Still, Jackson felt confident enough to make another prediction—on the upcoming National League championship series against the Cincinnati Reds.

"This is just the start," prophesized Jackson. "We get down to business on Tuesday. We have to do it Tuesday and Wednesday in Cincinnati and come back here and do it some more on the weekend. We won't be finished until we win the World Series.

"Oh, it's fun to sit here and watch. I was the same way the first time I won. But now I know that champagne burns when it gets in your eyes. You drink a little, have a beer and you're drunk. And it takes a little time for these things to strike me.

"The best thing about the playoffs is they bring out things you don't know you have in you. Guys who don't normally do certain things wind up doing them. Right now we have the best bullpen in baseball. We have a lot

of clutch hitters. If Dave Parker doesn't hit it, Willie Stargell does, or Phil Garner does, or Bill Madlock does. You can't pick one guy who has done it."

As is his custom after a game, Jackson tried to start a card game with Rennie Stennett. It wasn't possible. Within minutes, the cards became sticky from the loose flowing champagne, and anyway, Garner used the table as his stage for dancing. As usual, the Pirates were happy and fun-loving.

Stargell, Kison and Sanguillen were the only three Pirates' players remaining from the 1971 championship team. Kison was only a rookie then, but since that time, he had made a habit of winning games in September. In the nine years he had pitched in September, Kison's record for the month was 23-6. That's when pennants are won, and why Kison was looked upon as a money pitcher.

"This is the most emotional situation I've ever been in because we had to work so hard to get there," explained Kison. "Other years we ran away with it, but not this year. And it's even more meaningful because the last two years we played our hearts out and came out empty. We have that cohesiveness but it's more than that. We don't depend on any one guy. We have a lot of hitters hitting between .280 and .310. Stargell carried this team for years. Parker is capable of doing it. But we've gotten here this year by everybody making a contribution. I think every pitcher has made a contribution. This is the type of ballclub you want to be part of."

Stargell knew what Kison meant. He had been contributing longer than any other Pirates' player. His two runs batted in were the difference in the clinching victory over the Cubs. He was teary eyed when he spoke.

"I'm so proud of our unit, I just can't find the words," said Stargell. "This is the warmest feeling I've ever had about a team. It was a hard season. We had doubleheaders in a row, rain, lots of traveling, but we just got on the field and did it.

"We don't have many .300 hitters and we don't have any 20-game winners. What we have is 25 guys who play hard. What we have is a lot of junkyard dogs.

"It may sound funny, but the one thought that comes to my mind now is Dave Roberts standing on the mound in the 19-inning game in San Diego."

Stargell was referring to a tense, bases-loaded situation. Roberts had filled the bases with two out in the 16th inning and dug himself a hole when he ran the count to 3-0 on the San Diego pitcher. Dave Winfield, who was at second base, gave Roberts the choke sign. Roberts bore down and struck out the batter, ending the inning and extending the game.

"Roberts never gave up," exclaimed Stargell. "That's what strikes me about this team. It never gives up."

A short time later Roberts came by and hugged Stargell.

"You are the greatest man I've known," said Roberts.

John Milner looked over. Stargell's tears brought back memories to the former Mets' first baseman-outfielder.

"I watched Willie Mays cry in 1973 and we dedicated the playoffs to him," said Milner. "I watched Willie Stargell cry now and we're dedicating these playoffs to him."

The only thing that bothered the players for a while during the game was the scoreboard. As the scoreboard operator kept posting the score of the Philadelphia-Montreal game, the crowd in Three Rivers Stadium was reacting. Even the Pirates' players in the dugout stopped and looked. It didn't help concentration. It was an important game in that if the Pirates lost and the Expos won, the season would be extended another day. But the Pirates' players were merely concerned with winning the pennant against Chicago.

"We were upset with the guy who operates the scoreboard because he was making us stop the game when we were going," said Madlock. "We called upstairs and told them not to do it when the game was going on. When they would put up the score, everybody in the crowd would go 'ooooohhhh' and everybody on the bench would jump up to see the score."

So, the score of the final three innings of the Philadelphia-Montreal game was not posted on the scoreboard. It wasn't until Tekulve was facing the Cubs in the ninth inning that the

133

scoreboard beamed the information that the Expos had lost. All that was needed was for Tekulve to retire the Cubs and the Pirates would clinch the title.

"Once I saw that Montreal lost, I don't think I could have been higher and still kept on pitching," admitted Tekulve. "When I got 0-and-2 on (Bruce) Kimm, I tried to throw him a 500 mile-per-hour slider and just bury him for the third out. It went to the backstop. So I calmed down and threw him just a normal nasty slider."

Kimm popped up for the third out and the Pirates had won the Eastern Division crown. It was the first-third of a three-part season for Pirates' Executive Vice-President Pete Peterson.

"When the last out came," said Peterson, "I thought, 'It's been a struggle, but we won. But now it's only one-third over. The second third is the playoffs and the final third is the World Series.

The Cincinnati Reds represented the opposition for the second third of the season. The Pirates had little time to savor their title. They had to leave early the next morning for Cincinnati.

GAME ONE

A heavy fog consumed the Greater Pittsburgh Airport. Air traffic was delayed. It put a kink in the Pirates' schedule as well as others. The team had planned on arriving in Cincinnati in time for an afternoon workout before the best-of-five series opened on Tuesday night. There wasn't anything anybody could do but wait until the fog lifted. Nobody could predict when that would happen, not even Jackson. Most experts were predicting that the Reds would win the playoffs. The first two games were scheduled in Cincinnati with the final three assigned to Pittsburgh. All anybody could do until then was wait. The waiting is the worst part for ballplayers.

In the waiting room, John Candelaria, chosen to pitch the opening game, was sitting on the floor with his legs crossed. It wasn't a normal position for him. But he was sitting and

playing with Tim Foli's baby daughter. They were a study in contrast . . . Candelaria, a 6-7 left-hander and a tot dressed in blue pajamas.

Candelaria was a surprise starter. He had been bothered most of the season with rib and back problems. Candelaria had finished the season with a 14-9 record and a 3.22 ERA. However, in his last start, on September 16 against the New York Mets, he was shelled. In his last appearance, against the Cubs on Saturday, he faced four batters, got only one out and gave up two runs. His record against the Reds was unimpressive. He had hurled 19⅔ innings, yielded 13 runs and was 0-2. The Reds' scouts felt that if there was a weakness on the Pirates, it was their starting pitchers. Yet, Tanner defended his decision to open with Candelaria.

"He's a money pitcher," emphasized Tanner. "He's ready, well-rested and he's a great pitcher. Why wouldn't you want him to open this series?"

When the club finally arrived in Cincinnati four hours late, Candelaria did not say much. He was concerned about his back problems, and preferred not to discuss them.

"Injury?" he asked. "I'm fine. I stopped talking about it a month ago."

Ironically, that was about the time when the Reds stopped playing good baseball. Cincinnati had overcome a 10-game Houston lead on July 4 and appeared primed to pull away from the Astros. However, the Reds won only 13 of their remaining 27 games. They won the Western Division title only because the Astros' record was worse.

Still, in Tom Seaver, the Reds had their money pitcher working for them. After a slow start, Seaver had finished the season strong, with a 16-6 record and a 3.40 ERA. He was in such a good groove the final months of the season that he won 14 of his last 15 decisions. A crafty right-hander, Seaver always had been one of the premier pitchers in the National League starting when he had pitched for the New York Mets. In facing Candelaria in the first game, Seaver was making his first playoff appearance since 1973.

Seaver was well-rested for the opener. He

136

had an extra day to get ready, five days instead of the normal four he prefers between starts. An intelligent individual, Seaver had to make adjustments in his pitching style since his fastball no longer was as fast as in his younger days. He had started to rely more on his curve ball because early in June, Seaver was 2-5 and struggling. He adjusted well. Since that time, Seaver, who was voted the National League Cy Young Award winner three times, was 14-1. No pitcher in the majors could match that record.

"I still throw as hard as Nolan Ryan," joked Seaver, "but it just doesn't get to the plate as quickly as Ryan's fastball. I started to throw within myself. Pitching is like hitting a golf ball. If you overswing a golf club, everything goes wrong. If you overthrow a baseball, everything else goes wrong.

"Pitching now is more rewarding, more gratifying. I'm not overpowering anymore, but the games themselves are more rewarding. When I was with the Mets, I'd strike out 13 or 15 and maybe pitch a three-hit shutout. That's the physical effort. But it's much more enjoyable to be mentally fatigued. I know I have to constantly make adjustments in my pitching during a game and that's what makes it rewarding. You scratch and claw and all of a sudden you end up winning 4-3."

Seaver was the Reds' big hope. Their once-powerful hitting had been diminished during the final month of the season. The Big Red Machine was being referred to as the Little Red Wagon. It was enough to cause concern for catcher Johnny Bench.

"This club is a little unsure, a little bit guarded," revealed Bench. "This team has a different personality than our teams that won in '75 and '76. Those teams just blew away opponents; this team really hasn't done that often enough.

"We have to hope we get the real good pitching this series because our hitting just hasn't been there. The Pirates got a lot of weapons. They do everything well. They've got speed, power, defense, good relief pitching. On offense, you look at Parker, but then you've got Madlock. Stargell can do it with a

couple of swings. Robinson hits left-handers. You can't make a mistake on Ott or Garner, either."

Bench knew the Pirates well. Going in to the playoffs Pittsburgh was hot. In the final two weeks of the season, Madlock had batted .435 and finished with a 10-game hitting streak. Garner had a 14-game hitting skein; Foli an eight-game string; Stargell had smashed eight home runs down the stretch; and Parker had finished 21-for-39, a .539 mark.

The Pirates and Reds had met three previous times in championship play, in 1970, 1972 and 1975, and Cincinnati had won each time. During the 1979 regular season, Pittsburgh and Cincinnati had met twelve times with the Reds winning eight. That didn't bother the Pirates. This was a new season.

"We're here now, man," said Stargell, "and that's the important thing. If we aren't, then 8-of-12 would mean something."

Robinson felt the same way.

"People have been putting us down all year and I don't know why," he said. "We won 98 games that we HAD to win. Sometimes emotion is just as good as talent."

Tanner also was confident. He appeared quite relaxed sitting in the lobby of the hotel reading a newspaper despite the fact that his mother had been hospitalized with a stroke several days earlier.

"I'm dedicating the championship to my mother and father," said Tanner. "She suffered a stroke three or four days ago. It was . . . Gee, I don't know. What day is today?"

He wanted to talk about his ballclub. That was easier than the emotional strain from which he was suffering. He appreciated the talents of all his players, regulars and reserves. All the pieces fit and he made them work.

"Championship teams are formed by putting together the little pieces that are missing, just like a jigsaw puzzle," explained Tanner. "We didn't have all the pieces when we started the season. The ending was the greatest day in my life. We knew we had a few pieces missing and Harding Peterson went out and got them. What we needed was a shortstop who could play steady ball and another right-handed batter who could balance the attack. So we got Foli in April and Madlock in June.

"There are a lot of guys we could not have won without, but we definitely could not have won without those two trades. Foli cemented our infield and Madlock gave us the right-handed punch, plus the speed we needed. What we did with those two deals was add both defense and offense.

"In Foli, we wanted somebody who could do the ordinary things in an extraordinary way. He did just that for us. I still say no one comes across the bag and makes a double play better than he does. We got Foli to take shorter strokes at bat. Instead of hitting 350-foot fly ball outs, he hit 270-foot singles.

"You know, we didn't pick up two regulars in Foli and Madlock. We picked up two players who weren't playing regularly for other teams and we made them regulars. There's a difference. Peterson always liked Madlock and he had pursued him before, but we couldn't make the deal by the June 15th trading deadline. We couldn't close the deal until June 28 when the other clubs waived on him."

Tanner's observations were generally shared by the players. Parker didn't hide his feelings about the importance of getting Foli and Madlock. He also was happy because he was returning to his hometown for a few days.

"I'm here to get some of my mom's home

Omar Moreno slides safely into third base in third game.

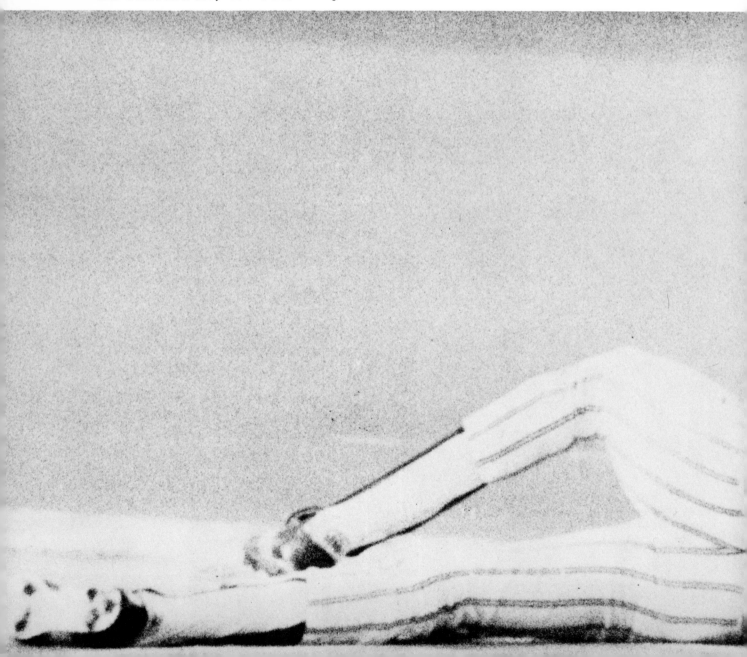

cooking and about ten home runs," mused Parker. "Hey, some people were ready to run me out of town this summer, but I started swinging the bat at an opportune time for myself and for the ballclub. I came through when they needed me.

"A lot of people wrote us off early. We had to struggle and we did. This club doesn't quit. We're just not like that. That's probably the biggest reason I stayed here. We never thought we weren't going to win the pennant. We've been under pressure all year. But getting a Tim Foli and a Bill Madlock synchronized this club. It's been a season of crises, but we took the bad days with the good ones and we stuck it out together."

Despite a chilly evening, a crowd of 55,006 filled Riverfront Stadium. While players from both clubs wore long sleeve sweatshirts under their uniforms, they were a contrast in dress styles and personalities. The Pirates were loud and colorful, displaying a great deal of facial hair and wearing eye-catching uniforms. The Reds were cool and businesslike, with knee-high stockings and their sideburns and hair neatly trimmed.

Seaver was well rested. The concern was Candelaria. It was feared that the cold weather might make his back condition worse. Yet, Tanner was not concerned. His bullpen, which he had utilized so often during the regular season, was ready. He had Tekulve,

Robinson, Jackson and Romo assigned to relief duty, to be ready at a moment's notice. Nobody knew how long Candelaria would last with his troublesome back. In the playoffs, Tanner was ready to move quickly.

Both starting pitchers worked quickly during the first inning. In the second inning, Madlock beat out a two-out dribbler to third base for the Pirates' first hit. A moment later, he stole second base. But Seaver, pitching to the corners, struck out Ott, ending the mild threat.

In the bottom half of the inning, Bench, who had lamented about the Reds' lack of offense during the closing weeks of the season, ripped one of Candelaria's fastballs off the left centerfield wall for a triple. But Candelaria, throwing hard, struck out Ray Knight and Dan Driessen, preventing the Reds from scoring. Candelaria didn't give any indication that his back was bothering him. All the Pirates needed were some runs.

Garner led off the third inning. He took a ball. Seaver threw again. It was another ball. On 2-and-0, Garner stepped out of the batter's box looking for a sign. Seaver fired a pitch on the outside corner. Garner swung and connected. He hit the ball on a line ino the right field stands for a home run, giving Pittsburgh a 1-0 lead.

After Candelaria struck out, Moreno drilled Seaver's offering into right field. Dave Collins charged the ball trying to make a one-handed catch. The ball hit sharply in front of him and bounced over his head. The speedy Moreno raced all the way to third base before the ball was finally returned to the infield.

The Pirates had a chance to score another run, and Foli delivered it with a sacrifice fly. The Pirates led 2-0. Seaver appeared shaky. He had trouble keeping his ball down and walked Parker and Stargell, offering the Pirates an opportunity to add to their lead. However, Milner swung under a pitch and popped it to Joe Morgan at second base, ending the inning.

Pittsburgh's lead was short-lived, as the Reds tied the score in the fourth inning. Dave Concepcion led off by ripping a single to left.

Power hitter George Foster, who had been in a mild slump, brought Cincinnati fans screaming out of their seats on the first pitch to him from Candelaria. Foster sent a drive to deep centerfield, the ball landing in the seats for a home run. The game now was tied 2-2.

Following Foster's blast, both pitchers settled down. After yielding a single to Foli in the fifth inning, Seaver retired the Pirates in order in the sixth and seventh innings, Candelaria was just as effective. He set down the Reds easily in the fifth. In the next inning, he pitched carefully to Foster with two out and walked him before getting the third out. In the seventh, he set down the Reds with nothing resembling a hit. Candelaria was pitching a strong game despite the pain which showed on his face.

Tanner sent Candelaria back to the mound in the bottom of the eighth inning. It was a ploy. Seaver was the first scheduled batter. Instead, Reds' Manager John McNamara sent up right-hand hitting Rick Auerbach to bat for Seaver. Tanner made McNamara commit to a pinch hitter before lifting Candelaria for right-hander Enrique Romo.

After Auerbach fanned, Collins singled and stole second. Morgan then coaxed a walk from Romo. That was all for Romo. Tanner called for Tekulve to try and subdue the Reds. He did on one pitch. Tekulve induced Concepcion to ground into an inning-ending double play, from Madlock to Garner to Stargell. It was a big pitch.

The Pirates' bats had been silent since the third inning. Seaver had retired ten batters in a row. Tom Hume came in to get the Pirates out in the ninth inning but not before surviving a scare. Hector Cruz climbed the centerfield fence to take at least a double away from Madlock. Tekulve took care of the Reds in the bottom of the ninth and the game went into extra innings.

With one out in the 10th, Garner singled to left. Tanner then sent up Mike Easler to bat for Tekulve. But Easler flied to left and Moreno took a third strike, ending the inning.

Jackson, the Pirates' new pitcher, then disposed of the Reds in order. In the 11th inning,

Manager Chuck Tanner is flanked by Pirate owners Dan and John Galbreath.

Foli, the first batter, dumped a single into left field. Tanner sent in Matt Alexander to run for Foli. Parker followed with a single to left as Alexander stopped at second base. As Stargell stepped in to bat, the crowd began to stir. Stargell pumped his bat in his usual windmill fashion while waiting for Hume's first pitch. Then as Stargell swung, the crowd moaned. The ball sailed over the right centerfield fence for a dramatic three-run homer, giving the Pirates a 5-2 lead. It was the first home run off Hume in 52 innings. "Pops" was hugged at home plate by both Alexander and Parker as Milner congratulated him on his way up to bat. The Pirates' players in the dugout were excited and came over to mob Stargell.

Jackson took care of the first two Reds' batters in the 11th, but Concepcion singled and Foster walked. Bench, the next batter, represented the tying run. Tanner replaced Jackson with hard-throwing right-hander Don Robinson.

Over the years, Bench had been a clutch hitter for the Reds. On several occasions, he had beaten the Pirates with ninth-inning home runs. Cincinnati fans were clamoring for Bench to hit another homer. Robinson was in a tight spot.

He threw a fastball on the first pitch and Bench fouled it back on the screen. The next two pitches were balls. Stargell called time and walked over to the mound. He wanted to calm

141

down the 22-year-old Robinson. Robinson came back with a strike, making the count 2-2. Again Robinson fired. Bench didn't swing. Garner excitedly jumped in the air thinking it was a strike. But the umpire yelled "ball" and the count was 3-2.

The crowd was roaring as Robinson stepped on the mound for the next pitch. Then he stepped off. The noisy fans yelled louder. Robinson threw a curve ball. It broke outside. Bench had walked, loading the bases. That brought up Ray Knight, another dangerous hitter. All the Reds needed now was a base-clearing double to tie the score.

Robinson fired his first pitch and Knight missed it. He fired again and Knight fouled it. Robinson came back with another fastball. It was low and outside. Then he tried a breaking pitch. That, too, was low and away, but Knight swung and missed. The ball bounced a couple of feet behind Ott. He pounced on it quickly, picked it up and threw to first base to Stargell, retiring Knight for the final out. The dramatic first game had ended.

Stargell tried to be low-key afterwards. The writers congregated around him. His home run had won the game. Winning the first game in a short series was important.

"A routine win for the Pirates, nothing special," deadpanned Stargell. "Oh well, maybe a little bit special. Actually, this has to be one of the most thrilling games I've ever been associated with if you want to know the truth. It was a big game, but all the ones we've played the last month were big games.

"Obviously winning a game that Seaver starts against you is important. But we feel we can go up against anybody. We don't give in to anyone. But I was glad Tom wasn't out there at the end. You know, before I stepped up to hit in the 11th inning, I looked at Joe Lonnett for a sign. It's strange, but when you get ready to bunt, for some reason you always get a pitch you can hit. I'm glad I was hitting."

Then Stargell revealed that the Pirates had been miffed before the game because of a story in a local newspaper in which Detroit Tigers' scout Jack Tighe had claimed that the Reds were better than the Pirates in six of the eight positions other than the pitcher. They were particularly angered by the fact that Tighe rated Knight over Madlock, Driessen over Stargell and Morgan over Garner.

"It sounded as if we didn't belong here," snapped Stargell. "We put it up on the locker room wall. We don't think we're better than anybody else, but we don't think they're better than us, either. Maybe now they'll think we belong here."

Candelaria certainly had showed that he belonged. While many had questioned Tanner's selection in naming him to pitch the opener, Candelaria had displayed courage in limiting the Reds to two runs in the seven painful innings he had worked, matching Seaver's effort.

"I told Chuck I'd go as long as I could, that I'd fire until I fell," said Candelaria. "I fired until I fell. Why be a hero? I did what I could. The thing is, it's just a pain to pitch in pain. The doctor said I might have a tear, but that at the end of the year I could get a rest. Well, I don't want to rest right now."

Bench could understand why. He had been impressed with Candelaria's pitching.

"He threw the fastball different tonight," pointed out Bench. "He used to throw risers that came straight at you, but tonight he was turning the ball over. 'Candy Man' had a hell of a game."

Actually, so did Robinson in his first playoff appearance. Robinson was bothered by a sore shoulder, but Tanner had faith in him. Robinson had been put in a pressure situation and he had come through. He was excited by it all, the meaning of the game and his performance.

"We beat Tom Seaver," Robinson said excitedly. "Well, we really didn't beat him but we got past him. That means they have a young pitcher with no playoff experience coming back tomorrow. There's going to be a lot of pressure on him. I know what it's like the first time in playoff pressure.

"When I went in there I was so pumped up, the adrenalin was flowing so much, I didn't know if there was any pain in my shoulder. I know I didn't feel any. But I know Candy did.

It was obvious he was in a lot of pain out there. I could hear him screaming from the bench.

"I went in there with one objective: don't let Bench hit it out of the park. He's beat the Pirates so many times in the ninth inning with home runs, I didn't want to give him anything good to hit. The first pitch was a fastball up and over the plate. Oh, a mistake pitch. I'm glad he didn't hit that one out. When I fell behind, 2-1, Stargell came over. He wanted to calm me down. He said, 'Why don't I pitch and you play first base.'"

"I thought I had Bench struck out on 2-2. It was close but I guess it was outside. The crowd noise didn't bother me before the 3-2 pitch. We just had some communication problems. Ed Ott kept signaling for a fastball. I wanted to throw a curveball. I grew up watching Johnny Bench hit too many clutch home runs, and I wasn't going to let him hit a three-run home run off me."

Ott explained why he wanted another fastball.

"Donnie had thrown two fastballs past Bench," reasoned Ott. "I thought we could get another one past him. The way he was throwing, I had a lot of confidence in him."

All the Pirates had confidence now. "Pops" had shown them how to win.

GAME TWO

Normally, during the regular season, Stargell doesn't play in day games after a night contest. But this was the championship playoffs. It didn't matter that the second game was scheduled for a day game. Stargell would play in the morning if it was necessary. As it was, he was at the ballpark early. He was being featured on a couple of television commercials and Stargell had to fulfill those commitments before getting ready to face the Reds again.

When Stargell arrived on the field dressed in sandals to do his interviews, some of the Reds already were there taking batting practice. Morgan looked at Stargell and pretended to spike his unprotected feet. Stargell joined in the fun, then asked Morgan to let him borrow some of his bats.

"This is a pea-shooter," chided Stargell. "I didn't know you swung a pea-shooter."

Morgan broke out in laughter. A few moments later, George Foster began conversing with Stargell. He, too, found reason to laugh. That's the way it is with Stargell. He is loved and respected by everyone in the league. In the tension of the playoffs, Morgan and Foster had found time to share a laugh with Pops.

Later, Stargell was standing in front of the Pirates' dugout. He was holding a microphone for another commercial. Spontaneously, Madlock hopped up on his back, just like a little child would jump on a father's back.

"Hey," somebody from the television crew yelled, "he's doing an interview."

Madlock immediately got down and apologized for the interruption. Stargell never moved. He wasn't the least bit annoyed. He just kept staring straight ahead at the camera.

"See what I got to put up with?" he exclaimed. "I'm going to play out my option this year and be the first black goalie in the National Hockey League with the New York Rangers."

Then he turned and looked at Madlock.

"Worst trade we ever made," he joked.

Somehow, Stargell finished the commercials. Then he left to finish dressing for the game as more players from both teams began to emerge from the clubhouse. Some of the Pirates still were reflecting on the previous night's victory.

"The first game is always a big one," said Tekulve. "Now they have to win three out of four to beat us. That's a whole lot better than us having to win three out of four from them."

Tanner said, "It means that we now have to play .500 ball to win it, that's all. It's a good feeling when you know you can win a series by playing .500 ball."

Parker's perspective was centered on Game Two. The way he viewed it, Game Two was important.

"This is not a long series," said Parker. "If we can beat them in the second game, there is no way they can win three from us at home."

Tanner designated veteran right-hander Jim Bibby to pitch the second game. Bibby was paired against rookie right-hander Frank Pastore, who was only 6-7 during the season. Pastore opened the season with the Reds and had pitched impressively until yielding five home runs in one game against the Los Angeles Dodgers. That hastened his exile to the minors. He was recalled by the Reds in August. In the final week of the season, he won two key starts.

After a scoreless first inning, The Reds scored the game's first run in the second inning. Dan Driessen opened the inning with a single. Ray Knight followed with a single, sending Driessen to second. Cesar Geronimo, playing centerfield instead of Hector Cruz, sacrificed the runners. Pastore then hit a sacrifice fly, scoring Driessen and the Reds led 1-0.

In the fourth inning, the Pirates tied the score despite some bizarre base running. Foli led off with a single, the first hit off Pastore. Parker also singled, and the Pirates had runners on first and second with none out. Stargell was at the plate. It was the first pressure situation for Pastore, the rookie left-hander. Everyone in Riverfront Stadium was aware of what Stargell had done the previous night with two runners on base in the 11th inning.

Stargell got good wood on the ball. He sent a deep fly ball to left field. George Foster went back on the warning track and appeared ready to catch the ball. Suddenly he turned away. He had lost the ball in the sun and it dropped safely behind him. Foli, anticipating that the ball would be caught, went back to second base to tag up. Parker, running cautiously, pulled up in front of second. When the ball hit the ground. Foli ran to third base and Parker glided into second.

However, Stargell, watching the ball all the way, ran hard toward second base after the ball dropped. When he got there, he was surprised to see Parker occupying the base. Quickly, Stargell retreated back to first. But the relay throw from Foster to first base was in time to nip Stargell. Instead of the bases being filled with none out, the Pirates had runners on second and third with one out. Milner walked loading the bases. The Reds then played their infield back in hopes of getting a double play. Madlock hit a ball on the ground to shortstop, but the Reds couldn't make the double play and Foli scored easily on the force play, tying the score 1-1.

In the next inning, Pittsburgh moved into a 2-1 lead. Again there was a bizarre play. Garner led off the inning with a sinking line drive to right field. Dave Collins broke in fast, dove for the ball, tumbled over and came up with it in his glove. He got up off the ground and held his glove high in the air to show that he had caught the ball.

However, umpire Frank Pulli signalled a hit. He contended that Collins had trapped the ball. Garner was safe at first with a single and the Reds began to scream. Collins pleaded with Pulli. Cincinnati manager John McNamara and second baseman Joe Morgan ran out to right field. Collins kept showing Pulli the ball in his glove. McNamara pleaded with Pulli to ask for help on the play by appealing to another umpire. But Pulli was adamant in his decision and ordered everyone to return to their positions so the game could continue.

After the argument, Bibby sacrificed Garner to second. When Moreno made the second out, it appeared that Pastore would get out of the inning. Foli wouldn't let him. He lined a shot past third base for a double, sending in Garner with the run that gave Pittsburgh a 2-1 lead.

Bibby held that advantage until the eighth inning. He was removed after developing a crick in his neck. Jackson came in and retired Morgan. Then Tanner surprisingly removed Jackson and called in Romo. Tanner was playing the percentages by having the right-handed Romo face Concepcion and Foster.

This time, the strategy backfired. Concepcion and Foster both singled. Tanner was out of the dugout again. This time he called for Tekulve to make his 96th appearance of the season. Tekulve threw a wild pitch, allowing the runners to reach second and third with only one out. But Tekulve fanned Bench for the important second out. With first base open, Tanner ordered an intentional walk for the left-handed swinging Driessen.

The drama grew in intensity when Tekulve went to a full count on Knight. However, on the next pitch, Knight lofted a fly ball to Moreno for the third out as the Pirates went into the final inning still ahead, 2-1.

Tekulve started the inning in fine style, striking out Geronimo. Cruz pinch-hit for Hume. On a 1-1 pitch. Cruz swung and missed. However, he got another chance. A baseball had gotten loose in the bullpen and rolled into the outfield. Jim Quick, umpiring along the left field, and third base umpire Dick Stello had called time before Tekulve had delivered his pitch.

So, instead of being behind, 1-2, Cruz had a great deal of pressure removed. He took advantage by whacking the next pitch for a double to right centerfield. Collins, who was involved in the controversial play in the fifth inning, was the next batter. He tied the score with another double.

Tanner made another move to his bullpen. He wanted left-hander Dave Roberts to pitch to Morgan. Roberts walked Morgan on four pitches as the fans yelled. With Concepcion and Foster the next two batters, Tanner decided on another pitching change. This time, he brought in Robinson, the pitching hero of the previous night.

Robinson fired the ball past Concepcion and struck him out. Then he got the dangerous Foster to ground out to Garner for the third out of the inning. For the second straight game, the teams went into extra innings.

The Reds brought in Doug Bair, a former Pittsburgh farmhand, to pitch the 10th inning. Moreno greeted him with a single. Foli sacrificed Moreno to second. Parker worked the count to 2-1, then lined a single to center. Moreno scored easily, giving the Pirates a 3-2 lead.

It was up to Robinson to preserve the victory. The first batter he faced was Bench. Robinson challenged him with fastballs and struck him out. He then retired Driessen and Knight without any problems. The Pirates had won the game and now had a commanding 2-0 lead, having beaten the Reds twice in Cincinnati.

Robinson, who had not worked much in relief, had a save and a victory in two appearances. Surprisingly, he was firing the ball hard despite the nagging pain in his shoulder.

"I felt pumped up and my shoulder didn't hurt anymore," exclaimed a happy Robinson. "I was careful with Bench at first, but then I decided to challenge everybody. If they hit it out of the park, I tip my hat to them. I'm just trying to throw as hard as I can. I tried to keep the ball away from Concepcion, and that curve on 0-2, I don't think any person in the history of baseball could have hit that one."

"That's the fastest curveball in the league," said Garner. "It looks like it's 100 miles an hour."

"Right now, because of my shoulder, it would be tough for me to start," Robinson admitted. "I'd probably get stiff after five or six innings, then be out for a week, like I was during the middle of the season.

"But this is fun. However, I wouldn't want to do this regularly. I'm glad I didn't have to go any further today. I want to be a starter. When you're coming in like this, you can't pitch around hitters, set them up, throw different kinds of pitches. I want to be able to make my pitch. I want to start."

Tekulve, who probably never will be a starter, knows the hazards of relief pitching. Situations can change rapidly as they did for him in the ninth inning.

"I made two mistakes," disclosed Tekulve. "I threw two high sliders, and they are professional hitters. They don't let you get away with mistakes."

Luckily, the Pirates' base running mistake in the fourth inning didn't hurt in view of the victory. Still, Stargell had to explain his gaffe.

"It was my fault," he said. "I should have been watching what the runners ahead of me were doing. But I saw that Foster didn't catch the ball, that's why I kept running. Foli thought he might catch it, so he stayed at second to tag up, but Parker knew it wouldn't be caught, so he went down to second. I was

145

watching the flight of the ball. I was a runaway beer truck out there. And when I looked up, we had three men on second base. We've never worked on going from second to first before. I'm gonna get on Chuck about that."

For Parker, supplying the game-winning hit was a sweet ending for him. Eight of his relatives were in the stands watching the game.

"I'm kind of surprised they're pitching me away," said Parker. "I know most people like to go with the hard stuff away, but I can reach that hard stuff outside. I'm not surprised they didn't walk me. I know they'd rather try to get me out than to deal with Willie Stargell, as hot as he's been. I know one thing, it is virtually impossible for Cincinnati to beat us three straight in Pittsburgh."

The Reds' clubhouse was heavy with disappointment. They knew they had to win. It was a must game for them and they had failed. They still weren't getting the big hits. The Big Red Machine wasn't so big anymore. They kept replaying Garner's drive to Collins that was ruled a hit. The fact that the instant replay showed that Collins had made the catch was no solace.

"I didn't have to see the replay," snapped Collins. "I caught the ball. I'm an honest person. If I had shoe-stringed it, you would have seen water come off the carpet because it was wet out there. If I hadn't caught it, I would have come up throwing to second base because I know Garner can run. I caught the ball. If there was a Bible here I'd swear on it."

McNamara believed his right fielder.

"He made a hell of a catch," said McNamara. "I saw him make it with my own naked eyes, and my eyes are pretty good. There's no doubt that he made the catch. I felt Pulli was shielded on the call by Collins' body angle. I thought he should have asked for help. That was my argument."

However, McNamara had no argument over another matter. No team ever had come back to win the playoffs after trailing by two games. The way the Reds were hitting, their chances were slim. The Reds were batting only .208 after the first two games.

"It's the toughest thing in the world to know

146

Willie Stargell is mobbed after hitting game-winning three run homer in 12th inning of first game.

Stargell gets a reception after hitting home run in game three.

that you had the opportunity to do the job and did not," sighed Bench. "You blame yourself. You feel the worst because that's the situation you want to be up in, and should be up in. I didn't do the job."

GAME THREE

Pittsburgh was in a festive mood. After the Pirates had won the first two games in Cincinnati, Pittsburgh fans were in a mood to celebrate. A case of pennant fever started to grip the fans. Downtown buildings displayed a myriad of signs exhorting the players onward to their first World Series appearance in eight years. The signs were in all shapes and sizes and gaily decorated the office buildings. Some were quite original, festooned with the head of a Pirate. There were messages like: "Babushka

Brigade," "Pittsburgh Backs Its Bucs," "No Doubt About It," "Pirate Fever," "Bucs #1," "Here's The Bucs," and "Let's Go Bucs." Just like the Steelers ten months earlier, the city had a love affair with the Pirates. Pittsburgh was a burgeoning city of champions.

A light drizzle dampened the Pirates' scheduled Thursday afternoon workout. The players took advantage of the weather to relax around the clubhouse. Friday afternoon would come soon enough, and besides, they couldn't do any celebrating until clinching the playoffs with another victory. Their chances of succeeding were excellent. No team in either league ever had lost the first two games of the championship playoffs and won. The fact that the Reds had beaten the Pirates in five of six regular-season meetings in Three Rivers didn't matter. Tanner dismissed any in-

ference that the Reds might hold something of a hidden edge despite their current predicament.

"This is the playoffs," emphasized Tanner. "It's a different season. I could go over the details of what happened in those games this season, but it just doesn't matter now."

Tanner selected Blyleven to face the Reds in the third game. Blyleven was the youngest pitcher ever to pitch in the playoffs. He was only 19 years old when he appeared in the 1970 playoffs in relief for Minnesota against Baltimore. The baby-faced right-hander had a 12-5 record during the regular season. He had shaved his beard for the playoffs, uncovering a youthful face. He threw what many consider the best curveball in the majors. Strangely, Blyleven was involved in 20 no-decision games during the season, or he might have been cre-

dited with more victories. Pitching coach Harvey Haddix knew why Blyleven had not won more games.

"Bert has as good stuff as anyone in the league," said Haddix. "But when someone gets on base, he gets in too big a hurry to deliver the ball. There are certain runners who make a pitcher fall into that habit. All you can do is keep talking to him about it."

For years, Blyleven had pitched under a shadow. Many observers contended that Blyleven couldn't win the big games and, indeed, lost too many one-run games. Blyleven had heard the insinuations. He didn't like them.

"People who say that have never pitched in the big leagues," said Blyleven. "I know that people have said those things about me. It's a bad rap. I've heard it and I don't like it. I think

over the years I've been a very consistent pitcher with a very good earned-run average. It's tough pitching for Tanner because he goes to the bullpen so often. I realize we have a good bullpen, but it is a lot different in the American League.

"I'm glad to get the chance to pitch in the playoffs. I'm a competitor. I don't like being taken out of a game. I know I've lost many one-run games over the years. But I didn't lose 6-5 or 7-6. I lost 2-1 and 3-2. When I look back, I got to think I pitched a pretty good game. You need runs to win."

Blyleven's pitching opponent, Mike LaCoss, was even more of a paradox. In fact, his problem was much more severe. LaCoss was in a slump. During the month of September, his earned run average was an atrocious 11.50! It was perplexing because LaCoss had started the season in excellent form. At the All-Star break, he was 11-4, and was selected to the National League team. LaCoss, only 23 years old, finished the season with a 14-8 record. He was only in his second year with the Reds and was making his first playoff appearance.

Friday was the start of a big weekend for the Galbreath family. Besides being emotionally involved in the basebll playoffs, they had their hearts in horse racing. The next day, the Galbreaths' pride of the Darby Dan Farm, Affirmed, was running against Spectacular Bid in the Jockey Club Gold Cup race at New York's Belmont Park. It was John Galbreath's "daily double" dream that his Pirates would clinch the National League pennant on Friday, which would give him plenty of time to fly to New York and watch Affirmed run—and hopefully win—the next day.

It wasn't a bright Friday morning. It was drizzly and cold and the Galbreaths were hoping that the game wouldn't be postponed until Saturday. That would really dampen their weekend. It also would give the Reds a breather in that their beleaguered pitching staff would benefit from an extra day of rest. This was especially meaningful to Seaver. If there was to be a fifth game, Seaver would get the pitching assignment.

Although the rain stopped at game time, the weather remained cold. Still, Pirates' fans braved the chilly conditions and began huddling outside the ticket windows as early as 11 o'clock to purchase whatever tickets remained for the three o'clock start. Steven Smith and Brian Hois of nearby Mount Lebanon claimed to be the first two in line and nobody cared to argue about it. Yet, Chuck Hardwick of Mount Washington was hoping that he would be one of the first to leave the stadium when the game was over. What he was worried about was that the game would go into extra innings. That would present a severe problem for Hardwick. He was a violinist with the Pittsburgh Symphony Orchestra and he had to be seated and ready to play for the ballet at eight o'clock.

But before anyone had arrived at Three Rivers Stadium, Stargell was there. Still dressed in his bathrobe, Stargell drove his automobile as close as he could to the press gate. He got out carrying an armful of roses. He gave them to an attendant who recognized him. The attendant was surprised.

"Every wife gets one of these," said Stargell. Then he got back into his car and drove away.

The crowd for the most part resembled a football gathering. A great many fans were dressed in heavy outerwear with a presence of black and gold trimmings, just like the Steelers. While the groundskeepers were going about their chore of drying the field, the fans were at work hanging their signs on the railings. There was a variety of them, such as "Madlock's Maniacs," "Omar's Amigos," "Garner's Gang" and "The Buc Brigade." When some over-enthusiastic sign-hangers unfurled their banners in dead centerfield, which would interfere with a batter's vision, they were instructed by the public address announcer to remove their wares. Only when Mayor Richard Caliguiri threw out the first ball was the game about to start.

Blyleven didn't experience any trouble in his first inning on the mound. However, LaCoss, who had been having difficulty in recent opening innings, again ran into trouble. Moreno patiently extracted a walk. On the first pitch to Foli, Moreno stole second base.

Pitcher Bert Blyleven shows joy after striking out Cesar Geronimo to end the third game.

Foli then hit a slow roller to shortstop. Concepcion fielded the ball cleanly and had a play at first. Instead, he decided to try and catch Moreno running toward third. Concepcion threw high and late to Knight, and Moreno slid in safely. Without the benefit of a hit, the Pirates had runners at first and third, with Parker, Stargell and Milner the next three batters.

Parker sliced a fly to medium-left field. Foster caught it and fired the ball to home plate, trying to catch the speedy Moreno, who had tagged up and tried to score. However, Moreno was too fast and slid safely past Bench for the the Pirates' first run.

After LaCoss retired the dangerous Stargell, he pitched himself into another jam by walking Milner and Madlock, loading the bases. Foster then caught Ott's fly ball to deep left field, but the Pirates had a 1-0 lead without getting a hit.

However, LaCoss ran into more difficulty in the second. Garner opened the inning with a curving line drive that got past Collins for a triple. After Blyleven bounced out to LaCoss, Moreno walked for the second straight time. It was the fourth walk issued by LaCoss. Fred Norman, the veteran 37-year-old left-hander, who had been in the bullpen warming up from the start of the game, began to throw harder. Foli scored Garner with a sacrifice fly to centerfield, giving Pittsburgh a 2-0 advantage.

LaCoss still looked unsteady. He continued to misfire, throwing two balls to Parker. McNamara called time, went to the mound and removed his young right-hander. Norman came in and retired Parker. Still, the Pirates had a 2-0 lead and Blyleven was throwing well.

Norman didn't have an easy time in the third inning. Stargell ripped Norman's 1-2 offering high into the second row of stands in right field for his second homer of the playoffs. Stargell circled the bases to a standing ovation. The fans were yelling, "Wil-lee." After reaching the dugout, that had the words "The Family" painted on its roof, Stargell came out into view again. He wanted to

acknowledge the fans' thunderous applause. He did, throwing them a kiss.

After Milner was retired, Madlock brought the crowd to its feet again. He propelled a home run off the green concrete wall in left field, and the Pirates' lead was increased to 4-0. The crowd of 42,240 gave Madlock a standing ovation. For a change, Blyleven had a comfortable lead after only three innings.

Blyleven wanted more runs. He opened the fourth inning with a single. Moreno sacrificed Blyleven to second base. Norman got Foli on a fly ball for the second out. Pitching carefully to Parker, Norman walked him. It was Stargell's turn to bat again. The noisy crowd gave him another big ovation. Stargell responded. He cracked a double into the right field corner that scored Blyleven and Parker. Pittsburgh's advantage was 6-0! The champagne was chilling in the clubhouse.

It wasn't until the sixth inning that the Reds finally scored a run off Blyleven. Bench accounted for the run with a homer over the left field wall. It was a ghost of the Big Red Machine, bringing back memories of Pete Rose and Tony Perez.

Still, Blyleven was in command. He wasn't in any immediate danger. The 6-1 lead appeared sufficient. Blyleven couldn't complain of not getting enough runs this time. By the seventh inning, the Pirates' wives began to sense the impending victory. Led by Patty Blyleven and Patty Nicosia, they left their seats and congregated behind the backstop screen. They formed a makeshift chorus line and began dancing to the delight and encouragement of the crowd.

The Pirates got another run in the eighth. Garner opened with a single and was sacrificed by Blyleven. After Moreno flied out, Foli hit a ball that Geronimo stood under for the apparent third out. But he dropped the ball for a two-base error. Garner scored, pushing the Pirates' lead to 7-1.

Blyleven finished strong. He wanted to complete his fine performance. He was determined to silence his critics. He did, too. Blyleven pitched the Pirates into the World Series, striking out nine batters during the game. It was a memorable effort, a well-pitched game. His joy was understandable as he leaped from the mound after getting Geronimo on strikes for the final out. What a finish!

It was champagne time for the Pirates for the second time in a week. Nobody was happier than Blyleven. This was his day. Tanner realized it. He gave Blyleven a kiss on the cheek. The look of satisfaction framed Blyleven's face. His fastball and curveball were his unfailing partners today. He had achieved fulfillment.

"It's upsetting to me when the news media people say that you can't win the big one," said Blyleven. "That's tough to swallow from someone who never pitched a ballgame. People can write what they want. I don't feel I had anything to prove. I don't feel I had to vindicate myself. You lose some 2-1 and 3-2 ballgames and people say you can't win the close ones. What are you supposed to do? Pitch a shutout every time you go out there? I'll settle for giving up two runs every time.

"All the runs we got helped. When you get ahead like that you don't have to worry about every pitch. You don't have to worry about making a mistake. If it's 2-1 and you make a mistake to someone like Foster, all of a sudden you're a goat. The big lead made it easy for me to relax and just pitch.

"In the first inning my fastball was good, but I couldn't get my breaking ball over. In the second inning, my breaking ball started to come around. By the fourth, I knew I was in control. I stuck with my fastball and used my curve when I got ahead. After the fourth inning, I think I threw only one change-up. I was so keyed up after striking out Foster in the sixth that I just wanted to blow my fastball past Johnny Bench. But instead he blew it by me and over the wall.

"I wanted to finish. That became the most important thing to me. I knew if I finished, we'd win. If I didn't finish, we might be in trouble. I really wanted to end the game with a strikeout. There's something about ending it with a strikeout. When I pitched my no-hitter with Texas, I got the last out on a strikeout, and

I wanted to do it again. There's something about seeing the last pitch go past the batter, and watch the catcher jump into the air.

"That's what happened today. Geronimo took the called third strike and Ott jumped up in the air. When he jumped, I jumped too. The last time I was involved with winning something was in 1969 in the Instructional League. It was the last day of the season. I pitched and we won, 1-0," recalled Blyleven.

"Then in 1970, we were on the plane going from Baltimore to Minnesota and our manager, Bill Rigney, came back to talk with me. He said since we were down, 2-0, he wanted to go with experience and was going to use Jim Kaat. I got in for a couple innings of relief.

"But this is great. I want to thank the good Lord for keeping us healthy and the Pittsburgh Pirates for giving us the ballplayers to win this. Bill Madlock and Tim Foli are the players we needed to put us over the top. In about four or five hours our guys will start letting out screams. I really don't think it's hit them yet. I really don't think we realize what's happened yet. I know I'll let out a scream."

Tanner had another kiss for Blyleven. It was really the first time he got close to him all afternoon. Tanner had not made one trip to the mound the entire game. That was a rarity. Even Tanner realized it.

"When was the last time I never made a single trip to the mound?" he asked. "I can't remember. It's been a while. Why didn't I go out this time? Because Blyleven told me to stay in the dugout."

Parker didn't know if he would make it to the dugout when the game ended. The thought crossed his mind as he began to run in from right field.

"My first thought was that, hey, I'm in the World Series," said Parker. "The second was, hey, how am I going to get into the clubhouse? It's my first World Series, baby, first one. The sweet taste of victory, my first one. I've never had the opportunity to play in a World Series. Ever since the first time I picked up a ball and bat as a baby, I dreamed about it. Now I'm here. This is better than everything else I've ever done."

153

Others shared Parker's sentiments. A World Series was something special.

"It's every ballplayer's dream," exclaimed Tekulve. "I think about guys like Ernie Banks who were in the game for so long and were never in a World Series. I have been here just five years and now I'm going."

Bibby had been around longer than that. This was his eighth year in the majors and he had not come close previously. He cherished the moment.

"This is the greatest moment of my career," said Bibby. "I was never close to winning. Now I'm in a World Series. I think the way we played in the playoffs was tremendous. I think because of it, we'll be more loose in the World Series. I know we have a lot of guys like me who had never been in games like this before. We were nervous because we didn't know how we would handle them. Now we know."

Everybody knew these were Stargell's playoffs. He was named the most valuable player after hitting .455 with two home runs and six runs-batted-in. As is his character, he remained humble. He was touched by the fans' overwhelming ovation that coaxed him to come out of the dugout for a bow after his third-inning homer.

"If they took a picture of my body, it would show goosebumps everywhere," revealed Stargell. "The good Lord lets us shed tears at touching moments and that's what transpired with me. I wish there was a way to thank every fan individually. Just like the wives. All summer long they take care of the homes and the children and put up with a bunch of high-strung athletes. Behind the scenes, they're as much responsible for what this team has accomplished as the players are. It occurred to me that someone should thank them and that was the reason for the flowers. The wives are mother and father most of the time. To look up there and see them dancing, letting it all go, I was very happy.

"We are family. I couldn't find the words to express the excitement and joy of being here. We have thousands of people looking over our shoulders while we work. It's important that I don't get fancy with my life. Really, the Man upstairs put each of us here for a purpose and regardless of what happens, I am blessed and grateful. Winning and losing, I could care less. I am joyful for living and being able to do what I dreamed of doing.

"This may sound corny, but I get on my knees every night and give thanks. If somebody thinks something is bigger than that, I feel sorry for them. The World Series will be like this whole season. We'll be out there playing good, country baseball. Nothing fancy. If we keep it up, it'll be a good series. We're not a fancy team. We just have an all-out, day-to-day effort. You can have all the outstanding players who make all the outstanding plays. I'll take all the guys who can move the runner from first to second, bunt, hit-and-run, do all the little things. I wish I could explain to everybody what a real close family all of us are on this ballclub. We love each other. I'm just so happy, not only for myself, but for all of the guys."

He didn't have to explain it too much. Players around the league knew that Stargell was someone special. Even in defeat, Joe Morgan found joy in the presence of Stargell.

"He is the greatest guy in baseball," said Morgan. "If you went to 600 major league players, you couldn't find one who didn't like Willie. He bubbles with life, like that champagne he's been drinking. He's fun and he cares about people. When I look at him, I don't see Willie Stargell, Superstar, and I don't see Willie Stargell, who might hit five home runs. I see Willie. I see a person who has feelings for people. Willie."

And the others players have feelings for him. That was demonstrated when the Pittsburgh ground crew made a presentation to Stargell. The crew gave him a trophy . . . first base, the bag that he covers. It didn't go unappreciated by Stargell.

"I'll cherish this always," claimed Stargell."

He will, too. But first, he had a World Series to play. All of the family would cherish that.

World Series

The rain cast a pall over the entire city of Baltimore. In the early days of October it appeared even drearier. The air had a chill to it. Dampness was everywhere. The streets were wet, and the trees and buildings of the old city dripped water. It certainly wasn't a setting for the opening of the World Series. The rain began to fall steadily on Monday. Although the Series wasn't scheduled to open until Tuesday, the weather forecast wasn't promising. Rain was forecast for Tuesday, threatening to delay the 76th World Series.

The weather created a deep concern for Baseball Commissioner Bowie Kuhn. The eastern seaboard was engulfed in a low pressure area, and it appeared the rain would continue past Tuesday. Before the first ball was even thrown, a serious scheduling problem loomed. The first two games of the Series were scheduled for Baltimore on Tuesday and Wednesday. After an off day Thursday, the next three games were scheduled for Pittsburgh beginning Friday. If the Series was forced to return to Baltimore, there would be

an off day Monday and the final two games were set for Tuesday and Wednesday.

Kuhn's concern was understandable. If the rain continued through Wednesday as anticipated, then the entire scheduling, which was carefully programmed to accommodate television, would be jeopardized. Kuhn's quandary was obvious. If the Series didn't open until Thursday, which loomed as a possibility in view of the long range forecast, what would happen to the Friday game that was scheduled for Pittsburgh?

The players of both teams didn't appear affected by the terrible weather. Simply, there wasn't anything they could do about it. They were ready to play at a moment's notice. The hardest part was waiting around, not knowing if the rain would cease. The only immediate decision confronting both Chuck Tanner, manager of the Pirates, and Baltimore Manager Earl Weaver was their pitching plans. Tanner had designated Bruce Kison to open the Series, while Weaver had named Mike Flanagan. The game-delaying rain and the loss of an off day could dramatically alter the

157

Tim Foli holds up 1979 World Series trophy after Pirates arrived in Pittsburgh.

pitching rotation soundly diagrammed by both managers.

It wasn't the first time that the Pirates and Orioles were facing each other in the World Series. In 1971, the two played an exciting seven-game series, won by the Pirates. Weaver remembered it as did his veteran right-handed pitcher, Jim Palmer. While the rain fell steadily on the playing field in Memorial Stadium, Weaver talked about the '71 Series. What he remembered most was the play of Roberto Clemente. The popular outfielder was named winner of the Series' Most Valuable Player Award. After the Pirates had lost the opening two games, Clemente, with his indomitable spirit, led them to victory. He batted .414 with 12 hits in 29 at-bats, including two home runs, a triple, two doubles, four runs-batted-in, and three runs scores. In the field, he also was magnificent. He made several outstanding plays and ran the bases with enthusiasm that belied his 37 years of age. Tragically, he died a little over a year later in a plane crash.

"It was almost a fitting eulogy for him," said Palmer.

"I remember Clemente running very hard to first base when the ball popped out of (pitcher) Mike Cuellar's glove," said Weaver. "He forced Cuellar to hurry his throw. It was wide, and it led to an important run. That was very impressive."

Brooks Robinson also recalled Clemente's brilliant play. Now an Orioles' broadcaster, Robinson played in the 1971 Series. The previous year, he had been the star of the Series with his magnificent fielding plays at third base that devastated the Cincinnati Reds.

"You hear about things a guy does," said Robinson, who also helped beat the Reds with his bat, "but to have a guy do those things against you in the World Series puts them on another plateau. It was just a fantastic performance by Clemente."

Dramatically, Clemente clubbed a home run in the seventh game that provided the Pirates with a thrilling 2-1 victory, giving Pittsburgh its fourth world championship in six appearances. Elrod Hendricks, the Baltimore catcher

at the time and now a coach with the Orioles, still vividly recalls the dramatic moment.

"I second-guessed myself on that pitch to Clemente," admitted Hendricks. "It was a screwball, and maybe I should have called a fastball. We had him set up for a fastball, but Cuellar had a good fastball. It's the only game in my life that I ever cried after it was over. You dream about things like that. After the game I stayed up all night and replayed it."

Nelson Briles understood. His memories were happier than those of Hendricks. In 1971, Briles was a pitcher with the Pirates. With the Series deadlocked 2-2, Briles responded with the finest pitching performance of his career. He shut out the Orioles on only two hits.

"There is so much emotion, so much excitement in the World Series that you never have to be frightened," said Briles, now a Pirates' broadcaster. "It is days later before you realize what you have done. It was a wonderful Series for all of us but especially for Roberto. He was very much a leader on our club, a brilliant player who finally got the attention he deserved. after that Series. He got the recognition he always craved. It was so tragic what happened afterward."

If there ever was an intangible that the Pirates carried into the 1979 World Series, it was the memory of Roberto Clemente and the pride he represented in being a member of the Pirates. It was reflected after the Pirates lost the first two games of the 1971 Series in Baltimore.

Before. Game Three in Three Rivers Stadium, Clemente warned, "We were embarrassed in Baltimore. We will not be embarrassed again. They will not beat us. Now we are playing on our own field. We do not have to worry about holes in the outfield and a bumpy infield."

It was a speech Stargell did not forget. In 1971, Stargell played left field. After Clemente's untimely death on December 31, 1972, in a plane crash in which he was bringing food to earthquake victims in Nicaragua, the leadership of the Pirates was passed to Stargell. Stargell has performed his role quietly in all his years with the Pirates.

"We are family," Stargell said in 1979. "All Pirates past and present are part of this effort. We played exceptionally well the whole month of September. We're not a fancy team. We just play hard and aggressive and try to make all the routine plays. We just get right to it. We're not going to do anything different now.

"The World Series is like a good meal you can seldom afford to enjoy. You save money all year, and each mouthful you chew it up real good. You digest real slow. And you get up the next day and you say, 'Damn, I got to do this again.'"

With Monday's workouts dampened by the rain, most of the pre-Series banter in 1979 revolved around the teams. The Pirates had arrived in Baltimore as the underdogs. Despite the fact that they had swept the Cincinnati Reds in three games in the National League playoffs, the oddsmakers and most of the experts connected with baseball felt that the Orioles would beat the Pirates. It was all conjecture, and it had little effect on the Pirates' players. They kept low profiles and didn't get involved in any verbal outbursts in the opinions expressed by others.

Sparky Anderson, for one, felt that the Orioles would win. Although having managed the Detroit Tigers in the American League in 1979, Anderson was quite familiar with the Pirates. He knew them well from the time he had managed Cincinnati for many years. In 1972, '74, and '75, he guided the Reds to playoff-game victories over the Pirates. Never pitching-rich when he managed the Reds, Anderson was impressed with Baltimore's hurlers.

"I think Baltimore is the best team our league can send against Pittsburgh because of their pitching," said Anderson. "They have the left-handers to beat the Pirates, and I believe left-handers are needed to stop Pittsburgh. To me, the key to beating the Pirates is stopping Omar Moreno. If you keep him off the bases, then you can beat them.

"You try to keep the Pirates from hitting home runs, and you try to put as many runs on the scoreboard as you can. If you don't do those two things, you're going to be in trouble because the Pirates are going to be whaling away, and that kind of game usually gets them their four or five runs. The Pirates are very aggressive. They're aggressive in everything they do: hitting, fielding, pitching, running.

"The Pirates aren't going to quit. You won't have them beat until you nail the last nail into the coffin. If you want to beat the Pirates, then you better make sure they don't get the long ball, the home run. That's their game. If they start bombing, the party could be over quickly. The Orioles have got to keep people like Dave Parker, Willie Stargell and John Milner within the playing field."

Bob Lemon, the deposed New York Yankees' manager, also favored the Orioles. Although he only managed the Yankees for parts of two seasons, he saw enough of Baltimore during his years as manager of the Kansas City Royals and the Chicago White Sox. As a former pitcher, Lemon liked the Orioles pitching staff. He always has been an advocate of strong pitching, dating back to his playing career with the Cleveland Indians when the pitching staff of Lemon, Early Wynn and Mike Garcia was the scourge of the league.

"The Pirates better have two things going for them when they play the Orioles," said Lemon. "First, their pitching has to be up. Second, they have to be able to cope with their pitching. In other words, when you're pitching against them or batting against them, playing the Orioles is no day at the beach. Don't ask me for any secrets on how to beat the Orioles because I don't know of any. They're just a real steady ballclub, probably the steadiest in baseball right now. They don't have any weaknesses as far as I can see. They score runs, and they don't allow very many."

Those were some of the experts. The bookies, experts in another area, established the Orioles as 5½-6½ favorites for the Series and 6-7 for the opening game. Certainly, the Orioles had the scheduling edge. If the Series went the full seven games, four games would be played in Memorial Stadium. Baltimore had won 55 of 79 home games on its way to the American League pennant. The Orioles were coaxed at times by frenzied fans, including a bearded taxi driver, Wild Bill Hagy, who stood on top of the Baltimore dugout and led the crowd in cheers.

On paper, the Orioles appeared to have the advantage. In analyzing both teams, the Orioles were given the edge in pitching and fielding while the Pirates were better in hitting. Still, the Pirates' bullpen was rated a little stronger than Baltimore's. That was one reason why Tanner went to his bullpen quickly and often during the season. Still, with all the numbers, there are many intangibles that do not show up on a computer. One was the spirit, the family theme, that the Pirates carried with them into the World Series. It was with them all year, and now, in the World Series, it would mean even more.

As the weatherman-had predicted, it rained Tuesday. There was no question that the game would be postponed. It not only rained, but it snowed! No one could remember the last time snow fell on, Baltimore during the first week of October. It wasn't the type of snow that stuck to the ground. Rather, it was the wet variety. But it was enough to send shivers through the warmest person. What now was of great concern was the playing condition of the field once the precipitation stopped and the Memorial Stadium ground crew got a chance to work on the field.

Only 48 hours earlier, the Baltimore Colts and the New York Jets had played a football game. The field was moist and soft then. At the game's conclusion, the field that was to be the setting for the World Series was pretty well chewed up with cleat marks and divots. The steady rain that had fallen since that time impeded the efforts of the ground crew. It presented somewhat of a problem.

Yet, Pat Santarone didn't appear worried. He was in charge of the playing field, entrusted with getting the diamond in shape for the opening game . . . whenever it would be played. He felt confident that he could get the field in shape if it stopped raining long enough before game time. He was proud of

the fact that the Orioles had played in rainy weather 17 times during the season and won 16 of those games.

Psychologically, he tried to shake Tanner, but the ploy failed. When Santarone's figures about the Orioles success in the rain were presented to Tanner at a news conference later, he didn't flinch.

"We were 35 for 35 in the rain," said Tanner. "I can only see some good in the bad weather. We all have to play at one time or another under these conditions. I know everybody is concerned with injuries, but you can get hurt on a dry field. I've seen ankles and knees twisted on a hot summer day. I don't think they'd let us play if it was dangerous."

It was typical of Tanner's attitude. He never has been known to panic. Rather, he lets situation present itself, then reacts to it accordingly.

Tanner looked at ease. He was sitting in his office, his feet comfortably at rest, chewing tobacco. He had an ample supply of Red Man tobacco on his desk along with dozens of paper cups, three telephones, and a stack of congratulatory telegrams. The cups were necessary. They were utilized by Tanner as a receptacle for his discarded tobacco juice.

"When I was young, my baseball heroes were the Gashouse Gang," Tanner recalled while arranging the cups. "Pepper Martin, Ducky Medwick, Dizzy Dean, what a wild, aggressive bunch of ballplayers. They always were swinging, running, and going for that extra base. This club reminds me a lot of what those old St. Louis teams used to be. They never think they're behind. They always go into the last inning feeling they're going to win."

Tanner's relaxed clubhouse was in evidence even now. Outside his door, portable stereos were alive with the sounds of disco and rock 'n' roll music, with even some sounds of country and western. A large television set was turned on, but instead of any commercial programs, it was showing tapes of the club's playoff vic-

160

Stargell finished Series with seven extra base hits to set a new record.

tories over Cincinnati. It wasn't anything new, nothing more than a replay. Yet, every time a Pirates' player got a key hit, or made a fine fielding play, a big roar went up throughout the room.

Despite the heavy rain outside, the Pirates' free team spirit was far from dampened. Stargell, sitting barefooted on a sofa, was playing cards with Jim Bibby, Rennie Stennet and Grant Jackson. They were playing a game called "pluck." Frequently, in a display of conquest, Stargell would bang a card on the table with a force that was heard on the other side of the room.

In a prankish mood, someone had hung the head of a roasted pig in Jim Rooker's locker. It didn't hang there unceremoniously. Instead, it was placed inside the pitcher's uniform.

Off in another corner of the clubhouse, rookie Matt Alexander was concentrating on cutting and styling Bill Madlock's hair. That was quite a responsibility for a rookie. However, Tanner, who was now looking around the clubhouse, gave the rookie a vote of confidence.

"Matt's out of barber school," pointed out Tanner. "He's good. Cuts all our hair. I've let him take a whack at me a couple of times."

Big Dave Parker shuffled some items in his locker. He wasn't at all perturbed by the weather. He was ready to play, if not this night, then the next night.

"I just put on the glove, pick up the bat, and go out there and attack," Parker said with a smile. "I know the turf will be wet. I'll apply some heat to my knee. I'll wear a knee brace, but I'll take the same approach as any other day."

One who couldn't wait to play was Omar Moreno. He was a bit piqued. The network televising the Series, in analyzing the teams position-by-position, had given the edge to Baltimore's Al Bumbry in centerfield. Moreno, a mild-mannered person not known to display his temper, didn't agree with the analysis.

"What do they know?" he snapped. "I'm going to play and do the best I can. I'm very proud to be in the World Series and very happy my people in Panama will get to see me play on television. When I first started playing baseball, I wanted to be in the World Series.

"I played against their catcher, Rick Dempsey, in the minor leagues, and I know that he has a good arm. But I will do my best, and I am happy to get the chance to play here. Every ground ball, every fly ball, you have to be careful on a wet field."

Moreno's fellow Panamanian, Manny Sanguillen, was in a different mood. He was quiet and somber because he knew he wouldn't play much, if at all, as the team's third-string catcher. The 35-year-old veteran didn't make an appearance in the playoffs, but he remembered the 1971 World Series in which he had hit .379.

"In a way, the Latin player is always in the shadow," claimed Sanguillen. "They say Clemente proved himself in the 1971 Series. He was 37 years old then. He had been great for a long time. He had been great for 17 years. Clemente was ashamed. Here he was 37 years old, and they said he had to have a great World Series or else people would not know how great he was. He was so ashamed. He'd tell me, 'Oh, when I was younger, I was so much better.'

"I remember the second game of the '71 Series. I remember when Dave Johnson knocked me down. Stargell made a bad throw from left field, and I had to jump. My mask was all over the place.

"But I'm glad I'm here, I thank God I'm one of the Pittsburgh Pirates. I can't complain."

There wasn't any game Tuesday night. The players were ready to leave and come back Wednesday night and try again to play the first game. Tanner was asked if he had any rules for his players during the rainout.

"Yes," he said. "Twenty-five. One for every man on the squad. Every man is different. Every many has to be treated differently."

There was one last question. Tanner was asked if he ever had earned one of Stargell's stars.

"Sure," replied Tanner. "One! That was when I gave the team an off day."

Tanner appeared unruffled. The postponement of the opening game didn't create any hardship. He still planned to use Kison in the first game and follow with Bert Blyleven in Game Two.

"The postponement is not an irritation," said Tanner. "It's not a disaster. It's just an inconvenience. Look, we're going to stay here until we play two games. Actually, we were concerned about the condition of the wet field. We're disappointed, but we didn't want anybody hurt on either side. The World Series is supposed to be fun.

"We have six pitchers who can start games, but if we were to have another postponement, then I'd have to take another look at my rotation. Meantime, no change, and losing the travel day would have no effect on us at all. We'll be going home.

"Coming out of the season we were playing as good as you can play. A true hot streak. We had to be hot because the Montreal Expos were smoking, too. We were playing .700 baseball down the stretch, and they were still gaining on us. Now we hope our guys will maintain that momentum. We will play our basic game regardless of who they pitch. The two teams are too evenly matched to change things around.

"The Orioles have a lot of depth on their pitching staff and power in the lineup. You might say they're a lot like us. If I were them, who would I pitch against the Pirates? I'd start my best pitchers, regardless of whether they were left-handed or right-handed. Look, we won 34 games against left-handers this season and lost 23. What's that? It's .570 baseball. If we play .570 baseball in the World Series, we'll be okay. Whatever, it should be a great Series. We're the two best teams in baseball. We have the two best records. That's how it should be."

Kison somewhat expected that the opening game would be rained out. He had that feeling Sunday when he was working out with the rest of the Pirates in Three Rivers Stadium. It drizzled that day, and Kison immediately thought about opening night.

"When we get rain, it usually means that they get it a day or so later in Baltimore," reasoned Kison. "I have a feeling that we're in for a long Series. I would have preferred playing, certainly. But we're not going to have that opportunity so we just have to deal with it and so do they. What can you do but wait until tomorrow?"

Stargell, one of the quickest players on the team in changing from his uniform to street clothes, was heading back to the hotel. He was calm as usual.

"I think it was good judgment to call the game," he said on his way out. "The field took an awful lot of water over the weekend, and anybody would hate to see a situation where one of your key players, on the Pirates or the Orioles, would get hurt. It's not the first time that we've had to do this."

The rain that fell late Monday and all day Tuesday still was falling early Wednesday. It appeared that the opener would be delayed another night. That would really cause havoc with the scheduling. With Tuesday's postponement, Thursday no longer was an off-day. It was penciled in for Game Two. The rain carried into the afternoon hours Wednesday, adding further gloom. But then surprisingly, several hours before game time, the rain stopped. Santarone and his ground crew went to work.

Weaver remembered Kison from the 1971 World Series when the lean right-hander was a 21-year-old rookie. He stopped the Orioles in the fourth game, tying the Series 2-2.

"It was that skinny kid who turned it all around for them," noted Weaver. "If it wasn't for him, it might have been a different ending."

Kison had only a 13-7 record during the season. Yet, Tanner remained unflappable in selecting him to open the Series. He counted on Kison to start at least two games.

"I have faith in him, that's why he is starting," Tanner snapped in answer to a challenging question. "He must get in a groove in September the way he's pitched."

Tanner's decision appeared sound. Kison's career record in September was a remarkable 23-6. In post-season appearances, he was 4-0. There wasn't any pitcher around with such impressive credentials. Even Kison was baffled by his amazing late-season success.

"I wish I knew why my record is so good in September and October," said Kison. "I wish I could give you an answer. If I really knew, I'd apply it in April, May and June. There are a lot of intangibles in baseball. You can look at the statistics, but black and white figures don't mean anything. I enjoy big games. I like meaningful games."

His regular catcher, Ed Ott, was pleased that Kison was designated as the opening-game pitcher.

"He's our most competitive pitcher," pointed out Ott. He'll bunt, steal, slide. He is very low-key off the mound, but when he hears that national anthem, he goes into a Dr. Jekyll-Mr. Hyde act. He'll scream and he'll holler at me. He'll blame me for not getting the glove down.

"Oh, it's not that he's nuts. It's not anything like that. He's just like some football players. Off the field, he's the gentlemen of all gentlemen."

Because the left-handed Flanagan, who was 23-9 during the year, was starting for Baltimore, Ott, who bats left-handed, would not be in the Pittsburgh lineup. The Pirates' right-handed hitting catcher, Steve Nicosia, a rookie, replaced Ott. Although this was Nicosia's first full season with the Pirates, he knew how much Kison meant to the club during the final month of the season when he won all three starts.

"He is one of the great competitors when he steps between those lines," said Nicosia. "He is out to beat you any way he can. He is very easy-going, but what I like is that he can get behind the batters and throw his slider for a strike. And his slider sets up his good fastball. When a big game is on the line, you have to give the ball to him."

A chilly wind brought even further discomfort. Its one redeeming factor was that it began to remove the rain-laden clouds from the atmosphere. The weather prediction was that the rain would stop by late afternoon. Actually, Santarone was only hoping for three hours to allow his 55-member ground crew time to get the playing field in shape. Weaver has a great amount of faith in Santarone. He brought Santarone with him to Baltimore in 1969 from a minor league team in Elmira, New York. Periodically, he checked with Santarone.

"Batting practice is off," announced Weaver. "I don't think that will make Willie Stargell happy, but it is. And infield practice is very questionable. I think, though, that if the rain stops by five o'clock we'll play. Damn right, we'll play."

The rain did indeed stop. Now it was up to Santarone and his gang to get the field ready. It was no easy task, but Santarone was confident.

"The snow didn't stick," said Santarone. "We've had the tarpaulin on the field since yesterday (Tuesday) afternoon, and the outfield is still in excellent condition. It is not mushy, and it is not dangerous. It would be slow and soggy, but the footing would be all right. We got lots of drains. We can sit and wait, but now we're going to try shallow pumps. I'm not sure they will work because we have never used them before. We're swamp rats by now."

Some four hours later, Santarone could have earned one of Stargell's stars. Amazingly, he had the playing field in good shape, surprising in view of the fact that his job was difficult because of the incessant rain that had drenched the playing surface. The World Series was ready to begin.

"I'm ready to play," exclaimed Parker. "I don't care how cold it is. I just want to get it started. This is the big showcase, right? We can't keep America waiting."

Parker had played most of the season with a strained knee. It hurt his base running because he wasn't as aggressive. It also affected his throwing from the outfield because he pushed off on the knee when throwing, but his adrenalin was flowing.

"At 90 percent, I'm still better than most guys," chided Parker. "I got it cranked up the last two weeks when we really needed it. I've waited seven years for this."

inning	1	2	3	4	5	6	7	8	9	TOTAL
Pittsburgh	0	0	0	1	0	2	0	1	0	4
Baltimore	5	0	0	0	0	0	0	0	x	5

GAME ONE

It seemed almost that long for the fans. Still, the excitement of the delayed opening pitch overcame the feeling of the cold dampness. As Omar Moreno walked up to the batter's box, the Pirates' fans in the crowd of 53,735 began to yell. Most obvious were the group of players' wives who were led by the shrill whistle-blowing of Moreno's wife. As soon as Moreno got set to face Flanagan, she stopped the whistle-blowing.

"C'mon Sweetie," she yelled above the crowd.

However, Moreno couldn't respond. He bounced to second baseman Billy Smith and was thrown out. Tim Foli was next. He drove a fly ball to left field that John Lowenstein caught. The sight of Parker aroused the crowd. Swinging freely, he sent a line drive down the right field line and wound up at second base with a double. The Pirates had a threat going, but Bill Robinson ended it by striking out.

Except for Parker's double, Flanagan pitched well. He didn't seem affected by the cold. Now it was up to Kison to match pitches with the Baltimore left-hander. The partisan Baltimore crowd cheered Al Bumbry, the Orioles' leadoff batter. Like Moreno, he was an important key to his team's attack. He didn't wait long to get the Orioles going. Bumbry swung at Kison's first pitch and lined it into left field for a single.

With Mark Belanger up next, the Pirates had to be ready for two things. One was the possibility of Bumbry stealing second. The other was a bunt by Belanger. The Pirates played for the sacrifice. Belanger carefully looked over Kison's pitches and worked him for a walk. Quickly, the Orioles had a serious threat. Ken Singleton, perhaps the Orioles'

best hitter and a candidate for the American League Most Valuable Player Award, faced Kison with runners on first and second. Kison challenged him, and Singleton hit the ball right back to the mound. Kison threw Singleton out as the runners advanced.

Baltimore appeared ready to break through. Kison, pitching cautiously to Eddie Murray, walked the Orioles' cleanup hitter, loading the bases. Kison was in trouble. He had to bear down on the next batter, Lowenstein, and hope for a double play. Kison managed to get the Baltimore left fielder to hit a ground ball to Phil Garner at second base. But in his anxiety to start a double play, Garner threw the ball into left field. Bumbry and Belanger scored on the error, and Murray wound up on third base. The Orioles led 2-0.

It quickly became 3-0. Kison fired a wild pitch with Doug DeCinces at bat, and Murray scored easily as Lowenstein moved to second base. Kison fell behind DeCinces. With the count 3-1, DeCinces was expecting a fast ball. He figured correctly. He swung and sent the ball over the left field fence for a two-run homer as the Orioles' fans went wild. The inning wasn't over yet and Baltimore was ahead, 5-0!

Kison was stunned. When Smith followed DeCinces' homer with a single, Baltimore fans wanted more, but that was all for Kison. Tanner slowly walked to the mound and replaced his right-hander with left-hander Jim Rooker. There still was only one out. Rick Dempsey, the catcher, was the first batter to face Rooker. He lined a ball toward shortstop. Foli speared it, but threw wildly past first base in an attempt to double up Smith. As Stargell retrieved the ball, Smith went to second. Flanagan then tapped the ball in front of the plate and was

Parker slides safely into second base while (below) Garner avoids a close pitch in opening game.

thrown out by Nicosia.

The Pirates' power remained short-circuited. Pittsburgh went out in order in the second and third innings. However, in the fourth inning, the Pirates awoke.

Foli opened the inning with a sharp single to center. Parker followed with a single to right, sending Foli to third. Pittsburgh's hopes quickly rose. It was up to Robinson again. But he grounded out to DeCinces as Foli held third and Parker advanced to second. Stargell managed to knock in the Pirates' first run when he hit a grounder to Smith at second. Running on the play, Parker easily reached third base. Madlock walked, but Nicosia ended the rally by forcing Madlock at second base.

It remained 5-1 until the sixth inning as the Pirates wasted Garner's leadoff double in the fifth. Again, Parker made his presence felt. He singled to center for his third straight hit. When Robinson followed with a single to center, Pirates' fans cheered. Stargell was up, and a home run would make the score 5-4. But Stargell struck out, and Madlock flied to Singleton in right field for the second out. Nicosia then slapped a routine ground ball to Belanger for what appeared to be the final out of the inning. But Belanger booted the ball, and the bases were loaded. Garner ripped a single to left, scoring Parker and Robinson, and the Pirates trailed, 5-3. With the tying runs on base, Tanner sent up Lee Lacy to bat for Enrique Romo, who had replaced Rooker in the fifth inning. DeCinces misplayed Lacy's ground ball for his second error of the inning and the bases again were loaded. Quickly, the compexion of the game had changed. A hit by Moreno would tie the score, but Moreno failed to deliver. He flied to Bumbry, ending the inning.

In the eighth inning, Stargell brought the crowd to its feet. He led off by walloping a 2-2 pitch into the right field stands. The score now was 5-4. After Madlock and Nicosia were retired, Garner collected his third hit. Rennie Stennett batted for reliever Don Robinson and looped a single to right as Garner sped to third. Moreno had another chance, but he failed again, striking out.

The Pirates weren't finished yet. With one out in the ninth inning, Parker produced his fourth hit of the game. Flanagan then had him trapped off first base, but Parker broke for second, slid hard into Belanger and knocked the ball loose for an error. A hit would tie the score, but Robinson grounded out and Stargell flied out as the Pirates lost the opener, 5-4.

Still, the Pirates were undismayed afterward. Their clubhouse was as noisy as ever. The players appeared relaxed despite the loss. They didn't make any excuses.

"We didn't get this far by making excuses," emphasized Parker. "I gave 100 percent. I'll sleep well and come back tomorrow. We knew we weren't out of it when they jumped out to a five-run lead. We went to work and started playing good Pirate baseball. We'll regroup, come back, and play them again.

"I tried to put my foot in Belanger's glove. The ball landed right in front of the bag. It was good aggressive play. That's the way I play baseball. Aggressively! You might ease up earlier in the season, but this is the World Series. This is for all the marbles.

"It was a clean play. I tried to help Belanger up, but he wouldn't take my hand. I don't know if he was upset or what."

Stargell wasn't upset. Neither he nor any of the other players had their heads down or spoke in low tones.

"I won't be jumping off a bridge," he said softly. "I did try to go to left field in the ninth; but I got under it, and that is the ballgame."

Kison admitted he was bothered by the cold, 41-degree weather, but he didn't want to use it as an alibi.

"My fingers were numb, and I couldn't feel the ball," explained Kison. "I felt in a very good groove in the bullpen, but how you feel in the bullpen and how you do in the game are two different things. In cold weather like that, it's tough to grip the ball. I'm not making excuses. It was the same for both sides, but the ball was slipping out of my hand. I was happy with the way the team played, coming back from five runs like that. I wish I could have done a better job."

inning	1	2	3	4	5	6	7	8	9	TOTAL
Pittsburgh	0	2	0	0	0	0	0	0	1	3
Baltimore	0	1	0	0	0	1	0	0	0	2

GAME TWO

It was up to Bert Blyleven to stop the Orioles in the second game. Already baseball historians were citing the fact that very few teams had come back and won the Series after losing the first game. But the Pirates didn't believe in history books that revealed such negativism.

The rap on Blyleven was that if a team stayed close to him, he would find a way to make a mistake that would cost him the game. It also was felt that the cold weather might bother the veteran right-hander.

"I pitched eight years in Minnesota, and I'm still in the big leagues," said Blyleven, "so I don't think the cold will be a problem."

Blyleven had no easy assignment. His mound opponent was Jim Palmer, a veteran right-hander who had produced eight 20-victory seasons in his 14 years in the majors. Bothered by shoulder problems a good part of the 1979 season, Palmer had only a 10-6 record. The ten victories gave him a lifetime total of 225. He had wanted to open the Series, but Weaver explained that he needed to start with Flanagan, a lefty, against Pittsburgh's left-handed power hitters. Despite the fact that Blyleven had a 12-5 record, the Orioles were favored to win the second game.

The scouting reports on Palmer emphasized that a team had to get to him early. He reportedly wasn't as effective in the early innings as he was when the game progressed. Also, at times when he wasn't sharp, he had a tendency to throw high pitches. That would be like batting practice for a free-swinging team like the Pirates. Still, Palmer was a smart pitcher and knew how to work on the batters.

Again the shrill of whistles greeted Moreno as he became the first batter of the game. Hitless the previous night, Moreno opened the game with a sharp single. However, he was quickly doubled off first when Foli fouled out to Murray.

After Blyleven easily retired the Orioles in their turn at bat, Pittsburgh broke through Palmer in the second. They did it with suddenness. Stargell, who was batting fourth against a right-hander, started the inning with a single to right. John Milner followed with a hit to center. Madlock stroked a single to right centerfield, and Stargell crossed home plate with the Pirates' first run. Ott then delivered Milner with a sacrifice fly. The Pirates led 2-0, but Palmer got out of the inning without any further damage.

Murray didn't wait long to get the Orioles on the scoreboard. As the first batter in the bottom of the second inning, he connected with a Blyleven fast ball and sent it into the right field stands, trimming Pittsburgh's lead to 2-1. Blyleven prevented further scoring by striking out Palmer with runners on first and third and two out.

The Pirates wasted Foli's two-out single in the third. He was stranded on second base after reaching there on a wild pitch, but the Orioles also wasted a scoring opportunity in their turn at bat. With one out, Belanger reached second base when Parker muffed his soft fly for a two-base error. He raced to third when Singleton grounded out. Pitching carefully to Murray with two outs, Blyleven walked him. However, he got DeCinces on a grounder to Foli, ending the threat.

After the second inning uprising, Palmer began to settle down. The Pirates couldn't get anything going, but Blyleven was matching Palmer with a fine effort until the sixth inning when the Orioles tied the score 2-2. They did it quickly. Singleton singled to left, and Murray drove in his second run with a sharp double up the alley in left centerfield. As Foli threw out DeCinces, Murray moved to .third.

With only one out, the Orioles were threatening to take the lead.

Lowenstein, a left-handed power hitter, stepped up to face Blyleven. A fly ball would easily score the fast-running Murray from third. Lowenstein did manage to hit the ball into the outfield to Parker. As soon as the big right fielder caught the ball, Murray broke for the plate. Parker quickly removed the ball from his glove and fired the ball toward Ott. It was a perfect throw, strong and accurate. Ott had the ball waiting for Murray for what turned out to be an easy out as the crowd roared at Parker's clutch throw.

When the Pirates came to bat in the seventh inning, it began to rain. An infield single by Madlock and two walks loaded the bases with two out. However, Moreno, who seemed to be pressing at bat, struck out.

Don Robinson replaced Blyleven, who had pitched six creditable innings. After getting the first out in the seventh, Robinson suffered control problems. He walked the next two batters before striking out Bumbry. Then he walked pinch hitter Terry Crowley, loading the bases. Dramatically, Robinson struck out the dangerous Singleton, thwarting the Orioles.

Robinson escaped another jam in the eighth. After the first two Orioles had reached base safely, he induced Lowenstein to crack into a double play. The game still was tied when the Pirates came to bat in the ninth inning. Tippy Martinez, who had retired the Pirates in order in the eighth, prepared to pitch in the important final inning.

Tanner made a change. He sent up Bill Robinson to pinch hit for Milner. He was playing the righty-lefty percentage against the hard-throwing Martinez. Robinson delivered a single to left. It didn't take Weaver long to move. He replaced Martinez with Dan Stanhouse as Matt Alexander went in to run for Robinson. With Madlock up, Alexander tried to steal second on the first pitch, but he was gunned down by Dempsey's strong throw. Madlock then flied to Bumbry for the second out.

However, Ott bounced a single off Smith's

chest. When Garner walked, the Pirates had a threat. Tanner again went to his bench. He designated Sanguillen, his seldom-used third-string catcher, to bat for Don Robinson. In the first game, Sanguillen had pinch-hit for Rooker and grounded out.

It was a classic confrontation this time. Sanguillen was a notorious bad-ball hitter, and Stanhouse was a notorious bad-ball pitcher who often was more effective after walking the bases full. Stanhouse got ahead on the count to Sanguillen, with one ball and two striikes. Sanguillen crouched, waiting for the next pitch. He swung at a slider and hit it cleanly into right field. Singleton picked up the ball and threw it home. At the last second, Murray cut it off, whirled and threw home. It was too late! Ott slid across the plate, giving the Pirates a 3-2 lead. Joy was all over Sanguillen's face as the Pittsburgh dugout stood and cheered.

It was up to Kent Tekulve to preserve the victory. He didn't fail. He made the Orioles' batters look futile as he struck out the first two before getting Bumbry to ground out, ending the game. The Pirates had evened the Series 1-1.

In the clubhouse, Sanguillen was teary-eyed. It was ironical that he was a hero. In 1976, the Pirates had sent the 35-year-old catcher and $100,000 to Oakland for Tanner. It was the first time in baseball history that a player had been traded for a manager.

"Anything we do in this Series we are doing for Roberto Clemente," Sanguillen said in his halting English. "Roberto was with me in spirit. My hit, all I do to help the ball club win, is for him. I wasn't thinking about Roberto when I was at the plate. But after the game, after we won, it came to mind. If Roberto was alive, he might be a coach or a manager, but he is still with us. God took him away from us. That is the way life is, and it will happen to us all sometime. But I still have Roberto in my heart.

"Roberto has always been an inspiriion to me. I never forgot the 1971 World Series. Roberto, he tells everybody, 'Get us in the World Series, and I hit .400 and win it for you.' That's what he did. I dedicate my win-

171

Stargell leaps for joy after recording final out of second game.

ning hit for Roberto. I hope we play the whole Series for Roberto. I pray before every game. I pray that we win this one for Roberto."

Sanguillen was deeply sincere. He had been a close friend of Clemente. Inspired by Clemente, whom he called his baseball idol, Sanguillen collected 11 hits in the '71 Series and batted .379. When Clemente's plane crashed into the ocean, Sanguillen rushed to the scene. He made several dives into the murky waters looking for Clemente's body. Finally, several friends convinced Sanguillen that his dives into the choppy waters were too dangerous.

Tanner explained why he sent Sanguillen up to bat in such a clutch situation. He had faith in Sanguillen despite the fact that the catcher had batted only .230 during the season.

"I felt he could handle Stanhouse," said Tanner. "I know Manny likes pitches that are off the plate. I know Stanhouse likes to throw that pitch. I told him if he got an inside pitch to jerk it out. I wanted somebody who could put the bat on the ball, and I knew Manny could make contact. He helped us win four or five games this year with hits.

"He was involved in every game. He was always on the bench encouraging the younger players. Like tonight. He gave them a big lift. He did not want to go back to Pittsburgh down two games."

Sanguillen agreed.

"That's what happened in 1971," he said. "We lost the first two games here, then went back to Pittsburgh and got hot. I didn't want that to happen this time. It would have been too much pressure on the younger players. I want to help this team any way I can. I wanted to do it especially for the young players because I know how they feel being in their first World Series. I am always ready to help.

"I told my wife after I went hitless last night that maybe I wouldn't get any more chances. She told me, 'You got to stop grounding out, Manny. If you don't stop grounding out, they won't let you hit any more.'"

Sanguillen's game-winning hit created some controversy. Many observers wondered if Murray had made a mistake in cutting off Singleton's throw instead of letting it go through to Dempsey in an attempt to beat the slow-footed Ott. It was a puzzle to Ott.

"I never knew the ball had been cut off until I had a slice of baloney in my hand later in the clubhouse. Somebody said, 'Can you believe they cut that ball off?' I said, 'Cut what ball off?'"

Murray defended his play.

"I thought the ball was off-line," he said.

Weaver didn't find any fault with Murray's move.

"Eddie has good instincts, and he did what he thought was right," said Weaver. "Even if it wasn't off-line, the ball may have stuck in the mud and stopped. It all-boils down to Sanguillen rising to the occasion and doing his job."

inning	1	2	3	4	5	6	7	8	9	TOTAL
Baltimore	0	0	2	5	0	0	1	0	0	8
Pittsburgh	1	2	0	0	0	1	0	0	0	4

GAME THREE

The weather wasn't much better in Pittsburgh. When the players awoke Friday morning after their night flight from Baltimore, it was raining. By afternoon, the rain had subsided, and Pittsburgh's ground crew quickly went to work, using more modern methods than the Baltimore crew had employed. The synthetic turf at Three Rivers Stadium underwent a vacuuming, as three trucks, with a total capacity of 1,750 gallons, siphoned the water off the field. Still the threat of rain hovered over the city.

Despite the inclement weather, John Rumisek of the Chamber of Commerce,

Foli goes down on knee to stop a ground ball.

found reason to smile. He realized that the city would enjoy an economic boom over the long weekend. By Rumisek's estimates, a third of the fans that would see the three games would be from out of town. That represented a total of $4.5 million to the city burghers. Rumisek based his contention on the fact that each visitor would spend an average of $95 for hotels, meals and entertainment. And that didn't take into account the added effect the dollars would have as they were passed from the hotel owner to the baker to the supplier and so on.

Restaurants, from the fast food chains to the posh establishments on Mount Washington overlooking the city, were prepared for the heavy traffic. Diners seeking window seats at Christopher's were snapping up reservations at a brisk pace, said maître d' Mario Amgheloni.

Meanwhile, downtown, night manager Dante Bongiorni of McDonald's, was thinking in terms of selling a record number of hamburgers.

"We're looking to break the store record this

Garner prevented a run from scoring by diving for Al Bumbry's in fifth inning of third game.

weekend," said Bongiorni as he increased his employees from the normal 25 to 40.

The ticket scalpers were around, too. With World Series fever gripping the city, the scalpers were looking to make a bundle of money. Since the seating capacity at Three Rivers Stadium was only 50,364, tickets were scarce.

"One guy wanted $30 for a $10 seat," fumed Mike Visconti of nearby Gibsonia. "I told him I hope he still had the ticket at game time and that he chokes on it. This isn't funny. These guys belong in jail."

There certainly were enough policemen available. Normally, some 45 officers work the downtown area after a game. But the police, remembering how past victory celebrations had gotten out of hand, planned to have 360 officers available this time should the Pirates win by Sunday evening. Superintendent Robert Coll also disclosed that the city's 50 K-9 dog patrol was ready.

About the only player ready for any form of celebration was Don Robinson. His wife, Rhonda, was expecting their first child at any

hour. He was happy that he had arrived home from Baltimore before she was taken to the hospital.

"I don't think about it when I am on the mound," said Robinson. "You don't think about that when Ken Singleton is up to bat with the bases loaded."

One Pirates' player who was doing a lot of thinking was Moreno. Worrying was more correct. He was not hitting. He had only one hit in 10 at-bats and had struck out four times. Moreno had stranded 11 baserunners.

"I feel bad. I worry, I worry," sighed Moreno. "I know I help the team when I get on base. I know they need me on base, and I will get there, but I can't hit every day. I know that. The big thing is winning the game.

"I don't got my strike zone. I'm surprised at the way I'm swinging. I'm going for bad pitches. Sometimes, I feel tired. It's hard for me to play center because I run more than anybody. I run everywhere."

Moreno and batting coach Bob Skinner planned a special hitting session before the game. Skinner had corrected a flaw in Moreno's swing near the end of the regular season when he helped the swift Panamanian snap a 1-for-31 slump.

"I don't want any airballs from him," said Skinner. "His swing is a little bit off. There's more pressure and anxiety now. He wants to do well so badly that he's getting away from what he does best. I'm interested in direction, especially. I just want him back hitting the ball on the ground.

"Omar has to hit sharp line drives. He's got to utilize his legs. He's a guy who can turn a single into a triple."

Stargell wasn't worried about Moreno. Neither was Parker.

"Hey," noted Stargell, "if Omar doesn't get another hit the rest of the Series, the man has had a tremendous year. And I'll tell you what, as far as I'm concerned he's our most valuable player. He's been the fire of our offense all year, and I don't even have to tell you what he does offensively."

Parker agreed.

"He had a great season," said Parker. "He's the best centerfielder around. He's the type who needs just one swing, one hit to get back on the track. That's all it will take."

Tanner was worrying more about John Candelaria than Moreno. He wanted the big left-hander to pitch the third game. The afternoon weather conditions prevented Tanner from taking a close look at Candelaria who was bothered by an aching rib cage. The injury put a lot of strain on Candelaria's back.

"It's a day-to-day thing with Candy." explained Tanner. "I don't know how much he can pitch, but we have a strong bullpen. and I've got a lot of live arms down there."

After the pre-game warmup, Candelaria said that he could pitch. His mound opponent was Scott McGregor, a fragile-looking left-hander who was 13-6 for the season. Despite Candelaria's questionable back, the Pirates were slight favorites in their home park. The only serious concern was the weather. Rain again was threatening postponement of the game.

In a determined effort to get more offense, Weaver presented an all right-handed hitting lineup against Candelaria. The Orioles had scored seven runs in the first two games, but five had come in the first inning of the opening game. That meant that Baltimore had scored only two runs in the last 16 innings. That fact did not get past Weaver.

Kiko Garcia, who had replaced the light-hitting Belanger at shortstop, opened the game with a double down the right field foul line. Benny Ayala, another new player in the lineup, singled to center as Garcia moved to third. Quickly, the Orioles were threatening to produce a big inning.

The Pirates' relievers began stirring in the bullpen. Candelaria had to bear down against the middle of the Orioles' batting order. He challenged Singleton and struck him out. Murray then lined the ball straight at Garner for the second out, and Candelaria struck out DeCinces, ending the inning without any damage as the fans gave him an ovation.

Moreno kept them cheering. He cracked a double leading off the Pirates' first inning. Facing Foli, McGregor committed a balk, and

Moreno moved to third base. He remained there as Foli fouled out to Dempsey, but Parker brought him home. He hit a sacrifice fly to Gary Roenicke in right field, giving the Pirates a 1-0 lead.

Candelaria was impressive in the second inning. He retired the Orioles on three ground balls to Foli. The crowd warmly greeted Stargell when the Pirates came to bat in the bottom of the inning. Swinging easy, Stargell singled to center. After Madlock struck out, Nicosia sent Stargell to second with a hit to left. Garner then brought the chilled crowd to its feet with a double up the left-centerfield alley, scoring both Stargell and Nicosia. However, Garner was a bit too aggressive on the bases and was trapped in a rundown as he tried to stretch his double into a triple. The mistake was magnified when Candelaria singled to left field. Still, the Pirates had a 3-0 lead.

Weaver allowed McGregor to bat in the third inning, and he became Candelaria's seventh straight out. Garcia, who began the game with the Orioles' first hit, worked Candelaria for a walk. Candelaria then reached a 3-2 count on Ayala. Ayala caught hold of the next offering and hit it over the fence in left-center for a home run, reducing Pittsburgh's lead to 3-2. Apparently ruffled by Ayala's blow, Candelaria yielded a single to Singleton and followed with a walk to Murray. After DeCinces was retired for the second out, Roenicke lashed a single to left. Robinson charged the ball, threw hard to home plate, and caught Singleton attempting to score, ending the inning as the rain started to come down heavily.

The fans in the open seating areas retreated to shelter as the Orioles took the field. The intensity of the rain forced the umpires to stop the game. The players could do nothing but wait. It was a question of whether the rain would stop so that the game could be resumed. After about an hour, the rain stopped, and the trucks began to vacuum the water from the field. The rain delay lasted 67 minutes.

Now it was a question of whether the delay would affect the starting pitchers. McGregor appeared unaffected by it as he gave up only a single before getting the Pirates out in the third.

Rich Dauer opened the Orioles' fourth with a double. Dempsey's single advanced him to third, and Candelaria was in a spot. Foli then let him down. He bobbled McGregor's grounder, and the Orioles had the bases loaded. Garcia unloaded them. He walloped a triple to right centerfield, giving the Orioles a 5-3 lead and knocking out Candelaria. Romo came in to try and quiet things down. He didn't. He hit Bumbry, who was batting for Ayala, with a pitch. Singleton then hit safely, scoring Garcia with Baltimore's sixth run. Murray hit a fly ball to Parker, and Bumbry didn't test the right fielder's arm. However, he scored when DeCinces grounded out. When the inning finally ended, Baltimore was ahead 7-3.

It remained that way until the Pirates came up in the sixth. After Robinson fanned, Stargell ripped a double to right. Madlock singled him home, trimming Baltimore's advantage to 7-4.

The Orioles got the run back in the seventh on a double by Dempsey and Garcia's single, his fourth hit of the game. Meanwhile, McGregor got stronger. He retired nine straight Pirates, sealing Baltimore's 8-4 triumph and giving the Orioles a 2-1 edge in the Series.

The Pirates were disappointed. They had hoped to sweep the three games in Pittsburgh. Now, that was an impossibility.

"You haven't seen the real Pirates," said Garner. "Absolutely not. The weather was miserable the first two games, but tonight we just played lousy. Hell, I've been looking for things to blame it on, and I can't find any."

Neither could Tanner.

"There was nothing wrong with Candy," insisted Tanner. "He was throwing good and had good velocity. He didn't hurt or anything, and he had good stuff, but he didn't hit the right spots with some of his pitches. His location was bad.

"Sometimes though, when you have good momentum going and then you stop, you lose it."

The rain delay definitely helped McGregor. A sinker ball pitcher, he throws a variety of off-speed pitches. He had a rocky start, but after the rain, he was more effective.

"I had a whole week to get strong," explained McGregor. "I had too much strength, so my change was too hard. Its speed was too close to my fastball's. The hitters weren't getting out in front of it the way I'd like them to. Besides, I guess I pitch pretty well after rain delays. We get enough of them in Baltimore."

inning	1	2	3	4	5	6	7	8	9	TOTAL
Baltimore	0	0	3	0	0	0	0	6	0	9
Pittsburgh	0	4	0	0	1	1	0	0	0	6

GAME FOUR

The Pirates didn't have much time to lament about the loss of Game Three. The fourth game was to be played the following afternoon. Not long after the players got to bed, they had to awake and get ready to report to the field. The Pirates certainly had not expected to lose the opener in Three Rivers Stadium.

"On the way back to Pittsburgh we were thinking, knowing we could take three in a row," said Ott. "We said four out of five is not bad. That's the way we felt. We felt we could win three straight at home."

Since it wasn't going to happen, the Pirates now had to concern themselves with tying the Series 2-2. Tanner chose veteran Jim Bibby as his pitcher. A hard-throwing right-hander, Bibby fashioned a 12-4 record, starting and relieving during the regular campaign. Weaver selected Dennis Martinez, also a right-hander, who was 15-16 for the Orioles.

At least it wasn't raining. Only now it was cold. The weather was more suited for football than baseball as the temperature hovered around 50 degrees.

But Bibby was hot. He retired the first six Orioles he faced, striking out four. The Pirates' bats also got hot, breaking loose in the bottom of the second inning. Stargell ignited the inning by blasting a 2-2 pitch deep over the centerfield fence. It was his second home run of the Series. Milner followed with a single and Madlock got a ground-rule double when his hit bounced into the Pittsburgh bullpen. Ott then belted a drive to deep center that bounced over the fence for another ground-rule double, and the Pirates had a 3-0 lead.

When Garner lined another hit, Pittsburgh fans went wild. However, Ott was caught in a rundown between third and home as Garner went to second. Weaver had seen enough hits. He yanked Martinez and replaced him with Sammy Stewart. Stewart snared Bibby's line drive for the second out. But Moreno delivered Garner with the fourth run, singling to center for Pittsburgh's sixth hit of the inning. The barrage ended when Stewart picked Moreno off first base.

For the second straight game, the Pirates had jumped into a big early lead. An error by Madlock on Dave Skaggs' grounder gave the Orioles a break opening the third inning. Stewart became Bibby's fifth strikeout victim. However, Bumbry got the Orioles' first hit, a single to center as Skaggs stopped at second. Garcia then scored both runners with a double to left-center, his fifth hit of the Series in only six at-bats. Singleton followed with another double cutting Pittsburgh's margin to 4-3. Bibby then settled down striking Murray and getting DeCinces on a fly ball.

Pittsburgh added a run in the fifth against relief pitcher Steve Stone. Foli walked and Parker rapped a single to left. After Stargell popped up, Milner drilled a double just inside the right field foul line, scoring Foli and advancing Parker to third. Madlock was purposely walked, loading the bases with only one out. However, Ott flied to short left, and Garner forced Madlock for the third out.

The Pirates increased their lead to 6-3 with another run in the sixth inning. With two out, Foli cracked a single to right. Parker followed with a double to left as Foli raced home.

Baltimore threatened in the seventh. With one out, Skaggs singled past Madlock. Then Pat Kelly pinch-hit for Stone and beat out a hit to Stargell. Tanner brought in Grant Jackson as Bibby received a well-deserved hand from the Pirates' fans. Jackson served up a double play ball to Bumbry, and the Pirates were out of the inning unharmed.

When the Orioles came to the plate in the eighth inning, they faced a new pitcher. In a surprise, Tanner lifted Jackson after he had faced only one batter and asked Robinson to save the game. The pesky Garcia began the inning with a looping single in front of Parker. Singleton followed with a hit to left. Robinson got the dangerous Murray on a force out. However, when he walked DeCinces to fill the bases, he was replaced by Tekulve.

Weaver sent up Lowenstein to bat for Roenicke, and he came through with a double past Stargell down the right-field line, scoring two runs. Pittsburgh's lead had shrunk to 6-5. Smith then batted for Dauer and was intentionally walked, again loading the bases. There still was only one out, and Baltimore was threatening to break open the game. Weaver was thinking that way when he inserted his third straight pinch hitter, Terry Crowley, to bat for Skaggs. Crowley delivered a double to right field, driving in DeCinces and Lowenstein, and giving Baltimore a 7-6 lead. Pirates' fans couldn't believe what was happening.

The Orioles continued their assault. Relief pitcher Tim Stoddard was allowed to bat and got the first hit of his professional career, a run-scoring single that bounced over Madlock's head, scoring Smith with Baltimore's eighth run as Crowley raced to third. Dempsey pinch ran for Crowley and scored the Orioles' ninth run when Bumbry forced Stoddard. Tekulve finally got the third out by striking out Garcia. The six-run uprising left the Pirates stunned. They held a glimmer of hope of at least tying the score in the ninth inning. Singles by Stargell and Madlock put the potential tying run at bat with two out. But Ott struck out. The longest game in Series history had taken three hours and 48 minutes to play.

The Orioles raced off the field in joy. Their comeback victory gave them a 3-1 bulge. Gloom settled over Three Rivers Stadium. It carried over into the Pirates' clubhouse. They couldn't believe what had happened. They had out-hit Baltimore, 17 to 12, and lost! The players sat on their stools, on the floor, a bit glassy-eyed trying to understand what had taken place. Tekulve knew that he didn't have his usual good stuff.

"I just got a couple of balls up in spots I didn't want," said the thin right-hander. "Everybody makes mistakes. I don't make all perfect pitches. But those two pitches to Lowenstein and Crowley were my only mistakes. I didn't think I was struggling. They're just good hitters. Other guys may have fouled them off."

Garner understood that part of the game. He sat on a trunk with his back resting against the wall, holding a cup of beer in his hands.

"He (Tekulve) has been very effective all year," said Garner. "But when he gets the ball up, he gets hurt. He got a couple up today. He hasn't let too many games get away. But, he's human."

What Garner couldn't understand were the Orioles' hitters. They appeared super-human to him.

"They are hitting bullets all over the place," sighed Garner. "It's like they have somebody up there pointing a finger, saying, 'When those boys in gold get out there, we're going to get them.'

"Kiko Garcia is the greatest hitter I've seen. You get two strikes on him and bam! It's a base hit. We might as well walk him with the bases loaded. Then we're only giving up one run. I've never seen so many hard-hit balls and chinkers in my life. These guys are hitting some balls that are hard to believe. We hit balls and there is somebody right there. But I never saw anything like what they do. They hit it hard, it's a base hit, they hit it easy, it's a base hit. They're hitting balls everywhere. You make good pitches, they break their bats and get hits. You make bad pitches, they hit rockets somewhere.

"Weve been down all year and we battled back. We'll be out there fighting tomorrow." Tekulve agreed as he headed for the shower.

"The harder the challenge, the harder the club works," he said. "There's no way we'll fold."

The Pirates could not afford another loss—and they knew it.

inning	1	2	3	4	5	6	7	8	9	TOTAL
Baltimore	0	0	0	0	1	0	0	0	0	1
Pittsburgh	0	0	0	0	0	2	2	3	x	7

GAME FIVE

Baltimore had the champagne ready. And, justifiably so. Only four teams in the 75 years of World Series play ever had come back from a 3-1 deficit and won the fall classic. Garner didn't care about those figures.

"That has nothing to do with us," he snapped.

Stargell concurred.

"Of course, we can still win," exclaimed the Pirates' captain. "Nobody can tell us we can't."

Tanner wanted Kison to face Flanagan in the fifth game, making it a rematch of the opening game. However, Kison informed Tanner that he couldn't grip a baseball. After pitching in the cold weather in Baltimore the first game, Kison's arm had become numb from the elbow to the wrist. It still was bothering him.

There was no diluting the severity of the situation Tanner and his club faced. Tanner was well aware of it.

"Our backs are against the wall," he conceded. "We have to put together a three-game winning streak, or we run out of tomorrows."

Tanner was putting his hopes on Jim Rooker, a 37-year-old left-hander who had not become a pitcher until his fifth year in organized baseball. Rooker's 1979 performance wasn't very inspiring. He was 4-7 with a 4.59 earned run average and had experienced arm trouble a great part of the season.

Tanner defended his choice.

"I don't care what people think," said Tanner. "I have confidence in Rooker. When he's healthy, he can beat any club."

Tanner was managing under a tremendous strain. When the players arrived at the park, they learned that Tanner's mother had died from a stroke she had suffered a week earlier.

The game was scheduled for a 4 p.m. start. The odd hour was no doubt predicated by the fact that the city's other favorites, the Pittsburgh Steelers, were playing an important football game in Cincinnati against the Bengals starting at 1 p.m.

The Orioles were overwhelming favorites to win the game and the Series. Not only were the Pirates near the end of the plank, but in Flanagan they were facing the Orioles' best pitcher who had beaten them with a gutty performance, 5-4, in the opening game of the Series. Although the weather still was chilly for baseball, it was the best day of the Series.

Rooker wasn't the least bit affected by the pressure surrounding the game. When he was informed after Game Four that he would start instead of Kison, he went straight home. He packed for an elk hunting trip he had planned with former Pirates' relief ace Goose Gossage of the New York Yankess. They were to leave when the Series ended.

"I cleaned my guns, then went to bed at about 11 o'clock," said Rooker. "Then I got up this morning, had a fight with my wife, and came to the ball park."

"It's been a case of us doing a lot of talking and them doing a lot of playing. Baltimore's been playing terrific, fundamental baseball. You look at the scoreboard and wonder how a team of .250 hitters could win the American

180

Nicosia stretches to tag out Orioles' Ken Singleton.

League pennant. But they don't make mistakes and they have a great manager in Weaver, who knows how to manipulate his club. They're giving us a baseball clinic and we're watching it.

"Pittsburgh's always been a loose, take-it-easy club. But you can't be that loose in a World Series. We've made some base-running mistakes, done the things which not only demoralize one club, but pick up the other.

"I think five or six innings is what Chuck is looking for. I want to keep the ball in the park, and I've got to have good control. Walking them has been a killer for us. I've got to give our hitters a chance to score some runs.

"Beating Baltimore in a seven-game series is a big enough challenge, let alone trying to come back like this. But there's not a quitter in our clubhouse. We'll see now what kind of a club we are. You never know, I might win and surprise everybody."

Tanner didn't make any lineup changes. He went with the same right-handed lineup that he had employed against Flanagan in Game One.

Rooker was impressive in the first inning. He retired the Orioles in order without anything resembling a base hit. He did the same thing in the second inning and again in the third. Rooker had faced nine batters and retired them all.

When Rooker walked out to the pitcher's mound for the fourth inning, the fans were encouraging him. He had pitched the best three innings in the Series, better than any of the more publicized hurlers. He got Garcia for his tenth straight out. However, Ayala became the first Baltimore runner when he coaxed Rooker for a walk. Unruffled, Rooker easily retired the next two batters. After four innings, the Orioles had failed to get a hit. Maybe, just maybe, Rooker would add his name to Series history. Sure, he had pitched only four innings, but nobody had thought he would hold the Orioles hitless.

The tension began to build when the fifth inning opened. However, it didn't grow any further in intensity. Roenicke ended Rooker's no-hit dream with a solid double to left center-field. DeCinces followed with a single to right as Roenicke went to third. But Rooker held tough. He induced Dauer to hit into a double play as Roenicke scored the game's first run. Dempsey singled and Flanagan walked. But Rooker bore down and got Garcia on a force play grounder.

Madlock tried to get the Pirates going with a single opening the bottom of the inning. Nicosia went down swinging and Garner sent Ayala back to the warning track in deep left field for his fly ball. Tanner then went to his bench. He sent up Lee Lacy to hit for Rooker. After five innings of three-hit pitching, Rooker was finished. Lacy came through with an infield hit, beating out a slow bouncer to DeCinces. However, the Pirates' threat died when Moreno struck out for the third out.

Blyleven, who had pitched well in the second game, replaced Rooker. He got past the sixth inning without any damage. But the Pirates needed runs. Foli, first up in the bottom of the sixth, walked. Parker sent him to second with a sharp single to center. Pirates' fans were clapping for a rally. Playing the percentages, Tanner had Robinson bunt, advancing the runners. That left it up to Stargell, and he delivered a sacrifice fly to Bumbry in center-field, sending Foli home with the tying run as Parker took third. Madlock didn't leave him there. He ripped a single to center, providing Pittsburgh with a 2-1 lead.

It was up to Blyleven to hold it. After the first two Baltimore batters in the seventh were retired, Dempsey doubled. Weaver now made a move. He lifted Flanagan for a pinch hitter. But Blyleven met the challenge and struck out Kelly, ending the inning.

Stoddard, who had stopped the Pirates' the previous day, was brought in to pitch. Garner outlegged a grounder to Garcia for a single. Attempting to sacrifice, Blyleven forced Garner at second. Moreno, in turn, forced Blyleven. It appeared as if the Pirates were going nowhere. But Stoddard, trying to pick Moreno off first, threw the ball away. Moreno easily went to second. Pittsburgh was looking for an insurance run, and Foli got it. He ripped a triple to right centerfield and the Pirates were in front, 3-1. Weaver yanked Stoddard and brought in left-hander Tippy Martinez to pitch to Parker. Parker smacked a double to left center, increasing Pittsburgh's lead to 4-1.

The Pirates weren't finished. Stargell got them started in the eighth inning with a single. That was all for Martinez, and Weaver brought in Dave Stanhouse. Madlock greeted him with a single, sending Stargell to third. After Nicosia fouled out, Garner drove in Stargell with a hit to left field for the Pirates' fifth run. Blyleven sacrificed both runners. Weaver decided not to pitch to Moreno with first base open and ordered him walked intentionally. However, Foli foiled the strategy. He smacked a ball over second for a single, scoring Madlock and Garner, and giving Pittsburgh a 7-1 lead. Pirate fans were elated.

Blyleven yielded two harmless singles in the final inning before repelling the Orioles completely. He recorded the victory with four good innings of relief. The Pirates still were alive. The Series was forced to return to Baltimore for the sixth game. The Pirates didn't mind going back.

"I knew there had to be some eyebrows lifted when we named Jim Rooker as the starting pitcher," confessed pitching coach Harvey Haddix. "But we had a pretty good idea of what we were doing. As I was going out on the field, some fan yelled at me. He said, 'Why are you pitching Rooker?' I said, 'If you only knew!' We started him because he was our best arm at the time. He's experienced. He knows how to pitch and, when he's healthy, he has good stuff."

Rooker wasn't healthy most of the year. He had been placed on the disabled list twice. He struggled most of the season. It took him 12 starts to finally record his 100th career victory. The Pittsburgh victory was especially meaningful.

"I didn't feel any special pressure," said Rooker. "There was no pressure on me because I wasn't supposed to win. We were down three games to one. There was more pressure when we were struggling against Montreal late in the season.

"Nicosia called a fine game. I know that when I throw my sinker, I have got to let it run in on the righthanded batters. I guess that there is a certain element of surprise about it. I know that I got a called third strike on Singleton.

"I'm glad I did my job. All I wanted to do was keep them from having the big inning. I just did it hitter by hitter and inning by inning. That's all I thought about. I never seriously thought about the no-hitter. That's a once-in-a-lifetime thing, and at the World Series that's beyond my wildest dreams. Besides, playing for Tanner, whose favorite song is 'I Love a Parade,' there's no way I'd be in there longer than six innings."

"Now, added Rooker, "If we win Game Six, I guarantee you we'll win Game Seven."

Tanner would believe it. After Game Five, he would believe anything.

"It was unbelievable the way Rooker and Blyleven did their job," he said. "Rooker's a great competitor. Like I said before the game, when he's healthy, he can pitch as good as anybody. I had all the confidence in the world in him. He's always been good against right-handers.

"Rooker was terrific. The only reason why we took him out, was that the way Flanagan was pitching, we figured we needed the run. I had Blyleven scheduled in the sixth game in Baltimore, but we couldn't go anywhere but home if we lost. So I told him before the game to be ready, that he'd be the first up."

It had been a long, emotional day for Tanner. His mother's death placed an extra personal burden on him, but he never really showed the strain. He kept it to himself, so it wouldn't affect the players.

"Of course I've been thinking about her a lot, ever since it happened," he said. "She would understand, and know that I've got a lot going for me. She would want me to play because she understands that. I have a lot of faith, and I honestly believe she is in heaven and that she's happy. You know, we're supposed to cry when we are born and laugh when we die, but we do it in reverse."

Stargell was quite impressed with Tanner's composure. He knew what he was going through under great pressure.

"It took a hell of a lot for this man to do what he did," said Stargell. "He's a hell of a man to do that. I don't know if it happened to me if I could do the same. I was the first one to go in the clubhouse and I could tell he was hurting. I really saw something in that man. This man walked extremely tall today."

The Pirates walked along with him. They had to win to get the momentum turned around.

"After we split down there, I did not want to go back to Baltimore," said Garner. "But under the circumstances, it's a beautiful place."

Indeed it was.

inning	1	2	3	4	5	6	7	8	9	TOTAL
Pittsburgh	0	0	0	0	0	0	2	2	0	4
Baltimore	0	0	0	0	0	0	0	0	0	0

GAME SIX

Before the Pirates left for Baltimore, they scheduled a workout Monday morning. Tanner did not attend. He met with his father and other members of the family to finalize funeral arrangements for his mother. The family agreed that the funeral services would be conducted Thursday, the day after the seventh game of the Series, if the Pirates got that far. The team was to leave for Baltimore at 3 p.m. If Tanner was through with his family business by then, he would join his team on the charter flight. If not, the Pirates' owners would make arrangements to fly Tanner to Baltimore the next morning on a private plane.

The Pirates appeared loose at the workout. One had the feeling that with Sunday's victory, they had turned things around even though they still trailed in games, 3-2, and were going back to Baltimore.

Good Morning America, the ABC television show, was interested in the Pirates. A group of Pirates' players, led by Garner, taped a brief segment for inclusion on the popular TV show.

Batting practice pitcher Joe Coleman playfully hit Stargell with a pitch on his right hip. He threw it a bit harder than he anticipated and it stung Willie.

"Damn you, Joe, you said you were going to do that," shouted Stargell.

"Go get some ice on it," said Coleman, who

had pitched briefly for the Pirates during the 1979 season.

"Way to catch him leaning in there on you, Joe," playfully encouraged Nicosia, "Hey Pop, you can't dig in there on Joe."

"Man, that felt good," kidded Foli as he rubbed his hip and limped around for all to see.

"Don't ask me for sympathy," yelled Coleman. "I can't even sit on the bench with you guys."

"Drill a man in the hip like that so early in the morning," chided Stargell.

"Hey, I'm just being a nice guy doing this," said Coleman. "I could be down in Florida right now, playing golf."

"You want me to get you a ticket, Joe?" asked Stargell.

A moment later, Stargell stepped back in to hit. He drilled a couple of baseballs into the seats in right field. He was satisfied.

"The workout is over," said Stargell and he walked away. "This is too damn much work."

The Pirates were loose all right. Later that afternoon, Tanner met his team at the airport for the return trip to Baltimore and the conclusion of the wet cold Series. The players also were greeted by a large parcel of flowers that was sent to them by the disco group Sister Sledge, whose song "We Are Family," had been adopted by the team. Tekulve felt that all the players should share in the gift and

186

Moreno scores the first run in seventh inning of sixth game.

handed flowers to the players and their wives as they boarded the plane.

Haddix was non-committal on who the Pirates would pitch in the seventh game if they won Tuesday night. Blyleven, who had pitched Sunday, was scheduled to start Game Six. He had been brought in to insure there would be a sixth game. It left the Pirates' pitching rotation scrambled. Haddix didn't seem troubled.

"If we have to, we'll use them all," he said about the seventh game. "That's just the way we operate. We don't worry about tommorow. It might rain then. We'll operate the way we did all year. We've done this all summer. We say to the guys, 'Hey, get this game and then we'll think about tomorrow.' We got to number six and we can make more adjustments in a hurry. We've got some gutty guys who'll go out there without rest and do the job. These guys even volunteer to work."

Candelaria was one of them. His physical condition made him questionable. His arm was sound, but he was throwing in pain because of his back. Tanner considered him a "money" pitcher, the one he preferred in a big game. Tanner was hoping that Candelaria could provide five or six strong innings.

"I can tell you now, there will be a seventh game," Candelaria insisted somberly. "If I can get Garcia out, I'll be doing all right."

In the third game, Candelaria had been unable to handle Garcia. The pesky Orioles' shortstop had driven in four runs with a triple, a double and two singles. Candelaria had pitched only three innings in a lackluster performance. The Orioles had clubbed him for six runs and eight hits. He would have to do much better than that to match Palmer, who was selected by Weaver to try and wrap up the Series for Baltimore.

"When Jim Palmer throws the ball, it looks like a big fat grapefruit on the way in and the world's smallest pea on the way out," observed Ott. "He assaults you so nicely you can't even get mad at him. It's like Phil Garner says, 'Going 0-for-4 against him is the most relaxed 0-for-4 you will ever have.'

"It's that high fastball of his that kills you.

He will throw you the fastball up, the breaking stuff and the change. The thing to do is to lay off that high fastball if you can . . . at least when you have two strikes on you. So what you do if you want to see that this game will go right at the start, is to watch the umpire. If he takes away the high pitch from Palmer, then Palmer is going to have to rely on a second game plan, and whatever it is it can't be as good as the first. This is one hell of a hitting team we have, so it's easier said than done. But we have to think about laying off that marshmallow until we see exactly how it's going to be called.

"The only person who can get him away from his plan is the umpire. Palmer is really that good. So if we have any sense, we'll let him get aggravated with the umpire. Let him fight the ump. Of course, the way we like to swing, that won't be the easiest thing in the world, either."

Palmer realized that the Pirates were free swingers. After facing them in the second game, he had observed them closely from the bench in the next three games.

"There isn't an out man in their lineup," Palmer said. "I know I can't afford too many mistakes. Come to think of it, they're not hitting mistakes. They've been hitting good pitches.

"As far as I'm concerned, they're all good hitters. Everyone talks about Stargell and Parker. But they've got Madlock in there, too. He's won a couple of batting championships. You have to respect all of them.

"You just can't make a bad pitch on them. They're going to get their hits because they all hit the fastball so well. So you have to keep your mistakes to a minimum."

"Higher up in the batting order they don't want to take a chance of walking you with Parker and Stargell coming up after you," explained Madlock. "But batting sixth in the order like I am they move the ball around more. If they don't want to pitch to you, they'll give you an 'unintentional' intentional walk. In other words, nothing to hit at. I don't think I hit a strike all afternoon on Sunday (when he became the 39th player in World Series history to collect four hits in a game).

Garner is hit in the head in fouth inning of sixth game. Below, Moreno slides safely into second base in seventh inning.

"If there is any team capable of winning three straight, it's us. We have confidence in ourselves, we don't get down. Saturday, after the game was over, some guys sat on the bench. They were ticked. I told them, 'Come on in, it's not over. You're acting like it's over and it's not.'

"Our defense is what won it for us the last month and a half of the season. We made every play possible. I don't think there was a better team than us defensively going down the stretch. The way we played defense our whole infield could have won Gold Gloves. But we haven't made the routine plays in the Series, and we've missed routine double plays."

What was foremost in Madlock's mind was how well the Pirates had hit the ball and still trailed by one game. In the first five games, they had collected 61 hits and scored 24 runs while hitting .339 against the best pitching staff in baseball. Yet, the Orioles had outscored them. 25-24, despite the fact that they were hitting only .251 as a team.

The nine fielding errors by Pittsburgh had hurt the Pirates. There also were several errors of omission that weren't recorded. What also had contributed to their position was their failure to run as aggressively as they had during the regular season. During the season, they had stolen 188 bases in 252 attempts. So far in the Series, they had yet to steal a base in four attempts.

"The only way the Pirates win is through aggressiveness," emphasized Foli. "This is not a team with a particular hero, no matter what you read. Aggressiveness is the difference. If you don't get dumped a couple of times covering second, you're not doing your job. I know I play better when I'm bleeding!"

Still, the Pirates were loaded with most valuable player candidates if indeed they could win. Madlock was hitting .500 with three runs-batted-in and playing well at third. Garner also was batting .500 with five RBI's and playing a solid second base despite committing a key error. Parker was hitting .429 with three RBI's and intimidating Orioles' runners with his arm although he had made a costly muff on a fly

ball in Game Four, and Stargell was batting .381 with two home runs and four RBI's.

The only Pirates' player who wasn't hitting as expected was Moreno. His average was a dismal .217. He had made the third out in an inning eight times and stranded 14 runners. He was being called "Omar The Outmaker."

"We have played poorly up to this point," admitted Parker. "We know we're much better. We have played so poorly you'd think we wanted it this way so we could win with a dramatic finish. I just hope the win we had Sunday was indicative that we're going to start playing our style of baseball.

"The stage is set for a very dramatic finish, for us to win in Baltimore, which is only fitting."

Weaver wasn't concerned about dramatics. He even dismissed the talk that after Sunday's victory, the Pirates might have the momentum for the rest of the Series.

"If Palmer can get the ball past those guys, there's no such thing as momentum," said Weaver. "What's gone is gone. Each game stands by itself. All we need to win this thing is one more one-game winning streak."

The Orioles were back home, and they had natural grass, which they prefer, under their feet. The oddsmakers favored Baltimore. A noisy Baltimore crowd of 53,739 turned out to see if the Orioles could finally end the Series.

Moreno opened the game with new vigor. He slapped Palmer's first pitch up the middle for a single. Sandy Moreno blew her whistle with renewed enthusiasm. Foli then rapped a sharp grounder off DeCinces' glove into left field for a double as Moreno sped into third base. Two batters, two hits and the Pirates had the heart of their batting order coming up— Parker, Stargell and Milner. Palmer got Parker to hit to DeCinces. The third baseman held the runners as he threw Parker out. Stargell, swinging perhaps a bit too anxiously, fouled to DeCinces. Palmer was only one out away from getting out of a big jam. Milner topped a ball to the left of the mound. Palmer fielded it cleanly and raced over to first base for the unassisted putout. The Pirates had wasted a golden scoring opportunity.

191

Parker singled home Pirates' first run in seventh inning.

The pendulum swung to Candelaria. He again experienced trouble with Garcia, who began the Orioles' first inning with a single to centerfield. After Ayala flied out to Moreno, Singleton singled to left field as Garcia stopped at second base. Candelaria hung tough. He induced the dangerous Murray, who was battling a hitting slump, to ground to Madlock. Madlock stepped on third and threw to first base, completing an inning-ending double play.

Any thoughts of a wild hitting, high-scoring contest were quickly dispelled. After the first inning, both pitchers settled down. Throughout the next five innings, neither team seriously threatened except in the fourth when the Pirates loaded the bases on two walks and a hit batsman. Palmer was working smoothly. Candelaria was pitching on guts. Pain was visible on his face with practically every pitch he threw. He did more than he was asked. He not only kept the game close, he blanked the Orioles over six innings, allowing only six hits. In the sixth inning, Tanner went out to the mound to check Candelaria after Ott had indicated the pitcher might be hurt.

In the seventh inning, Tanner removed Candelaria for a pinch hitter. He was more than satisfied with Candelaria's performance. For the final three innings, he could turn to his bullpen with the rested Robinson and Tekulve.

Lacy, pinch-hitting for Candelaria, became Palmer's fifth strikeout victim opening the seventh inning. Moreno got his second hit of the game and reached second base when Foli outlegged a grounder up the middle. Parker had another chance to knock in a run. This time he produced. He singled past the lunging Dauer, driving in Moreno with the game's first run as Foli hustled to third. Stargell then came through with a sacrifice fly to deep left field, scoring Foli with the Pirates' second run. At that point of the game, each run loomed big.

Having warmed up while the Pirates were batting, Tekulve was ready to face the Orioles over the final three innings in an attempt to save the victory for the gutty Candelaria. Tekulve yielded a pinch-single to Smith after

two were out in the seventh, but escaped further damage. Now, only two innings were left for Tekulve to hold the Orioles and the Pirates would deadlock the Series.

With one out in the Pittsburgh eighth, Ott dumped a single to right. Garner then smashed a ground-rule double that bounced over the left field fence. Tactically, Bill Robinson who had been inserted into the lineup for Milner, was placed in the pitcher's spot in the batting order. Instead of Tekulve coming up, Robinson appeared and hit a sacrifice fly that scored Ott with the third run. Moreno drove in the fourth run with his third hit of the game. Now Tekulve had a 4-0 cushion.

He retired the Orioles in order in the eighth. There was only one more inning left. In the ninth, Tekulve was even sharper. He struck out two of the three batters he faced for his second save of the Series, as the Pirates won 4-0. More important, Pittsburgh had deadlocked the Series 3-3.

The disco sound in the Pirates' clubhouse seemed even louder. Nobody cared. The players had a right to celebrate. They had evened the Series, carrying it to the final game after having been so close to elimination. It all seemed so routine to them. One had to like their style. They were a relaxed, close-knit team that had an ingredient of togetherness that was lacking in so many other professional teams. Maybe it was the city of Pittsburgh that nurtures such an atmosphere. The Pittsburgh Steelers also reflect the family theme and they also have been champions.

Perhaps it was frustration or perhaps it was just being unobserving or insensitive to the emotions of the Pirates' players, but a Baltimore columnist criticized the thought of such an atmosphere on a professional team. He assaulted the family concept, labeling it "a cheap grandstand play." He even suggested that "any team that tries to compare itself to a family is straining for attention."

Stargell was told about the column. He said that he had not read it. He was told the gist of the article. He had an answer for the critic.

"They don't live with us," Stargell said angrily. "They don't know our feelings about

Garner collides with Baltimore's first baseman Eddie Murray.

each other. And we don't care what other people say. The family unit has never left us. It's a constant thing that's been with us all year long."

Madlock was nearby. He also was riled. He joined "the family" in midseason and felt its impact immediately.

"It was just that good ol' family togetherness that you guys don't like to hear about," he snapped to reporters.

Tanner savored the victory. He was moved by the way Candelaria had pitched.

"This Pittsburgh team has never given up," said Tanner. "We've had our backs to the wall before and came back. We were out of it after Saturday's game, but now we're all even again. When you look at the job Candelaria, pitching in pain, did tonight, you know what I'm talking about. He's had a problem with his side and has been pitching in pain.

"Ott pointed to his side and motioned for me to come out in the sixth inning. I went over to Candy and he told me he was okay. 'The Candy Man' is a money pitcher. He's been working in pain, but any chance I have to start him in a big game I will. To my mind, he's one of the greatest money pitchers of all time. Every time that I have called on him in a big game, he has done the job for me."

Tekulve agreed.

"He showed us all something tonight," the sidearm reliever said without mentioning his own fine performance. "Nobody will ever know how much he was hurting out there, but he kept getting them out. He kept coming up

with the big pitch."

Ott was concerned with Candelaria in the sixth inning. He saw him grimace and grab his side when he was warming up. It was at that point that he motioned to Tanner and pointed to his side to indicate that Candelaria might be hurting.

"Candy didn't have to tell me, I saw it on his face," revealed Ott. "He said he was okay and I told him he was a bad liar. I called out Tanner then. Candelaria was missing quite a lot of his velocity. But he had control of both his fastball and breaking ball, mixed them up, spotted the ball and made some great pitches when he had to."

Candelaria played down his performance.

"It was a do-or-die situation for us," said Candelaria. "If I had gotten in trouble early, I'm sure Chuck would have gone to the bullpen right away. The whole staff was ready to pitch. My side was bothering me a little when I warmed up, but fortunately it never got worse when I threw in the game.

"I'm happy. I'm at peace inside myself because we're going seven games. It would have been a real bummer if we went home tonight. I'm not smiling now, because if you were in the pain I am in right now, there'd be no reason to smile. They said the cure was rest. Rest? Now is hardly the time to rest. I just try to block out the pain. It's like pins sticking into my side when I push off the mound and turn toward the batter."

All the Pirates had to turn to now was Game Seven.

inning	1	2	3	4	5	6	7	8	9	TOTAL
Pittsburgh	0	0	0	0	2	0	0	2	4	
Baltimore	0	0	1	0	0	0	0	0	1	

GAME SEVEN

Maybe it was an omen. But while the Orioles were in a quandary about how to halt the Pirates' surge, one local vendor was worrying how she could sell 20 dozen birds of a different color. Mrs. Barbara Marder, an elementary schoolteacher, was excited about hawking stuffed toy Orioles outside the stadium. It was an enterprising idea. But there was one very unfortunate thing. The merchandise she ordered was completely wrong. Instead of the

194

Oriole birds she had ordered and expected, the manufacturer sent her 240 black and yellow Pirate parrots.

"They sent me Pirate birds, can you believe that?" she cried by the stadium long before the seventh game was to begin. "I almost had a heart attack when I saw them."

Undaunted, she cleverly glued a bright orange ribbon on each of the birds. Imagine selling a black and yellow parrot with an orange ribbon? She tried.

"Hey, ten bucks a bird. Charge-a-bird. I take Visa or Master Charge," she yelled in her best selling voice.

A potential buyer came by. He looked perplexed. He shook his head and sneered.

"Now if that ain't the damndest looking Oriole I've ever seen," he said.

She had a quick answer.

"Look, they're not Pirate birds, they're . . . oh, forget it," said Mrs. Marder.

But, she didn't give up easily. She spotted a carload of Pirates' fans and tried to convince them to buy a bird. She was determined.

"Hey, take the ribbon off and it's a Pirate bird," she shouted. "We have the only convertible birds anywhere."

She wasn't successful. But she knew she had to keep trying even though that hawking in the middle of a parking lot wasn't something one would expect of a schoolteacher. In fact, Mrs. Marder admitted that her husband and children had looked the other way.

"I'm a black sheep," she conceded. "But this is a lot more lucrative than teaching, and when the family goes on one of our big, expensive trips, no one talks about where the money came from."

One Pirates' fan who came from Pittsburgh was Harry Smail. It was tough for him to be impartial. But he was wearing a Pirates' hat that had been given to him by Bibby and he had six stars on it that had been presented to him by Stargell. That's how much the Pirates liked him.

Smail lived in Greenburg, Pennsylvania, a half hour's drive from Pittsburgh. During the umpires' strike earlier in the season, Smail was contracted to umpire 16 Pirates' games. It was quite a thrill that late in his life. The last time that Smail had umpired was 20 years ago in the Pacific Coast League. Since that time, he had been officiating small college football games. He knew he would never again umpire a Pittsburgh game so it didn't matter that he displayed his Pirates' cap proudly on his head. He was happy.

So was Scott McGregor, whom Weaver delegated to pitch the deciding seventh game. McGregor, who won the third game, 8-4, was looking forward to the challenge.

"Pitching the seventh game of the World Series is something I've always dreamed about since I was a kid," exclaimed the small left-hander. "You always watch the seventh game of the World Series and now I get a chance to pitch it and that doesn't happen to everybody. It's unfortunate that somebody has to lose, but after the game somebody's going to be crying and somebody's going to be pouring champagne. I think we'll be the ones with the champagne."

The Orioles had had the champagne ready ever since the fifth game. They still hadn't opened it. Tanner designated Bibby as the pitcher who would help the Pirates pop their champagne corks. While most figured Tanner would use Kison in the final game, Tanner decided that Bibby was a better choice.

"He is my only rested pitcher," explained Tanner. "That's why I'm starting him. I'll have Kison and Blyleven available for a couple of innings if we need them."

Bibby was ready.

"I'm the only one who is fresh," said Bibby. "I'm going to approach this game like I've approached every other game this year. If I don't do that I'll put too much pressure on myself. I'm going to treat this like any other game.

"I really don't think there is any more pressure than there has been all year. Ever since spring training I've looked to make it to the World Series. This is the top of the baseball season. We've come to the end of the line as far as professional baseball is concerned.

"I didn't try to put too much thought on the game last night. I went over the hitters by myself. I reminisced in my mind what guys can hit and the way I want to pitch to them

and then fell asleep. I won't promise anything. I'm just going out there and do my best."

Bibby, a veteran, hard-throwing right-hander, was approaching his 35th birthday. Before joining the Pirates in 1978 as a free agent, he had toiled in St. Louis, Texas and Cleveland. He had a good fastball and a slider. His pitches had been clocked at better than 90 miles an hour. Baltimore coach Frank Robinson remembered Bibby from the time when he was managing Cleveland and he was one of his pitchers.

"When I had him, he was more of a thrower," recalled Robinson. "Now he's learned to pitch."

Ironically, the Orioles were one of the teams that Bibby had considered signing with when he was a free agent in 1978.

"I had a chance to sign with Baltimore," admitted Bibby. "However, I thought I'd fit in better here (in Pittsburgh). They offered me more security, a better contract."

Ott was convinced that Bibby would pitch a good game. He had a reason for his optimism.

"Jim was too strong on Saturday," recalled Ott. "And when he's too strong, he has a tendency to overthrow his slider. He made too many mistakes Saturday and he just got away with them. I think he'll be better because he'll be a little weaker."

If Bibby was on, well and good. If not, then somebody else would pick up the slack. In his brief tenure with the Pirates, Madlock noticed that tendency.

"The key with us is that we don't put any pressure on anyone to do more than they are capable of doing," pointed out Madlock. "Look, Omar was going bad but it was no problem. He went 1-for-32 during the season and we still won. We got so many guys who can do it. Everybody takes turns carrying us, but at the same time we can play very bad at times. We did in a couple of games and came back. Sometime you can't believe some of us, the way we've come back."

Although the game was rated as even by the bookies, many observers felt that the Orioles had the home field advantage. They reasoned that since Baltimore had lost two in a row, it

197

Stargell crosses plate after delivering dramatic two-run homer in sixth inning of final game, to give Pirates 2-1 lead and eventual World Series triumph.

wasn't likely that they would be beaten three straight times.

Danny Sheridan, a sports analyst in Mobile, Alabama, who has won acclaim for his predictions of college and professional football games, liked the Pirates. Over the years, he had been uncanny in selecting the winner of the Super Bowl, compiling a 10-2-1 record.

"You have to go with the Pirates," suggested Sheridan. "They are like a football team in that they have the momentum. People don't think of momentum in such a short series as baseball, but it's there. The Pirates are like a football team, winning the games they have to in critical situations.

"And another thing. They have won without any significant contributions from their two biggest hitters, Parker and Stargell. They are the money hitters. To say that one of them is due, that's one thing. But with two of them due, the odds are that one of them will come through."

Now, it was up to Bibby and McGregor. The entire Series came down to one game. There wasn't any concern about tomorrow now. The champagne couldn't wait any longer.

As he had done the previous night, Moreno opened the game with a single. It was his fourth hit in his last six at-bats. It was clear that he had shaken his slump. Foli sacrificed Moreno to second. But Parker and Robinson both popped out.

Bibby didn't have any problems in the first inning. He set down the Orioles without a ball being hit out of the infield. Stargell tried to get the Pirates going in the second inning with a single. He took second when Lowenstein bobbled the ball. But he did not advance another base.

Bibby fanned the first two batters he faced in the second inning. He then surrendered a single to DeCinces before getting Dempsey to ground out.

However, after the Pirates were retired in the third inning, the Orioles broke through for the first run. It happened quickly. Dauer, the first batter Bibby faced, caught hold of a fastball and drove it into the left field stands for a home run, giving Baltimore a 1-0 lead.

The Series' first controversy occurred with Pittsburgh at bat in the fourth inning. After Robinson popped up, Stargell looped a double to left field. Madlock then grounded to Garcia who attempted to cut down Stargell at third. However, his throw was bad and the Pirates had runners at first and third with only one out. Nicosia hit a line drive to Dauer for the second out. Garner then hit a pop fly to Murray, who let the ball drop when Garner collided with him on the base line. However, first base umpire Bob Engel called Garner out because of interference. The Pirates argued but to no avail.

After Bibby disposed of the Orioles without difficulty in the fourth, he surprisingly was taken out for a pinch hitter in the fifth inning. Still, Pittsburgh couldn't score. Bibby had pitched well. He had allowed only three hits in the four innings, but one was Dauer's home run.

Tanner brought in Don Robinson, who immediately was touched for a single by De-Cinces. After two fly ball outs, Robinson lost his control and walked McGregor. That was all for Robinson. Tanner replaced him with Grant Jackson, who closed the inning unharmed.

McGregor appeared in command when he got Parker out on a ground ball opening the sixth inning. It was the sixth straight batter he had retired. Bill Robinson broke the string with a single to left. Stargell, who already had a single and a double, was the next batter. He rocked in the batter's box, pumped his bat several times and awaited McGregor's first pitch. The tension began to mount. McGregor threw and Stargell swung. The crack of the bat on the ball sounded good. Stargell's timing was perfect. The ball rocketed off his bat and it didn't stop until it landed over the right field fence into the Pirates' bullpen. Stargell had hit his third homer of the Series, and put the Pirates ahead, 2-1. The Pirates' dugout was alive with excitement. "Pops" had hit a big one.

It was up to Jackson to hold the lead. He did his job in the sixth and seventh innings, disposing of the Orioles without travail. He had retired all seven Baltimore hitters he had faced. Jackson, almost forgotten in the Pirates' bullpen with Robinson, Tekulve and Romo, was rising to the challenge.

When Stargell came to bat in the eighth inning with two out, he was greeted by loud applause from the Pirates' fans in the crowd of 53,733. Stargell kept them cheering. He doubled off the left field wall for his fourth hit of the game. What a night for the popular 38-year-old star!

In the bottom of the eighth inning, Jackson got Dauer for his eighth straight out. The streak was snapped when Lee May, batting for McGregor, walked. Bumbry also walked. Suddenly, Jackson was having trouble with his control. When Ayala was sent up to hit for Garcia, Tanner made a move. He signaled to his bullpen for Tekulve. Weaver then called back Ayala and ordered Crowley to bat instead.

It was a tense moment. The Orioles had the tying run on second base and the potential winning run on first. Orioles' fans were out of their seats yelling. Crowley hit a slow roller to Garner. Garner charged the ball, fielded it cleanly and tossed out Crowley as the runners each moved up a base. Tanner went out to the mound to talk with Tekulve. With first base open, they decided to intentionally walk Singleton and pitch to the slumping Murray. The Orioles' slugger was overdue. He connected with one of Tekulve's fast balls and drove it deep to right field. Pittsburgh fans held their breaths. Parker ran hard and caught up with the ball, making a fine running catch for the third out. Baltimore fans sighed.

Stoddard was picked to face the Pirates in the ninth. Garner opened with a double into the left field corner. Tekulve tried to bunt him to third but failed. Weaver made a change. With the left-handed hitting Moreno up, he replaced Stoddard with Flanagan. Moreno met the challenge. He singled to center for his third hit, scoring Garner with the Pirates' third run. Weaver again went to his bullpen and called in Stanhouse, who had been bothered by a sore shoulder and wasn't expected to pitch in the Series after having worked in Game Five. When Foli singled to

left center, Moreno advanced to third and Weaver replaced Stanhouse with Tippy Martinez. Martinez didn't last long either. The first batter he faced was Parker and he hit the Pirates' slugger with a pitch, loading the bases. There still was only one out when Dennis Martinez came on to pitch.

Martinez also missed the plate. On his first pitch, he hit Bill Robinson on the left hand. Moreno scored Pittsburgh's fourth run and the bases remained filled. Stargell's appearance at the plate brought a roar from the crowd. He already had a big game with a two-run homer, a double and two singles. But the fans wanted more. They wanted a grand slam. Electricity filled the ball park. But Stargell grounded into a double play, ending what assuredly was the Pirates' last time at bat in the 1979 World Series.

All Tekulve had to do was protect a 4-1 lead. Roenicke struck out swinging. DeCinces struck out swinging. Kelly then batted for Dempsey. The Pirates were only one out away from an amazing comeback, one out away from the world championship. Kelly hit a soft fly ball to Moreno. Moreno clutched it in his glove and ran all the way to the Pirates' dugout. The Pirates rushed onto the field, jumping with joy as the crowd made its way onto the playing area. It was 1971 all over again! It was an unbelievable ending. The Pirates had beaten the odds. Somewhere Roberto Clemente was smiling.

Within minutes after the game, a legion of Pirates' fans jammed the corridor outside the Pittsburgh locker room. They were gaudy and bold, most of them wearing black and yellow baseball caps and all singing "We Are Fam-a-lee." They cheered and yelled to their heroes every time the door was opened to the steamy Pirates' clubhouse.

Inside, the room was hot and crowded with well-wishers as the Pirates' players 'received congratulations. There were cases of champagne, an army of visitors, and in an unusual move, the wives of the players were allowed to participate in the celebration that even left President Carter smiling on a makeshift stage. The President was there, along with baseball

Commissioner Bowie Kuhn, to make the championship trophy presentation to John Galbreath and his son Dan, the owners of the Pittsburgh team.

The word filtered down from the press box that Stargell had been voted the Series' most valuable player. At 38, he was the oldest player in the fall classic to receive the honor. It wasn't a sentimental choice either. Stargell had earned the award. He had batted .400, hit three homers, drove in seven runs, set a Series record of seven extra base hits and tied another mark with 25 total bases.

As usual after a game, Stargell sipped from a green bottle of California white wine as he talked to the hundreds of writers and announcers who were surrounding him. He stood behind a microphone with a white towel draped around his neck and he didn't talk about himself and his moment of World Series glory. Instead, he spoke about something else that was close to him.

"I'd like to talk about a columnist here who wrote that we aren't a family," began Stargell. "I thought that was unfair. That man didn't live with us all year. He didn't understand that we depend on closeness, that we are a family. No words can express what we've done. We've overcome. We've worked hard. We've scratched and clawed. We took that song, 'We Are Family' and identified with it. We weren't trying to be sassy or fancy. We're just a ballclub that is a family in our clubhouse. And that's why we won the World Series. That's why we came from behind."

Stargell had to make his point. Then he talked about the game, about baseball.

"Howard Cosell kept telling me how many men I was leaving on base," said Stargell. "But I told Howard that when I leave a man on base, give the pitcher some credit. I wish like hell I could deliver every run that's on base every time I came up. But when I hit that homer tonight, I wanted to rise to the occasion."

One writer wanted to know if Stargell ever had a moment in baseball that was higher than this?

"One other time," answered Stargell.

"When the Pirates signed me in 1959, they gave me a $1,500 bonus and $175 a month. I was elated then. But then and now, it's hard to find the words to say how I feel."

Another writer pointed out that Stargell also scored the winning run in the 1971 World Series and wanted to know how did this game rated with the game eight years earlier?

"To tell you the truth, that never occurred to me until somebody else mentioned it to us in the clubhouse," replied Stargell. "But to go back to that year, I thought 1971 was Roberto Clemente's moment of glory. He had started something with his winning, driving attitude. Whatever contributions I've made have been merely an extension of what he started.

"These guys are trying to use me as an excuse. They have great ability and great character and I'm proud of each and every one of them. Dammit, I'd go to war with them. It's such a joy to be able to do this. How can thoughts of pressure enter your mind when you're doing what you want and you're getting paid for it?

"We go out to have fun because we only have a few years to play this game and you can't be tied up in knots if you're going to be loose like you should be. When you come into the game without ulcers you should leave without ulcers. And what you saw in this World Series was an outstanding bunch of guys who enjoyed playing baseball.

"What we did this year goes back to 1978 when we came hard at the end but finished second to the Phillies in our division. When we got to spring training this year, everyone was there early because it was so important to us not to watch the 1979 World Series on television. I knew we were not going to be denied. We didn't go to spring training and then play 162 games to lose.

"You know, on that last out of the game, I saw Tim Foli jumping up and down before the ball came down and I couldn't help doing the same thing. I flashed back to so many things. We kept driving all year. We should all give thanks to the Almighty for giving us the chance to have the courage, the desire and the drive. I'm just so pleased to have been given this chance to enjoy this moment. To be part of this, the Good Man above has given us the right to shed tears at this point."

Then Stargell reached out and grabbed his sister Sandra. They embraced and wept together. Stargell is family all the way. At that moment, the stereo blasted Sister Sledge singing, "We Are Family." Stargell heard it. He turned and smiled.

"There it is," he exclaimed.

And he and his sister began to walk away, arms around each other. He was happy. Someone wanted to know what the President had said to him. And Stargell smiled again.

"He said congratulations and talked to me about the records I broke," disclosed Stargell. "He said it was a thrilling game between two outstanding teams. I wanted to ask him if he had any peanuts on him, but there were too many Secret Service men around."

Madlock and Jackson were quite exuberant in pouring champagne over their heads. Stargell smiled at them.

"You just expect that from Willie when he hit the homer," said Madlock. "He can handle the pressure and it takes a certain kind of guy to do that. I don't know if I could have handled it."

Perhaps more than anyone, Parker was happy for Stargell. He places him in a special light.

"That Willie should win it is only right," said Parker. "The man is a legend. Right now, to me, he's like a god."

He was something like that to losing pitcher Scott McGregor.

"Pittsburgh is a helluva ballclub and Mr. Stargell is an amazing guy," said McGregor.

Meanwhile, the fans in Pittsburgh also were celebrating. Just in case the downtown crowd got a little too frivolous, the police department was ready. Shortly after the final out, police officers in riot gear and took up positions around Market Square. They were reinforced by the department's canine corps. The police took the extra duty in stride.

"We expect people to be loud, profane and throw paper," said inspector Horace McDaniel. "I guess if we weren't in police work we'd do the same thing."

Yet, after the long night, police termed the jubiliation orderly. Naturally there were arrests; over 100. But there also were 10 cases of dog bites, damaged street signs, busted windows and several uprooted trees. But nobody was seriously injured.

"I gave the last call for drinks at 12:30, just as soon as things started getting out of hand," said bartender Kevin Carroll of The Press Box. "There was a television camera outside our door and everybody was pushing to be near the camera. As soon as someone opened the door to try to leave, somebody else was pushed in and they'd stay to have a drink. I'm surprised the door didn't get ripped off."

When the Pirates arrived home, shortly after 3:30 in the morning, there were more than 1,000 fans waiting to greet them at the airport. It was just too late for the players to do any more celebrating. That would have to wait for later in the evening.

Chuck Tanner had to wait even longer to celebrate the sweetest triumph of his career. Early Thursday morning he had to attend the funeral of his mother. Somewhere, Ann Tanner was smiling, too.

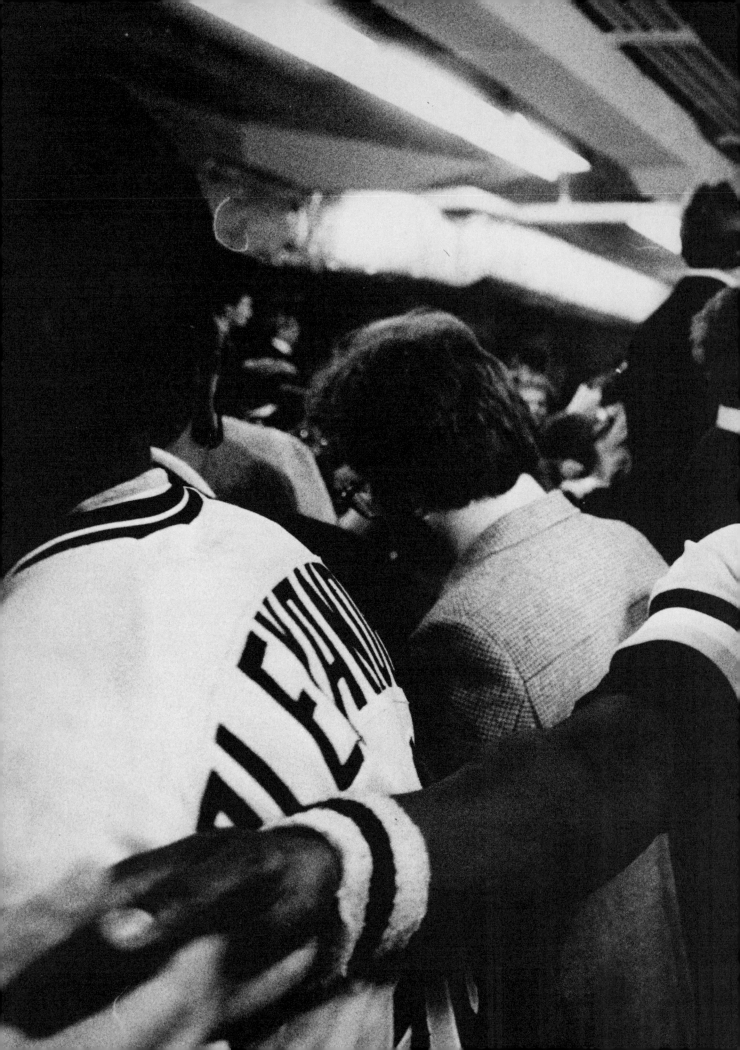

Appendix

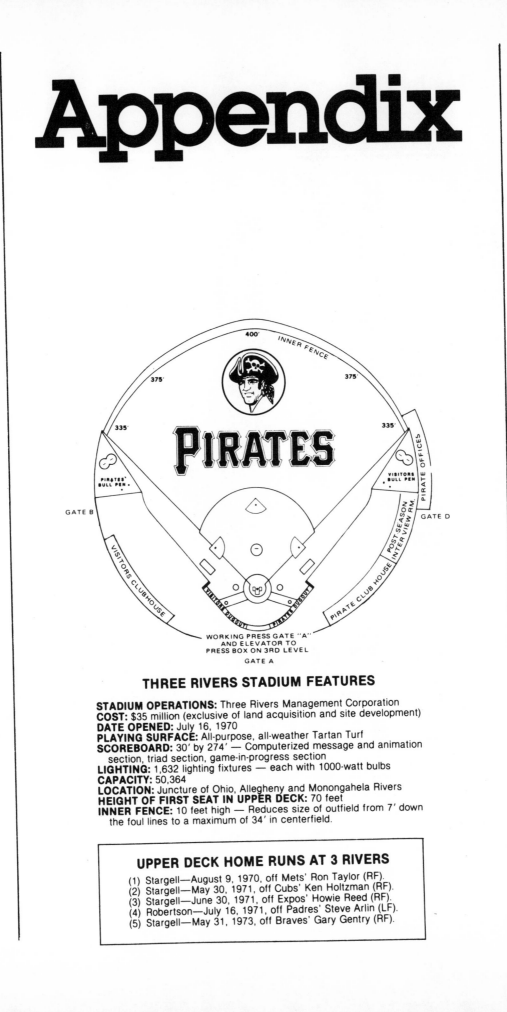

THREE RIVERS STADIUM FEATURES

STADIUM OPERATIONS: Three Rivers Management Corporation
COST: $35 million (exclusive of land acquisition and site development)
DATE OPENED: July 16, 1970
PLAYING SURFACE: All-purpose, all-weather Tartan Turf
SCOREBOARD: 30' by 274' — Computerized message and animation
  section, triad section, game-in-progress section
LIGHTING: 1,632 lighting fixtures — each with 1000-watt bulbs
CAPACITY: 50,364
LOCATION: Juncture of Ohio, Allegheny and Monongahela Rivers
HEIGHT OF FIRST SEAT IN UPPER DECK: 70 feet
INNER FENCE: 10 feet high — Reduces size of outfield from 7' down
  the foul lines to a maximum of 34' in centerfield.

UPPER DECK HOME RUNS AT 3 RIVERS

(1) Stargell—August 9, 1970, off Mets' Ron Taylor (RF).
(2) Stargell—May 30, 1971, off Cubs' Ken Holtzman (RF).
(3) Stargell—June 30, 1971, off Expos' Howie Reed (RF).
(4) Robertson—July 16, 1971, off Padres' Steve Arlin (LF).
(5) Stargell—May 31, 1973, off Braves' Gary Gentry (RF).

Day by Day
1979

Date	Game No.	Opp.	W/L	Score	Winning Pitcher	Losing Pitcher	Season Record	Pos.	Gbl.
4/6	1	Mont.	L	2-3	Sosa	Tekulve	0-1	2	1
4/7	2	Mont.	W	7-6	Jackson	Sosa	1-1	2	1
4/8	3	Mont.	L	4-5	May	Romo	1-2	4	1½
4/10	4	at Phil.	L	3-7	Ruthven	Romo	1-3	4	1½
4/11	5	at Phil.	L	4-5	Carlton	Blyleven	1-4	4	3
4/12	6	Stl.	W	3-1	Robinson	Denny	2-4	4	2½
4/13	7	Stl.	W	7-6	Bibby	Schultz	3-4	5	2½
4/14	8	Stl.	W	7-4	Whitson	Forsch	4-4	4	2
4/15	9	Stl.	L	4-9	Littell	Tekulve	4-5	4	2½
4/17	10	Phil.	L	2-13	Carlton	Blyleven	4-6	4	3½
4/18	11	Phil.	L	2-3	Lerch	Robinson	4-7	4	4½
4/20	12	at Hou.	L	4-5	Sambito	Bibby	4-8	5	4½
4/21	13	at Hou.	L	4-5	Andujar	Tekulve	4-9	5	4½
4/22	14	at Hou.	L	2-3	Andujar	Candelaria	4-10	5	5½
4/24	15	at Cin.	W	9-2	Robinson	Pastore	5-10	6	5½
4/25	16	at Cin.	W	3-2	Tekulve	Tomlin	6-10	6	5½
4/27	17	Hou.	L	8-9	Riccelli	Whitson	6-11	6	6½
4/29	18	Hou.	W	10-5	Kison	J. Niekro	7-11	6	6½
5/1	19	Atl.	L	2-5	P. Niekro	Tekulve	7-12	6	7½
5/2	20	Atl.	W	10-2	Candelaria	M. Mahler	8-12	6	7
5/4	21	at Stl.	L	3-4	Sykes	Robinson	8-13	6	7½
5/5	22	at Stl.	W	6-5	Jackson	Vuckovich	9-13	6	6½
5/6	23	at Stl.	L	2-4	Martinez	Kison	9-14	6	6½
5/7	24	at Atl.	W	4-2	Candelaria	M. Mahler	10-14	6	7½
5/8	25	at Atl.	L	1-4	Solomon	Rhoden	10-15	5	8½
5/9	26	at Atl.	W	17-9	Bibby	Garber	11-15	5	8½
5/11	27	Cin.	L	4-8	Tomlin	Whitson	11-16	5	8½
5/12	28	Cin.	W	3-2	Bibby	Pastore	12-16	5	8½
5/13	29	Cin.	L	3-7	LaCoss	Candelaria	12-17	5	9
5/15	30	N.Y. +	L	0-3	Swan	Robinson	12-18	5	9
5/16	31	N.Y.	W	4-3	Romo	Lockwood	13-18	5	9
5/17	32	N.Y.	W	6-3	Tekulve	Orosco	14-18	5	9
5/18	33	at Chi.	W	9-5	Candelaria	Holtzman	15-18	5	8
5/19	34	at Chi. +	W	3-0	Rooker	Krukow	16-18	4	7
5/20	35	at Chi.	W	6-5	Robinson	McGlothen	17-18	4	6
5/21	36	at Mont.	W	4-2	Blyleven	Sanderson	18-18	4	6
5/22	37	at Mont.	L	3-6	Grimsley	Whitson	18-19	4	7
5/23	38	at Mont.	L	0-3	Rogers	Candelaria	18-20	4	7
5/25	39	at N.Y.	T	3-3				4	6½
5/26	40	N.Y.	L	8-10	Lockwood	Tekulve	18-21	4	6½
5/27	41	at N.Y.	W	2-1	Jackson	Murray	19-21	4	6½
5/28	42	at N.Y.	W	6-1	Candelaria	Falcone	20-21	4	5½
5/29	43	Chi. +	W	8-0	Robinson	Holtzman	21-21	4	5½
5/30	44	Chi.	W	9-2	Rooker	McGlothen	22-21	5	5½
5/31	45	Chi.	W	4-3	Kison	Sutter	23-21	4	5½
6/1	46	S.D.	W	9-8	Tekulve	Shirley	24-21	4	4½
6/2	47	S.D.	L	3-1	Perry	Candelaria	24-22	4	4½
6/3	48	S.D.	W	7-0	Kison	Owchinko	25-22	4	3½
6/4	49	L.A.	L	2-4	Sutcliffe	Rooker	25-23	4	4½
6/5	50	L.A.	W	3-1	Blyleven	Sutton	26-23	4	3½
6/6	51	L.A.	W	5-4	Romo	Welch	27-23	3	3½
6/8	52	S.F.	W	3-2	Romo	Curtis	28-23	3	2½
6/9	53	S.F.	L	2-6	Blue	Kison	28-24	3	2½
6/10	54	S.F.	L	4-7	Lavelle	Romo	28-25	3	3½
6/12	55	at S.D.	L	3-6	Perry	Candelaria	28-26	4	4½
6/13	56	at S.D.	L	2-3	Owchinko	Kison	28-27	4	4½
6/14	57	at S.D.	L	1-2	D'Acquisto	Candelaria	28-28	4	5½
6/15	58	at L.A.	W	6-2	Blyleven	Sutton	29-28	4	4½
6/16	59	at L.A.	W	6-3	Robinson	Welch	30-28	4	4½
6/17	60	at L.A.	W	5-1	Whitson	Reuss	31-28	4	4½
6/19	61	at S.F.	W	9-4	Candelaria	Montefusco	32-28	3	4
6/20	62	at S.F.	W	8-5	Jackson	Lavelle	33-28	2	4
6/22	63	Chi.	W	7-2	Blyleven	Holtzman	34-28	2	4
6/23	64	Chi.	L	3-4	Krukow	Robinson	34-29	3	4½
6/24	65	Chi.	L	0-5	Reuschel	Kison	34-30	3	5
6/25	66	at N.Y.	W	8-1	Candelaria	Swan	35-30	2	5
6/25	67	at N.Y.	L	0-4	Falcone	Rooker	35-31	2	6
6/26	68	at N.Y.	W	2-1	Blyleven	Hausman	36-31	2	6
6/27	69	N.Y.	L	9-12	Twitchell	Jackson	36-32	2	6
6/28	70	N.Y.	L	2-3	Allen	Bibby	36-33	2	6½
6/29	71	Mont.	W	6-5	Kison	Lee	37-33	2	5½
6/30	72	Mont.	L	3-5	Sanderson	Blyleven	37-34	2	6½
7/2	73	at Stl.	W	5-4	Romo	Knowles	38-34	2	6½
7/3	74	at Stl.	W	4-1	Candelaria	Forsch	39-34	2	5½
7/4	75	at Stl.	W	6-4	Blyleven	Vuckovich	40-34	2	5½
7/5	76	at Stl.	L	0-2	Fulgham	Rooker	40-35	2	6½
7/6	77	at Cin.	L	1-2	Bair	Jackson	40-36	2	6½

Date	Game No.	Opp.	W/L	Score	Winning Pitcher	Losing Pitcher	Season Record	Pos.	Gbl.
*7/19	87	Hou.	W	9-5	Roberts	Forsch	47-39	2	3
7/19	88	Hou.	W	4-2	Kison	Niekro	48-39	2	1
7/20	89	Hou.	W	9-3	Candelaria	Richard	49-39	2	½
7/21	90	Hou.	W	6-5	Romo	Sambito	50-39	2	1½
*7/22	91	Atl.	W	5-4	Robinson	Solomon	51-39	2	1½
7/22	92	Atl.	W	3-2	Bibby	Mahler	52-39	2	½
*7/23	93	Atl.	W	7-1	Blyleven	Hanna	53-39	2	½
7/23	94	Atl.	L	0-6	Niekro	Rooker	53-40	2	1
7/24	95	Cin.	L	5-6	Norman	Kison	53-41	2	1
7/25	96	Cin.	L	5-6	Bair	Tekulve	53-42	2	1½
7/26	97	Cin.	L	7-9	Soto	Roberts	53-43	2	2½
*7/27	98	at Mont.	W	5-4	Tekulve	Sosa	54-43	2	1½
7/27	99	at Mont.	W	9-1	Blyleven	Sanderson	55-43	2	1½
7/28	100	at Mont.	W	5-3	Bibby	Schatzeder	56-43	1	½
7/29	101	at Mont.	L	3-5	Rogers	Kison	56-44	2	1½
7/30	102	N.Y.	W	8-5	Jackson	Bernard	57-44	2	.002
7/31	103k	N.Y.	L	1-2	Twitchell	Blyleven	57-45	2	1
8/1	104	Stl.	W	4-3	Romo	B. Forsch	58-45	2	1
8/2	105	Stl.	L	4-5	Frazier	Jackson	58-46	2	1
*8/3	106	Phil.	W	6-3	Romo	McGraw	59-46	2	½
8/3	107	Phil.	W	5-1	Bibby	Christenson	60-46	2	½
8/4	108 +	Phil.	W	4-0	Candelaria	Espinosa	61-46	2	½
*8/5	109	Phil.	W	12-8	Tekulve	Eastwick	62-46	1	½
8/5	110	Phil.	W	5-2	Romo	Noles	63-46	1	½
8/7	111	at Chi.	L	2-15	Reuschel	Rooker	63-47	1	½
8/8	112	at Chi.	W	5-2	Tekulve	Tidrow	64-47	1	1½
8/9	113	at Chi.	L	3-11	Lamp	Candelaria	64-48	1	1½
*8/10	114	at Phil.	L	3-4	Eastwick	Jackson	64-49	1	1½
8/10	115	at Phil.	W	3-2	Kison	Lerch	65-49	1	1½
8/11	116	at Phil.	W	14-11	Romo	Eastwick	66-49	1	1½
8/12	117	at Phil.	W	9-1	Bibby	Christenson	67-49	1	2½
8/14	118	S.D.	W	7-1	Candelaria	D'Acquisto	68-49	1	3½
8/15	119	S.D.	W	5-1	Blyleven	Jones	69-49	1	3½
8/16	120	S.D.	W	5-4	Kison	Perry	70-49	1	4
8/17	121	L.A.	L	6-7	Patterson	Bibby	70-50	1	3
8/18	122	L.A.	L	5-1	Reuss	Robinson	70-51	1	2
8/19	123 +	L.A.	W	2-0	Tekulve	Hooton	71-51	1	2
8/20	124	S.F.	W	6-5	Romo	Lavelle	72-51	1	2
8/21	125	S.F.	L	1-5	Knepper	Kison	72-52	1	2
8/22	126	S.F.	W	8-6	Tekulve	Lavelle	73-52	1	2
8/24	127	at S.D.	L	2-3	Jones	Romo	73-53	1	2
8/25	128	at S.D.	W	4-3	Roberts	D'Acquisto	74-53	1	3
8/26	129	at S.D.	W	9-2	Kison	Shirley	75-53	1	3
8/27	130	at L.A.	L	2-4	Brett	Tekulve	75-54	1	3
8/28	131	at L.A.	W	4-1	Candelaria	Hough	76-54	1	3
8/29	132	at L.A.	W	4-1	Blyleven	Reuss	77-54	1	3
8/31	133	at S.F.	W	6-4	Robinson	Curtis	78-54	1	3
*9/1	134	at S.F.	W	5-3	Kison	Montefusco	79-54	1	3
9/1	135	at S.F.	W	7-2	Bibby	Knepper	80-54	1	3½
9/2	136	at S.F.	W	5-3	Candelaria	Blue	81-54	1	3½
*9/3	137 +	Phil.	L	0-2	Carlton	Blyleven	81-55	1	2½
9/3	138	Phil.	W	7-3	Rooker	Lerch	82-55	1	2½
9/5	139	at Stl.	W	7-5	Roberts	Thomas	83-55	1	2½
9/6	140	at Stl.	L	6-8	Martinez	Bibby	83-56	1	2
9/7	141	at N.Y.	W	6-4	Jackson	Allen	84-56	1	1
9/8	142	at N.Y.	L	2-3	Ellis	Rooker	84-57	1	1
9/9	143	at N.Y.	W	6-5	Tekulve	Glynn	85-57	1	1
9/11	144	Stl.	W	7-3	Roberts	Denny	86-57	1	½
9/12	144 +	Stl.	W	2-0	Candelaria	Forsch	87-57	2	.001
9/15	145	N.Y.	W	5-4	Roberts	Glynn	88-57	1	½
9/16	146 +	N.Y.	L	0-3	Falcone	Candelaria	88-58	2	.001
9/17	148	at Mont.	W	2-1	Robinson	Rogers	89-58	1	1
9/18	149	at Mont.	W	5-3	Jackson	Murray	90-58	1	2
*9/19	150	at Phil.	W	9-6	Tekulve	Eastwick	91-58	1	2
9/19	151	at Phil.	L	5-6	Kucek	Romo	91-59	1	1
9/20	152	at Phil.	L	1-2	Lerch	Tekulve	91-60	2	½
9/21	153	at Chi.	L	0-2	McGlothen	Robinson	91-61	2	1
9/22	154	at Chi.	W	4-1	Kison	Riley	92-61	2	½
9/23	155	at Chi.	W	6-0	Bibby	Reuschel	93-61	2	½
*9/24	156	Mont.	W	5-2	Blyleven	Schatzeder	94-61	1	½
9/24	157	Mont.	L	5-1	Grimsley	Jackson	94-62	2	½
9/25	158	Mont.	W	10-4	Rooker	Sanderson	95-62	1	½
9/26	159	Mont.	W	10-1	Kison	Rogers	96-62	1	1½
9/27	160	Stl.	L	5-9	Forsch	Roberts	96-63	1	1
9/28	161	Chi.	W	6-1	Bibby	Reuschel	97-63	1	2
9/29	162	Chi.	L	6-7	Caudill	Robinson	97-64	1	1
9/30	163	Chi.	W	5-3	Kison	McGlothen	98-64	1	2

8/4-Candelaria and Tekulve
8/19-Candelaria and Tekulve
9/3-Carlton and McGraw
9/12-Candelaria and Tekulve
9/16-Falcone and Allen

+ Combined shutouts: 5/15-Swan and Lockwood
5/19-Rooker, Jackson and Romo
5/29-Robinson and Jackson

Bold Face — Complete Game
*Double Header

PIRATE TOP 10 BATTING

GAMES
Roberto Clemente 2,433
Honus Wagner 2,432
Max Carey 2,171
Bill Mazeroski 2,163
Paul Waner 2,154
Pie Traynor 1,941
Lloyd Waner 1,803
Tommy Leach 1,548
Fred Clarke 1,442

AT-BATS
Roberto Clemente 9,454
Honus Wagner 9,046
Paul Waner 8,429
Max Carey 8,406
Bill Mazeroski 7,755
Pie Traynor 7,559
Willie Stargell 7,542
Lloyd Waner 7,256
Tommy Leach 5,909
Fred Clarke 5,471

RUNS
Honus Wagner 1,520
Paul Waner 1,492
Roberto Clemente 1,416
Max Carey 1,414
Pie Traynor 1n183
Willie Stargell 1,159
Lloyd Waner 1,151
Fred Clarke 1,017
Tommy Leach 1,007
Arky Vaughan 936

HITS
Roberto Clemente 3,000
Honus Wagner 2,970
Paul Waner 2,868
Max Carey 2,416
Pie Traynor 2,416
Lloyd Waner 2,317
Willie Stargell 2,145
Bill Mazeroski 2,016
Arky Vaughan 1,709
Fred Clarke 1,638

SINGLES
Roberto Clemente 2,154
Honus Wagner 2,101
Paul Waner 2,018
Lloyd Waner 1,906
Max Carey 1,827
Pie Traynor 1,823
Bill Mazeroski 1,522
Willie Stargell 1,235
Tommy Leach 1,229
Arky Vaughan 1,218
Fred Clarke 1,212

DOUBLES
Honus Wagner 556
Paul Waner 556
Roberto Clemente 440
Willie Stargell 405
Max Carey 375
Pie Traynor 371
Bill Mazeroski 294
Arky Vaughan 291
Al Oliver 276
Gus Suhr 276

TRIPLES
Honus Wagner 231
Paul Waner 186

Roberto Clemente 166
Pie Traynor 164
Fred Clarke 155
Max Carey 148
Tommy Leach 137
Arky Vaughan 116
Jacob P. Beckley 114
Lloyd Waner 114

HOMERUNS
Willie Stargell 461
Ralph Kiner 301
Roberto Clemente 240
Frank Thomas 163
Bill Mazeroski 138
Al Oliver 135
Richard Hebner 121
Dick Stuart 117
Paul Waner 108
Donn Clendenon 106
Bob Robertson 106

TOTAL BASES
Roberto Clemente 4,492
Honus Wagner 4,234
Paul Waner 4,120
Willie Stargell 4,041
Pie Traynor 3,289
Max Carey 3,285
Lloyd Waner 2,898
Bill Mazeroski 2,848
Arky Vaughan 2,484
Fred Clarke 2,286

RUNS BATTED IN
Willie Stargell 1,476
Honus Wagner 1,475
Roberto Clemente 1,305
Pie Traynor 1,273
Paul Waner 1,177
Bill Mazeroski 853
Ralph Kiner 801
Gus Suhr 789
Arky Vaughan 764
Al Oliver 717

EXTRA-BASE HITS
Willie Stargell 920
Honus Wagner 869
Paul Waner 850
Roberto Clemente 846
Pie Traynor 593
Max Carey 589
Bill Mazeroski 494
Arky Vaughan 491
Ralph Kiner 486
Al Oliver 467
Gus Suhr 467

BATTING AVERAGE
Paul Waner 340
Kiki Cuyler 336
E. E. (Mike) Smith 328
Honus Wagner 328
Matty Alou 327
Arky Vaughan 324
Clarence Beaumont 321
Pie Traynor 320
Lloyd Waner 319
Roberto Clemente 317
Dave Parker 317

STOLEN BASES
Max Carey 678
Honus Wagner 639
Fred Clarke 261
Tommy Leach 249

Omar Moreno 217
Frank Taveras 204
Carson Bigbee 182
Ginger Beaumont 169
Pie Traynor 158
Kiki Cuyler 130

PIRATE TOP 10 PITCHING

STRIKEOUTS—Pitcher
Bob Friend 1,682
Bob Veale 1,652
Wilbur Cooper 1,191
Vernon Law 1,092
Babe Adams 1,036
Steve Blass 896
Dock Ellis 868
Deacon Phillippe 853
Sam Leever 845
Roy Face 842

INNINGS PITCHED
Bob Friend 3,481
Wilbur Cooper 3,201
Babe Adams 2,991
Vernon Law 2,673
Sam Leever 2,645
Deacon Phillipe 2,283
Rip Sewell 2,108
Ray Kremer 1,955
Bob Veale 1,869
Howie Camnitz 1,754

WINS
Wilbur Cooper 202
Sam Leever 194
Babe Adams 194
Bob Friend 191
Deacon Phillippe 165
Vernon Law 162
Rip Sewell 143
Ray Kremer 143
Bob Veale 116
Howie Camnitz 115

GAMES—Pitcher
Elroy Face 802
Bob Friend 568
Vernon Law 483
Babe Adams 483
Wilbur Cooper 469
Dave Giusti 410
Sam Leever 388
Rip Sewell 385
Kent Tekulve 363
Bob Veale 340
Deacon Phillippe 330

THREE RIVERS STADIUM FIRSTS

FIRST Day Attendance—48,846
FIRST Pirate Pitcher—Dock Ellis
FIRST Opposing Pitcher—Gary Nolan
FIRST BATTER—Ty Cline
FIRST Put-out—Al Oliver
FIRST Hit—Richie Hebner
FIRST Double—Al Oliver
FIRST Triple—Roberto Clemente
FIRST Homerun—Tony Perez
FIRST Base-on-balls (Batter)—Gary Nolan
FIRST Base-on-balls (Pitcher)—Dock Ellis
FIRST Strikeout (Batter)—Willie Stargell
FIRST Strikeout (Pitcher)—Gary Nolan
FIRST Stolen Base—Lee May
FIRST Doubleplay—Alley to Mazeroski to Oliver
FIRST Relief Pitcher—Clay Carroll
FIRST Pinch-hitter—Angel Bravo
FIRST Error—Woody Woodward

1979 Pirate Roster

Manager: CHUCK TANNER (7)
Coaches: JOE LONNETT (32), AL MONCHAK (42), BOB SKINNER (48), HARVEY HADDIX (57)
Trainer: TONY BARTIROME—Traveling Secretary: CHARLES MUSE
Team Physician: DR. JOSEPH FINEGOLD—Equipment Manager: JOHN HALLAHAN

No.	NAME	B-T	HT.	WT.	BIRTHDATE	BIRTHPLACE	RESIDENCE
	PITCHERS (11)						
26	Bibby, Jim	R-R	6-5	250	10/29/44	Franklinton, NC	Madison Heights, VA
22	Blyleven, Bert	R-R	6-3	207	4/ 6/51	Zeist, Holland	Villa Park, CA
45	Candelaria, John	L-L	6-7	232	11/ 6/53	New York, NY	Pittsburgh, PA
23	Jackson, Grant	LR-L	6-0	204	9/28/42	Fostoria, OH	Upper St. Clair, PA
25	Kison, Bruce	R-R	6-4	173	2/18/50	Pasco, WA	Churchill, PA
49	Roberts, Dave	L-L	6-3	192	9/11/44	Gallipolis, OH	Houston, TX
43	Robinson, Don	R-R	6-4	231	6/ 8/57	Ashland, KY	Kenoa, WV
15	Romo, Enrique	R-R	5-11	185	7/15/47	Santa Rosalia, MX	Torreon, Coahuila, MX
19	Rooker, Jim	R-L	6-0	193	9/23/42	Lakeview, OR	Library, PA
27	Tekulve, Kent	R-R	6-4	160	3/ 5/47	Cincinnati, OH	Bethel Park, PA
	CATCHERS (3)						
16	Nicosia, Steve	R-R	5-10	185	8/ 6/55	Paterson, NJ	North Miami Beach, FL
14	Ott, Ed	L-R	5-10	190	7/11/51	Muncy, PA	Allentown, PA
35	Sanguillen, Manny	R-R	6-0	193	3/21/44	Colon, PAN	Pittsburgh, PA
	INFIELDERS (5)						
10	Foli, Tim	R-R	6-0	175	12/ 8/50	Culver City, CA	Ormond Beach, FL
3	Garner, Phil	R-R	5-10	177	4/30/49	Jefferson City, TN	Pittsburgh, PA
5	Madlock, Bill	R-R	5-11	185	1/12/51	Memphis, TN	Foster City, CA
8	Stargell, Willie	L-L	6-3	225	3/ 6/41	Earlsboro, OK	Pittsburgh, PA
6	Stennett, Rennie	R-R	5-11	188	4/ 5/51	Colon, PAN	McMurray, PA
	OUTFIELDERS (7)						
36	Alexander, Matt	LR-R	5-11	170	1/ 3/47	Shreveport, LA	Shreveport, LA
24	Easler, Mike	L-R	6-1	196	11/29/50	Cleveland, OH	San Antonio, TX
17	Lacy, Lee	R-R	6-1	175	4/10/48	Longview, TX	Calabasas, CA
34	Milner, John	L-L	6-0	182	12/28/49	Atlanta, GA	East Point, GA
18	Moreno, Omar	L-L	6-3	170	10/24/52	Puerto Armuelles, PAN	Puerto Armuelles, PAN
39	Parker, Dave	L-R	6-5	230	6/ 9/51	Cincinnati, OH	Pittsburgh, PA
28	Robinson, Bill	R-R	6-3	197	6/26/43	McKeesport, PA	Turnersville, NJ

PIRATE HIGHS AND LOWS 1979

TEAM: PITCHING
MOST STRIKEOUTS: (Game) . . . . 12 vs. Mont. 4/8, vs. L.A. 8/20, 12 at S.D. 8/25
FEWEST WALKS: (Game) . . . . 0 — many times
FEWEST HITS: (Game) . . . . 1 vs. S.D. 6/3 (Kison)

TEAM FIELDING
MOST DP'S: (Game) . . . . 4 — 3 times
MOST ERRORS: (Game) . . . . 5 vs. Mont. 4/6

INDIVIDUAL: BATTING
MOST HITS: (Game) . . . . 5 — Garner at S.F. 6/19
MOST RUNS SCORED: (Game) . . . 4 — Garner at Mont. 2nd game 7/27
MOST AT-BATS: (Game) . . . . 9 — Parker at S.D. 8/25
MOST DOUBLES: (Game) . . . . 3 — Foli vs. Atl. 5/1
MOST TRIPLES: (Game) . . . . 1 — several times
MOST HOMERUNS: (Game) . . . . 2 — 7 times
MOST RBI'S: (Game) . . . . 5 — Ott at Phil. 8/11
MOST STOLEN BASES: (Game) . . . . 2 — 11 times

INDIVIDUAL: PITCHING
LONGEST WINNING STREAK: . . . . Romo — seven (7/2-8/24)
MOST STRIKEOUTS: (Game) . . . . . . 11 — Bibby vs. Chicago (9/28/79)
MOST WALKS: (Game) . . . . 9 — Robinson vs. N.Y. 5/15
FEWEST HITS: (Game) . . . . 1 — Kison vs. S.D. 6/3

TEAM: MISCELLANEOUS
LONGEST GAME: (Time) . . . . 3:42 at Atl. 5/9 (9 inn.)
LONGEST GAME: (Innings) . . . . 19 at S.D. 8/25
SHORTEST GAME: (Time) . . . . 1:54 vs. Stl. 9/12
LARGEST MARGIN OF VICTORY . . . . 9 runs vs. Mont. 9/26

TEAM: BATTING
MOST RUNS: (Game) . . . . 17 at Atl. 5/9
MOST RUNS: (Both Clubs) . . . . 26 at Atl. 5/9 Pgh. 17 Atl. 9
MOST RUNS: (Innings) . . . . 7 at Atl. 5/9
MOST RUNS: (Opponent) . . . . 7 at Atl. 7/13
MOST HITS: (Game) . . . . 23 at Phil. 8/11
MOST HITS: (Both Clubs) . . . . 38 at Phil. 8/11
MOST HITS: (Innings) . . . . 6 — five times
MOST HITS: (Opponent) . . . . 6 — twice
FEWEST HITS: (Game) . . . . one vs. Phil. 9/3 1st game
MOST DOUBLES: (Game) . . . . 5 — twice
MOST TRIPLES: (Game) . . . . 3 vs. Stl. 8/1
MOST HOMERUNS: (Game) . . . . 5 vs. S.D. 6/3
MOST EXTRA BASEHITS: (Game) . . . . 8 — twice
MOST MEN LOB: (Game) . . . . 15 at N.Y. 5/26
FEWEST MEN LOB: (Game) . . . . 1 vs. Phil. 9/3 1st game
MOST STOLEN BASES: (Game) . . . . 4 — six times

DOWN THE YEARS WITH THE BUCS

Year	W	L	Pct.	Pos.	Manager	Home Attendance
1887	55	69	.444	6	H. B. Phillips	
1888	66	68	.492	6	H. B. Phillips	
1889	61	71	.462	5	Phillips & Hanlon	
1890	23	113	.169	8	Guy Hecker	
1891	55	80	.467	8	Hanlon & McGunnigle	
1892	80	73	.527	6	Buckenberger & Burns	
1893	81	48	.628	2	A. C. Buckenberger	
1894	65	65	.500	7	Buckenberger & Mack	
1895	71	61	.538	7	Connie Mack	
1896	66	63	.512	6	Connie Mack	
1897	60	71	.454	8	P. J. Donovan	
1898	72	76	.486	8	W. H. Watkins	
1899	75	72	.510	7	W. H. Watkins, P. J. Donovan	
1900	79	60	.568	2	Fred Clarke	
1901	**90**	**49**	**.647**	1**	**Fred Clarke**	**251,955**
1902	**103**	**36**	**.741**	1**	**Fred Clarke**	**243,826**
1903	**91**	**49**	**.650**	1**	**Fred Clarke**	**326,855**
1904	87	66	.569	4	Fred Clarke	340,615
1905	96	57	.627	2	Fred Clarke	369,124
1906	93	60	.608	3	Fred Clarke	394,877
1907	91	63	.591	2	Fred Clarke	319,506
1908	98	56	.636	2t	Fred Clarke	382,444
1909	**110**	**42**	**.724**	1***	**Fred Clarke**	**534,950**
1910	86	67	.562	3	Fred Clarke	436,586
1911	85	69	.552	3	Fred Clarke	432,000
1912	93	58	.616	2	Fred Clarke	384,000
1913	78	73	.521	3	Fred Clarke	296,000
1914	69	85	.448	7	Fred Clarke	139,620
1915	73	81	.474	5	Fred Clarke	225,743
1916	65	89	.422	6	Jimmy Callahan	289,132
1917	51	103	.331	8	Callahan, Wagner & Bezdek	192,807
1918	65	60	.520	4	Hugo Bezdek	213,610
1919	71	68	.511	4	Hugo Bezdek	276,810
1920	79	75	.513	4	George Gibson	429,037
1921	90	63	.588	2	George Gibson	701,567
1922	85	69	.552	3t	Gibson & McKechnie	523,675
1923	87	67	.565	3	W. B. McKechnie	611,082
1924	90	63	.588	3	W. B. McKechnie	736,883
1925	**95**	**58**	**.621**	1***	**W. B. McKechnie**	**804,354**
1926	84	69	.549	3	W. B. McKechnie	798,542
1927	**94**	**60**	**.610**	1**	**Donie Bush**	**869,720**
1928	85	67	.559	4	Donie Bush	495,070
1929	88	65	.575	2	Bush & Ens	491,377
1930	80	74	.519	5	Jewel Ens	357,795
1931	75	79	.487	5	Jewel Ens	260,392
1932	86	68	.558	2	George Gibson	287,262
1933	87	67	.565	2	George Gibson	288,747
1934	74	76	.493	5	Gibson & Traynor	322,622
1935	86	67	.562	4	Pie Traynor	352,885
1936	84	70	.545	4	Pie Traynor	372,524
1937	86	68	.558	3	Pie Traynor	459,679
1938	86	64	.573	2	Pie Traynor	641,033
1939	68	85	.444	6	Pie Traynor	376,734
1940	78	76	.506	4	Frank F. Frisch	507,934
1941	81	73	.526	4	Frank F. Frisch	482,241
1942	66	81	.449	5	Frank F. Frisch	448,897
1943	80	74	.519	4	Frank F. Frisch	604,278
1944	90	63	.588	2	Frank F. Frisch	498,740
1945	82	72	.532	4	Frank F. Frisch	604,694
1946	63	91	.409	7	Frisch & Davis	749,962
1947	62	92	.403	7t	Herman & Burwell	1,283,531
1948	83	71	.539	4	William A. Meyer	1,517,021
1949	71	83	.461	6	William A. Meyer	1,499,435
1950	57	96	.373	8	William A. Meyer	1,166,267
1951	64	90	.416	7	William A. Meyer	980,590
1952	42	112	.273	8	William A. Meyer	686,673
1953	50	104	.325	8	Fred G. Haney	572,757
1954	53	101	.344	8	Fred G. Haney	475,494
1955	60	94	.390	8	Fred. G. Haney	469,397
1956	66	88	.429	7	Robert R. Bragan	949,878
1957	62	92	.403	7t	Bragan & Murtaugh (26-26)	850,732
1958	84	70	.545	2	Daniel E. Murtaugh	1,314,988
1959	78	76	.506	4	Daniel E. Murtaugh	1,359,917
1960	**95**	**59**	**.617**	1***	**Daniel E. Murtaugh**	**1,705,828**
1961	75	79	.487	6	Daniel E. Murtaugh	1,199,128
1962	93	68	.578	4	Daniel E. Murtaugh	1,090,648
1963	74	88	.457	8	Daniel E. Murtaugh	783,648
1964	80	82	.494	6t	Daniel E. Murtaugh	759,496
1965	90	72	.556	3	Harry W. Walker	909,279
1966	92	70	.568	3	Harry W. Walker	1,196,618
1967	81	81	.500	6	Walker & Murtaugh (39-39)	907,012
1968	80	82	.494	6	Larry Shepard	693,485
1969†	88	74	.543	3	Larry Shepard (84-73) Alex Grammas (4-1)	769,369
1970	89	73	.549	1*	Daniel E. Murtaugh	1,341,947
1971	**97**	**65**	**.599**	1***	**Daniel E. Murtaugh**	**1,501,132**
1972	96	59	.619	1*	William C. Virdon	1,427,460
1973	80	82	.494	3	William C. Virdon (67-69) Daniel E. Murtaugh (13-13)	1,319,913
1974	88	74	.543	1*	Daniel E. Murtaugh	1,110,552
1975	92	69	.571	1*	Daniel E. Murtaugh	1,270,023
1976	92	70	.568	2	Daniel E. Murtaugh	1,025,945
1977	96	66	.593	2	Charles W. Tanner	1,237,349
1978	88	73	.547	2	Charles W. Tanner	964,106
1979	**98**	**64**	**.605**	1	**Charles W. Tanner**	**1,435,427**

(t) Denotes Tie for Position
(†) Denotes Beginning of Divisional Play — Eastern Division
(*) Denotes Eastern Division Champions
(**) Denotes National League Champions
(***) Denotes World Champions

1979 Batting

Player	Avg.	G	AB	R	H	2B	3B	HR	RBI	SH-SF	BB	SO	SB-CS	HB	E
Alexander	.538	44	13	16	7	0	1	0	1	0-0	0	0	13-1	0	0
Berra	.211	44	123	11	26	5	0	3	15	2-2	11	17	0-0	0	12
Boyland	.000	4	3	0	0	0	0	0	0	0-0	0	2	0-0	0	0
Easler	.283	54	53	8	15	1	1	2	11	0-0	8	13	0-1	0	0
Foli w/Pgh.	.291	133	525	70	153	23	1	1	65	19-6	28	14	6-5	9	15
Overall	.288	136	532	70	153	23	1	1	65	19-6	28	14	6-5	9	15
Garner	.293	150	549	76	161	32	8	11	59	2-3	55	74	17-7	3	22
Lacy	.247	84	182	17	45	9	3	5	15	0-3	22	36	6-1	1	3
Lois	.000	11	0	6	0	0	0	0	0	0-0	0	0	1-1	0	0
Madlock w/															
Pgh.	.328	85	311	48	102	17	3	7	42	2-5	34	22	21-7	1	6
Overall	.298	154	560	85	167	26	5	14	85	3-7	52	41	32-10	1	13
Milner	.276	128	326	52	90	9	4	16	60	0-6	51	37	3-5	1	8
Moreno	.282	162	695	110	196	21	12	8	69	6-2	51	104	77-21	3	13
Nicosia	.288	70	191	22	55	16	0	4	13	1-0	24	17	0-2	0	3
Ott	.273	117	403	49	110	20	2	7	51	6-4	26	62	0-1	0	4
Parker	.310	158	622	109	193	45	7	25	94	0-9	67	101	20-4	9	15
Robinson, B.	.262	147	421	59	111	17	6	24	75	4-5	24	82	13-2	1	3
Sanguillen	.230	56	74	8	17	5	2	0	4	3-1	2	5	0-0	0	2
Stargell	.281	126	424	60	19	19	0	32	82	0-6	47	105	0-1	3	3
Stennett	.238	108	319	31	76	13	2	0	24	2-3	24	25	1-4	0	12
Others	.203	—	59	5	12	3	0	0	1	4-0	1	7	2-1	0	3

1979 Pitchers' Batting

Player	AVG.	G	AB	R	H	2B	3B	HR	RBI	SH-SF	BB	SO	SB-CS	HB	E
Bibby	.178	34	45	3	8	1	0	2	5	6-0	0	25	0-0	1	0
Blyleven	.129	38	70	1	9	1	0	0	3	15-0	0	33	0-0	0	0
Candelaria	.132	33	68	0	9	4	0	0	6	8-0	1	18	0-0	0	0
Coleman w/															
Pgh.	.200	10	5	0	1	1	0	0	0	0-0	0	3	0-0	0	1
Overall	.200	15	5	0	1	1	0	0	0	0-0	0	3	0-0	0	1
Ellis w/Pgh.	.000	3	1	0	0	0	0	0	0	0-0	0	0	0-0	0	0
Overall	.074	20	27	0	2	0	0	0	1	1-0	1	7	0-0	0	0
Jackson	.000	72	9	0	0	0	0	0	1	0-0	0	2	0-0	0	0
Kison	.145	36	55	8	8	2	0	1	6	7-0	1	19	0-0	0	1
Roberts w/															
Pgh.	.000	21	5	0	0	0	0	0	1	0-1	0	1	0-0	0	1
Overall	.000	47	10	0	0	0	0	0	1	0-1	0	3	0-0	0	1
Robinson, D.	.204	29	49	4	10	0	0	0	3	4-0	3	9	0-0	0	2
Romo	.167	84	12	0	2	0	0	0	1	4-0	0	2	0-0	0	1
Rooker	.121	19	33	1	4	0	0	0	0	2-0	1	13	0-0	0	2
Tekulve	.133	90	15	3	2	0	0	0	1	1-0	1	8	0-0	0	2

Team Batting Totals

AVG.	G	AB	R	H	2B	3B	HR	RBI	SH-SF	BB	SO	SB-CS	HB	E
.272	—	5661	775	1541	263	52	148	710	98-56	482	855	188-64	32	134

1978 Pitching

Pitching	W-L	ERA	G	GS	GF	CG	IP	R	ER	H	BB	SO	HR	SHO	SAV
Bibby	12-4	2.80	34	17	2	4	137.2	51	43	110	47	103	9	1	0
Blyleven	12-5	3.61	37	37	0	4	237.1	102	95	238	92	172	21	0	0
Candelaria	14-9	3.22	33	30	2	8	207.0	83	74	201	41	101	25	0	0
Coleman w/															
Pgh.	0-0	5.57	10	0	2	0	20.2	17	13	29	9	14	1	0	0
Overall	0-0	4.88	15	0	3	0	24.1	19	13	33	11	14	1	0	0
Ellis w/Pgh.	0-0	2.57	3	1	0	0	7.0	2	2	8	2	1	1	0	0
Overall	3-7	5.77	20	15	3	1	92.0	62	59	119	36	42	10	0	0
Jackson	8-5	2.96	72	0	29	0	82.0	32	27	67	35	39	9	0	14
Kison	13-7	3.14	33	25	2	3	172.1	70	61	157	45	105	12	1	0
Roberts w/															
Pgh.	5-2	3.23	21	3	5	0	38.2	18	14	47	12	14	1	0	1
Overall	5-4	2.89	47	4	16	0	80.2	33	26	89	30	38	4	0	4
Robinson, D.	8-8	3.86	29	25	1	4	160.2	74	69	171	52	96	12	0	0
Romo	10-5	3.00	84	0	25	0	129.1	50	43	121	43	106	11	0	5
Rooker	4-7	4.59	19	17	0	1	103.2	58	53	106	39	44	11	0	0
Tekulve	10-8	2.82	94	0	67	0	134.1	44	41	109	48	75	5	0	31
Others	2-4	4.60	—	8	4	0	62.2	40	32	58	38	33	6	0	1

Team Pitching Totals

W-L	ERA	G	GS	GF	CG	IP	R	ER	H	BB	SO	HR	SHO	SAV
98-64	3.41	—	163	139	24	1493.1	642	565	1424	503	906	124	7#	52

LEFT ON BASE: PIRATES 1,128 OPPOSITION 1,142
DOUBLEPLAYS: PIRATES 163 OPPOSITION 156
TRIPLEPLAY: PIRATES 1

Awarded First on Catcher's Interference: Berra, 2.

Note: Stats include figures from tie game on 5/25 . . . Total Earned Runs do not agree with individual totals due to provision of scoring rule 10:18 (i).

#Includes combined shutouts by: Rooker, Jackson & Romo @ Chi. on 5/19; Robinson & Jackson vs. Chi. 5/29, Candelaria & Tekulve vs. Phil., L.A., & Stl. on 8/4, 9/19 & 9/12.